Sheffield Hallam University
Learning and IT Services
Collegiate Learning Centre
Collegiate Crescent Campus
Sheffield   S10 2BP

101 871 188 0

Sociology for Nurses

Sheffie
Learning a
Withdra   Stock

D0581168

ONE WEEK LOAN

- 9 JUN 2008

16 OCT 2009

16 FEB 2011

18 MAR 2014

10 APR 2014

21. 11-08

20 APR 2009

18 JUN 2009
25 JUN 2009

26 MAY 2010

14 SEP 2010

-6 JUN 2011

-3 JUN 2013

25 MAR 2014

For J. J. E. and J. E., and in memory of Mary Garvey, a dedicated nurse from 1939 to 1984

Sociology for Nurses

Edited by
Elaine Denny and Sarah Earle

polity

Copyright © Polity Press 2005

First published in 2005 by Polity Press
Reprinted 2007

Polity Press
65 Bridge Street
Cambridge CB2 1UR, UK

Polity Press
350 Main Street
Malden, MA 02148, USA

All rights reserved. Except for the quotation of short passages for the purpose of criticism and review, no part of this publication may be reproduced, stored in a retrieval system, or transmitted, in any form or by any means, electronic, mechanical, photocopying, recording or otherwise, without the prior permission of the publisher.

ISBN-10: 0-7456-3100-2
ISBN-13: 978-07456-3100-4
ISBN-10: 0-7456-3101-0 (pb)
ISBN-13: 978-07456-3101-1 (pb)

A catalogue record for this book is available from the British Library.

Typeset in 10.5 on 13 pt Quadraat Regular
by Servis Filmsetting Ltd, Manchester
Printed and bound in Hong Kong by SNP Best-set Typesetter Ltd.

The publisher has used its best endeavours to ensure that the URLs for external websites referred to in this book are correct and active at the time of going to press. However, the publisher has no responsibility for the websites and can make no guarantee that a site will remain live or that the content is or will remain appropriate.

For further information on Polity, visit our website: www.polity.co.uk

SHEFFIELD HALLAM UNIVERSITY
WL
306.461
DE.
COLLEGIATE LEARNING CENTRE

Contents

Contributors

Geraldine Brown works as a researcher for the Centre for Social Justice at Coventry University. She has had considerable experience of researching a variety of social policy issues. Her interests include the working relationships between partners in health provision, and the relationship between the experience of social exclusion and institutional attempts at inclusion across a range of social policy areas.

Pat Chambers is a lecturer in the School of Social Relations at Keele University, teaching social work and gerontology. She works within a life-course perspective, and her published works and current research interests encompass age, gender and disability. Before teaching in further and higher professional education, she worked for a number of years in a variety of statutory and voluntary agencies.

David Cox is Professor and Associate Dean in the Faculty of Health and Community Care at the University of Central England. Since 2002 he has also been Chair of South Birmingham Primary Care Trust. He teaches and has written about the sociology of policy implementation and reorganization in child care and the NHS.

Lorraine Culley is Reader in Health Studies in the Faculty of Health and Life Sciences at De Montfort University. Her research interests are in ethnicity, health and health care and she is currently leading a major study of infertility and UK South Asian communities. She has published recently in nursing and social science journals on nurse education and on equal opportunities policies. She is co-editor (with Simon Dyson) of *Ethnicity and Nursing Practice*, Palgrave, 2001.

Elaine Denny is Head of Division, Health Policy and Sociology, School of Health and Policy Studies at the University of Central England in Birmingham. She has taught health sociology to pre- and post-registration nursing students for 15 years. Her research interests focus around women as recipients and providers of health care, and she has published work on women's experience of IVF, and on the occupation of nursing. Her current research is on women's experience of living with endometriosis.

Simon Dyson is Director of the Unit for the Social Study of Thalassaemia and Sickle Cell (http://www.tascunit.com) at De

Montfort University, Leicester. He is the author of *Mental Handicap* (Croom Helm, 1987) and co-editor (with Lorraine Culley) of *Ethnicity and Nursing Practice* (Palgrave, 2001). His most recent research has involved a project for the NHS Sickle Cell/Thalassaemia Screening Committee involving work on developing an ethnicity question for antenatal screening as part of the NHS maternity data set.

Sarah Earle is Lecturer in Health and Social Care at the Open University and teaches sociology of health and illness. Her current research interests include women's reproductive health, the sociology of sexuality and the role of sociology within health education and practice. With Gayle Letherby, she is editor of *Gender, Identity and Reproduction: Social Perspectives* (Palgrave, 2003) and, with Keith Sharp, author of the forthcoming *Sex in Cyberspace* (Ashgate).

Mike Filby is Head of the School of Health and Policy Studies at the University of Central England in Birmingham. His interests are in the sociology of health work and organization and he has a long-standing interest in the sociology of primary care. Recent consultancy has included a project working with community nurses across the 'surgery walls' in a Midlands health authority, from where he was able to observe the unfolding politics of organizational change in primary care. Recent publications include commentaries on organizational development in primary care.

Barbara Green is Senior Lecturer at the University of Central England in Birmingham with a first degree in sociology with history and a Master's degree in nursing. The theme of her research dissertation was the relationship between sociology and nursing. Her clinical background is as a registered nurse in acute medicine, working as a ward sister in this speciality for eight years. She currently teaches sociology to pre-registration student nurses.

Alistair Hewison is Senior Lecturer and Director of Postgraduate Studies in the School of Health Sciences at the University of Birmingham. He worked as a nurse and manager in the NHS and now teaches management at undergraduate and postgraduate level. His research interests also centre around the management and organization of health care.

Gayle Letherby is Reader in the Sociology of Gender, Associate Head of Subject and Deputy Director of the Centre for Social Justice at Coventry University. Her scholarly interests include: reproductive identity and experience; motherhood and non-motherhood; and feminist research and epistemology. She is author of *Feminist Research in Theory and Practice* (OUP, 2003) and co-editor (with Sarah Earle) of *Gender, Identity and Reproduction: Social Perspectives* (Palgrave, 2003).

Douglas McCarrick was Senior Lecturer in the Institute of Health and Welfare at the Open University between 1990 and 1992. Currently he is Senior Lecturer in the Faculty of Health and Community Care, University of Central England. He is an active local politician, interested in health inequalities and democratic control of health services. He has chaired various committees, including Urban Renewal, Joint Housing, and Health and Social Services Scrutiny.

Terry O'Donnell is Senior Lecturer at Leeds Metropolitan University. She is a health sociologist and is interested in health inequalities and risk. She has contributed a chapter on health and health promotion in L. Merriman and W. Turner (eds), *Clinical Skills in Treating the Foot* (Elsevier, forthcoming).

Keith Sharp is Head of the School of Contemporary Studies at De Montfort University. He is interested in the sociology of sexuality and social theory. He is a co-author of *Sociology in Focus* (1995) and *Psychology in Focus* (2002) (Causeway Press) and, with Sarah Earle, co-author of the forthcoming book, *Sex in Cyberspace* (Ashgate).

Philip Shelton is a Health Sociology and Policy lecturer at the University of Central England. He also works as an associate lecturer at the Open University. His current interests focus on the application of sociological knowledge to nursing practice.

Nick Watson is Professor at Strathclyde Centre for Disability Research. He has published on many aspects of disability and is currently researching the history of the wheelchair. He is co-editor with Sheila Riddell, of *Disability and Culture* (Palgrave, 2003), *Reframing the Body* (with Sarah Cunningham-Burley, Palgrave, 2001) and *Organizing Bodies: Policy, Institutions and Work* (with Linda McKie, Macmillan 2000). He is active in the Disabled People's Movement.

Corinne Wilson is a PhD student and part-time lecturer at the Centre for Social Justice, Coventry University. She teaches on a number of modules which explore the relationships between gender, the family and health. Her research interests include teenage pregnancy, lone motherhood, feminist methodology and epistemology.

Acknowledgements

The editors and publishers are grateful to the following for permission to reproduce copyright material:

John Arlidge for the extract in Activity 10.3 on p. 190;
Audit Commission for figure 11.1 on p. 203;
Blackwell Publishing for the extract in Activity 6.3 on p. 113;
BMJ Publishing Group for the letter from I. McKenzie to the *British Medical Journal*, 25 November 1998, in Activity 4.4 on p. 79;
Controller of HMSO and the Queen's Printer for Scotland for the table in Activity 1.3 on p. 23, figure 6.1 on p. 108, the figure in Activity 8.1 on p. 147, the figure in Activity 8.2 on p. 149, table 9.1 on p. 165. Crown copyright material reproduced under class licence no. CO1W0000283;
Guardian Newspapers Ltd for the extract in Activity 10.4 on p. 194, © Observer;
Policy Studies Institute for table 9.2 on p. 166;
US Department of Health and Human Services, Office on Women's Health – National Women's Health Information Center, www.4woman.gov, for the extract in Activity 5.3 on p. 93.

Every effort has been made to trace the copyright holders, but if any have been inadvertently overlooked, the publishers will be pleased to make the necessary arrangements at the first opportunity.

Introduction

Sarah Earle and Elaine Denny

Teaching sociology to nurses has become a significant issue within health sociology, as reflected in the workshop 'Teaching sociology to healthcare professionals in training' at the British Sociological Association's Medical Sociology Conference in York, 2001. The new nursing curriculum acknowledges the need for the twenty-first-century nurse to utilize knowledge from a range of disciplines when assessing patients/clients and deciding on an approach to care. Nursing is no longer (if it ever was) the sum of its tasks – or what nurses 'do' – but has become a complex set of relationships. Society has changed since the inception of the NHS, deference towards health professionals has lessened and individuals are more willing to challenge 'experts'. Professional boundaries are becoming less rigid, and many client groups are demanding a more active part in decision-making. The NHS itself has seen many reorganizations, and nurses, along with other health care workers, have had to adapt to changing structures and ideologies of health care.

The impact of these changes has been immense and many nurses have found themselves at a loss to know how to prepare themselves for the new demands made of them. There are probably few nurses who would turn to sociology to provide answers, as it is a discipline frequently perceived to be not of direct relevance to nursing work. This book has, therefore, deliberately set out to demonstrate the usefulness of sociology by relating the concepts and theories of sociology and health policy to nursing practice, with examples from all four branches of nursing. The aim of the book is to provide an accessible sociological textbook on health, illness and health care based on the needs of pre-registration nursing courses. It is also of relevance to post-registration students on 'top-up' degree programmes, particularly those who are new to the study of sociology.

The book is divided into four parts:

Part I considers the contribution that sociological knowledge can make to the delivery of nursing care. It starts by introducing the key sociological theories and approaches that underpin many of the concepts discussed later in the book. It then turns to the frequently raised question of why nurses need to study sociology, and how a knowledge of these theories may make a difference to nursing practice. One of the tasks of sociology is to encourage us to apply a 'sociological imagination' to things we may take for granted; the concepts of 'health' and 'nursing' are explored here using just such an approach.

Part II explores diversity and inequality in health and health care, demonstrating the link between client groups and the structures of society. These structures will advantage some groups and disadvantage others, resulting in wide variations in the incidence and experience of morbidity and mortality. A continuing theme here will be the role of nurses in challenging inequality and becoming advocates for patients and clients. Confronting and questioning your own beliefs and values may be the result of engaging with the issues raised in this section.

Part III questions where care takes place, and although the hospital is the visible face of the NHS, it is argued here that increasingly the location for health care is outside of institutions. Formal care in the primary and community care setting is providing a much wider range of services than ever before, and nurses are expanding their role in these settings, particularly within the fields of mental health and learning disability. The family has always been a major source of informal health work, although the relationship between the family, health and illness is a complex, and not necessarily a positive, one.

Part IV moves on to policy influences on health and health care, and considers the relevance of policy and management issues to nurses at all levels, not just those in senior roles, and the opportunity for nurses to engage in policy debate. The book finishes by moving outside of the NHS and direct patient/client care and introducing the reader to the crucial link between the environment and health, particularly the importance of housing.

The chapters are similarly structured and designed to enable you to reflect on the sociological issues raised and to relate them to nursing practice:

- each chapter begins with the key issues, giving you signposts on what to expect;
- learning outcomes enable you to assess whether you have understood and learnt from what you have read;
- key terms are explained in the glossary boxes to aid understanding at a glance;
- there are activities to carry out with colleagues from your own, or different, branches of nursing, enabling reflection and encouraging you to relate theory to practice;
- at the end of each chapter there are summary points;
- and, to expand your knowledge, annotated further reading and questions for discussion are included at the end of the chapter.

Once you have read this book, and engaged with the activities and discussion questions, we hope that you will feel equipped to use a sociological approach as one of your tools for formulating and delivering optimum nursing care. You may also wish to enter into the debates about the future of nursing, and its place in determining health policy. Most of all you should be able to look beyond the simple explanations of everyday issues and problems to gain a deeper, more meaningful understanding.

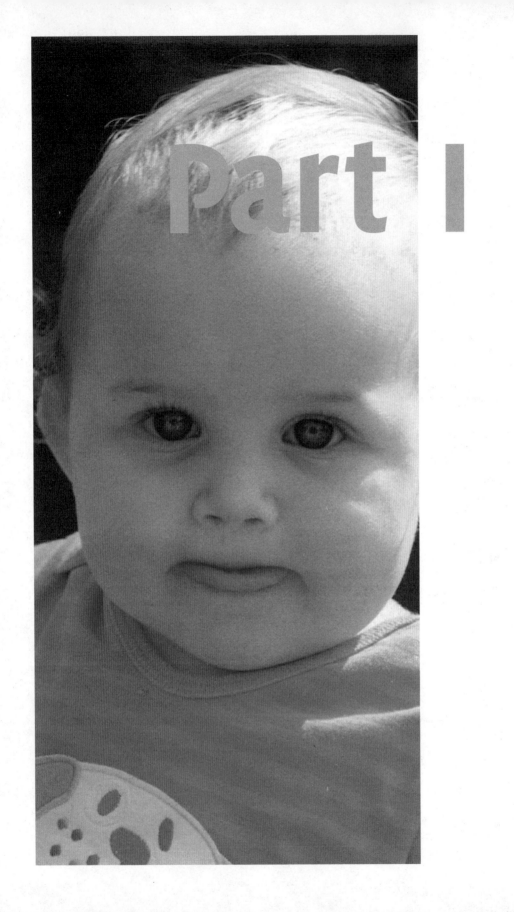

Part 1

Nursing and the Sociology of Health and Health Care

Sociology is not always easy to understand – even for sociology students – and its relevance to nursing, and nurses, is not readily apparent. There is considerable controversy regarding whether nurses should study sociology and we have attempted to reflect this within part I of this book. Some commentators have suggested that sociology should not be included in the nursing curriculum, arguing that it can add no value to nurse education and training. Others have suggested that sociology is vital to nurse education and to the future of nursing as a profession!

Student nurses often ask 'Why do we have to do sociology?', and it is as a response to this question that we have written this book and, more specifically, chosen to include the chapters in this part. Each of these chapters examines key concepts and debates in relation to nursing, and the sociology of health and health care.

The first chapter, 'What is Sociology?', introduces you to key sociological approaches, concepts and theories. With this in mind, you may find it useful to start with this chapter, or to come back to it after reading the other chapters within this part. The chapter begins by outlining the distinction between sociological knowledge and other forms of knowledge and considers the role of sociology within society. Sociology is often criticized as 'just common sense', and this chapter challenges this interpretation. It examines the distinction between social 'structure' and social 'action', outlining key sociological theories and their relevance to our understanding of health and health care. The chapter then explores methodological approaches and some of the research methods commonly used by sociologists to explore health and illness.

In chapter 2, we specifically address the question 'Why Should Nurses Study Sociology?' and explore the role of sociological knowledge within nursing practice. Following on from the discussion begun in chapter 1, this chapter examines how, far from being 'just common sense', sociology can help to develop a range of thinking skills which are vital to contemporary nursing. This chapter highlights the problem of the 'theory–practice gap' and focuses on the sociology of nursing as well as the role of sociology in nursing. By drawing on a variety of empirical studies, the chapter explores the value of sociological knowledge to nurses. We also explore the importance of sociological research methods as both a tool for carrying out research and a resource for evaluating published research.

Nurses are involved in caring for people who are ill or dying, as well as in promoting health and well-being. Whichever is the case, understanding what being 'healthy' means is important – although it is a challenging task, to say the least. In chapter 3, 'What is Health?', we consider the range of ways that health has been defined, looking at 'official' definitions of health, as well as the distinction between professional and lay definitions. Models of health are explored and, here, we contrast the biomedical model, which has been influential within medicine and health care, with the social model, which focuses on the social causes of disease. We consider the social construction of health and illness, examining how normal healthy processes become medicalized, and discuss the iatrogenic effects of medicalization on individuals and on society. The chapter also considers a more holistic approach to care within nursing and offers some sociological reflections on this.

Chapter 4, 'Nursing as an Occupation', provides a brief historical overview of nursing, mapping the development of nursing and nurse registration from the nineteenth century onwards. Just as other chapters within this section consider issues of definition, this one explores the debates which attempt to define what nursing is: is it an art or a science? We consider the process of becoming a nurse and the socialization of students into nursing. Following on from the debate identified in chapter 2, this chapter further highlights the tension of the 'theory–practice gap' within the socialization of student nurses. The gendered nature of nursing is considered together with the role and status of men within nursing. Power relations are explored and elitism within nursing and the relationships between nurses and other health care workers are considered. Drawing on the concept of emotion work, relationships between nurses and patients are also discussed.

1 What is Sociology?

Keith Sharp

Key issues within this chapter

- The nature of sociological enquiry and the role of sociology.
- Sociology and 'common sense'.
- An introduction to sociological theory.
- An introduction to research methods.

By the end of this chapter you should be able to . . .

- Understand some of the debates concerning the role of sociology within society.
- Recognize the distinction between sociology and 'common sense'.
- Discuss some of the different sociological theories.
- Recognize different research methods and understand the relationship between theory and method.

1 Introduction

Sociology is concerned, in the broadest sense, with the study of human society. As this implies, its scope is almost limitless: it is possible, in principle, to have a *sociology of* any activity in which human beings engage. Inevitably the sorts of things which have concerned sociologists have changed somewhat over time. The principal concerns of the 'founding fathers' of sociology, writing in the nineteenth century, were the major social, political and economic changes which had taken place across Europe since the late middle ages. Early sociological writing was dominated, for example, by attempts to chart and explain the rise of industrial capitalism, to explain the changing nature and role of religion in society and to understand the new forms which social and political institutions had taken since the Industrial Revolution (Giddens, 1986). Today, the concerns of sociologists have changed in ways which largely reflect the changing nature of society. Changing sexual attitudes and behaviours, changing gender relations, globalization, new communications technologies, changing patterns of criminality and social aspects of health and illness – the subject of this book – have all loomed large in recent sociological literature (see, for example, Jewkes, 2003; Annandale, 1998; Weeks and Holland, 1996).

There are a number of key questions and issues which lie at the heart of sociological enquiry, whatever the specific topic to which it is directed. The aim of this chapter is to introduce the most important of these. Before we do this it is important to make a few general points about the nature of sociological enquiry, and how it may differ somewhat from other disciplines. The remainder of this chapter is devoted to two main issues. The first is the range of what can be called 'theoretical debates' in sociology. We shall consider the main competing theoretical positions adopted by sociologists, and illustrate the implications of these different positions for the ways in which sociology can shed light on the nature of society and its institutions. An appreciation of these debates will be helpful in understanding many of the chapters which follow and in evaluating the contribution which sociology can make to nursing practice. The second issue is the methodological tools which are used in sociological research, and some of the debates which surround them. We shall introduce the main approaches to the conduct of sociological research, and the controversies which surround these.

2   The nature of sociological inquiry

The first thing we need to note about the discipline of sociology is that it is characterized by diversity. Whilst in any discipline we will find a degree of disagreement between practitioners, this is especially marked in the case of sociology. Unlike disciplines such as chemistry or biology, sociologists disagree even about the most fundamental principles of how to go about their work. We shall examine some of these disagreements later in this chapter. What this means is that sociology cannot, in general, be used to 'solve' technical problems in the way that knowledge from other 'scientific' disciplines may be able to.

Sociology and other disciplines

A second point worth noting about sociology is that many of the things it is concerned with are also of interest to researchers from other disciplines. It is therefore prone to 'boundary disputes'. A good example of this is the relationship between sociology and psychology. In broad terms it is possible to say that whilst sociology is concerned with understanding *societies*, psychology is concerned with understanding *individuals*. But very quickly the value of this distinction starts to break down. Rather obviously, societies are made up of individuals and so it seems silly to suggest that societies can be understood entirely without reference to individuals. Let us take a concrete example. Sociologists often like to use the term

socialization processes by which individuals acquire the roles, norms and cultures of society

◄ socialization. However, the processes by which individuals are socialized seem fairly clearly to fall within the domain of psychology, and the whole sub-field of learning has a great deal to say about this. Unfortunately, sociologists rarely seem to take much notice of the wealth of psychological literature which details the complexity of the socialization process; similarly, psychologists are often accused of failing to give proper attention to the insights of sociologists on the complex effects of wider social processes on individual learning.

The role of sociology within society

Finally, we should note that sociology must confront a particularly wide range of ethical issues. Not only must sociologists deal with the sorts of issues around the avoidance of individual harm in the course of conducting research which any human scientist must confront, but there are also a wider set of ethical concerns about the role of sociology in society. Is it the role of sociology, for example, to make recommendations about the kinds of social arrangements which are most desirable? Or should it, as the sociologist Max Weber argued, avoid such essentially political questions and focus, instead, on developing a neutral understanding of the social world, leaving questions of how society *should* be organized to politicians? As you will see from part II of this book, sociology has been particularly influential in identifying social inequalities in health. Is it the role of sociology to comment on the extent to which such inequalities *should* be eradicated (bearing in mind that even beginning to do so would entail massive costs which would have to be funded somehow) or should sociologists be content merely to describe and explain the extent of the inequality that exists?

Sociology versus 'common sense'

An often voiced criticism of sociology is that it is just 'common sense', and that sociologists do little more than state the obvious. So it is important to explain why sociology is, and must be, more than just common sense (see also chapter 2). The first point to make about this is that there is often more than one 'common-sense' view on any given issue. For some people it is just 'common sense' that the poor are poor because they are lazy, stupid and work-shy. For others, it is just common sense that poverty results from historical inequalities in society, and hence has nothing to do with individual attributes. Clearly both views cannot be correct, and so little will be gained in this case by relying on common sense. In fact the explanation of poverty is a highly complex example, which requires sophisticated sociological research and analysis (see chapter 8).

Similarly, 'common sense' often conceals positions of self-interest. It might be common sense for the rich to regard the poor as lazy, stupid and work-shy, but it seems most unlikely that such a view would be regarded as common sense by someone in poverty.

The role of sociology is to challenge the obvious, and to assess the evidence and arguments for and against any particular position which is advanced.

Genetically

Cartoon © Jacky Fleming
(www.jackyfleming.co.uk)

3   Major theoretical debates in sociology

The aim of this section is not to provide you with a comprehensive summary of debates in sociological theory, but rather to highlight some of the most important and to sketch out their implications for how sociologists concerned with health and illness go about their work. The distinction between **structure**, on the one hand, and **action**, on the other, is fundamental to theoretical debates within sociology and these are discussed below.

structure   organized patterns of social behaviour and the social institutions within society

action   purposeful and conscious behaviour

Structural theories

A question often posed by sociologists is: what is society? Although this may appear rather simple at first sight, we can quickly see that it does in fact raise a number of different possibilities. One general view of society can be called structural. This view tends to see societies as systems of interconnected parts, which influence each other in a variety of complex ways. The focus is less on the specific actions of individuals, than on the roles which they occupy and the ways in which these roles relate to each other.

Let us consider the example of a hospital. A structural view of a hospital might focus, first of all, on how power and authority are distributed throughout the organization. At the top of the hospital (or in modern Britain the Trust) might be a Chief Executive who has ultimate responsibility for the operational and strategic management of the hospital. The hospital's administration might be organized into a number of departments – human resources, finance, estates, etc. – each of which has a head, who is accountable to the Chief Executive and to whom staff of the department are responsible. The various clinical services provided by the Trust will similarly be organized into units, with heads, each of whom will be responsible to the Chief Executive for the effective and efficient delivery of their own particular service.

role the expected behaviours of holders of particular positions within society

Within these structures individuals occupy a particular **role**. Notice that in talking about roles, we are not talking about the individuals who occupy them. Take, as an example, the role of a consultant surgeon employed by an NHS Trust in a large metropolitan hospital. To a very significant extent, the behaviour and performance of any consultant surgeon employed in such a context will be substantially the same. The same job needs to be done, the same standard of professional performance is expected, even similar codes of dress and personal demeanour are expected (and usually found) amongst the individuals who occupy these roles. Plainly these similarities do not derive from essentially similar personalities just happening to find themselves in the same job; rather they derive from the expectations associated with the role in question.

We can see, too, that there are a variety of social mechanisms which tend to ensure that individuals conform to the expectations of the roles they occupy. Some of these are very formal. For example, it is a (not unreasonable) expectation that anyone occupying the role of consultant surgeon will take all reasonable steps to ensure that their patients are operated on in a safe and competent manner. If in a particular case a surgeon does not do this, then there exist various formal and legal sanctions which either ensure future conformity to this aspect of the role, or remove the individual from that role altogether. Others are much more informal. For example, a surgeon who reports to work unshaven, unwashed and dressed in a dirty track suit will probably suffer the disapproval of his colleagues and superiors, which may or may not be enough to cause a change in behaviour before more formal sanctions are invoked.

The concept of role allows sociologists to think about societies and organizations within societies as having a life independent of the individuals who make them up. In a very real sense, then, individual people, their hearts, minds and personalities, do not really figure in the sort of sociology that emphasizes structure. Hospitals, governments, prisons, families or whatever, operate in the way they do, with the consequences they have, not because of anything to do with the individuals who make them up, but because of the structures, rules and roles which define them.

'Structural' sociologists share a common view of how we should conceptualize society. Whilst at one level this is true, it is important to point out that there are a number of different approaches, which exhibit some quite fundamental differences, that fall under the general umbrella of structural sociology. We shall now consider two of these: functionalism and Marxism.

Functionalism The origins of sociology lie in the nineteenth century, and no one was more significant in its development than the Frenchman Émile Durkheim. Although the term 'sociology' had been coined by the French philosopher Auguste Comte, it was Durkheim who established it as a serious academic discipline. It was, moreover, Durkheim who established the principles of the theoretical approach known as functionalism.

The starting point for Durkheim, and for functionalist sociology in general, is the idea that societies are complete systems and that their component parts cannot be viewed in isolation from each other. Sometimes an analogy with a living organism is used. Consider a dog. It is composed of various limbs, organs, connective tissues, etc. In itself, each of these constitutive parts does very little; it is only when they are all connected together to form an actual living dog that we can appreciate the functions of each part and, crucially, how each part contributes to the overall functioning and performance of the dog. For functionalists like Durkheim, this is how we should view societies. We cannot take each part in isolation but rather need to consider each element of a society in relation to the whole.

Durkheim was fond of illustrating this point with seemingly unpromising examples. For example, in his classic text *The Rules of Sociological Method* (1964), he sought to illustrate that even crime – something we are accustomed to regarding as a social problem – makes a positive contribution to the overall functioning of society. Durkheim makes two important points about crime: first, that without crime (that is, the breaking of legally sanctioned social norms) there would be no innovation and societies would stagnate; secondly, that crime (and, importantly, its punishment) serves to

Émile Durkheim
(1858–1917)

heighten society's collective commitment to certain core values without which no society could exist. In other words, by punishing law-breakers, societies reinforce the boundaries of acceptable conduct and the commitment of their members to upholding these.

Although Durkheim had little to say about health care (he was, after all, writing at the turn of the nineteenth and twentieth centuries), later 'functionalist' sociologists have applied the idea of 'function' to various aspects of health and its management. Most famously perhaps was the work of Talcott Parsons on the 'sick role'. This is explored in more detail in chapter 3, but in essence Parsons argued that there was a socially defined 'role' which, in modern societies, individuals adopt when they become sick. The sick role has both rights and obligations attached to it: the sick individual has the *right* to refrain from work and other normal social duties, but also the *obligation* to seek appropriate medical advice and seek a speedy return to full health. For Parsons, this role – and note, it is the *role* and not the individuals who occupy it – ensures the smooth functioning of

Talcott Parsons
(1902–1979)

Photograph courtesy
American Sociological
Association

society. Disease and ill-health are potentially disruptive to society, and so the existence of the sick role ensures that this disruption is kept to a minimum.

Whilst there is something very appealing about the functionalist view of the world, it is not without criticisms. First of all, by concentrating almost exclusively on the positive social functions of institutions and roles, functionalists like Parsons have been accused of ignoring their negative or harmful consequences. For example, we might criticize the sick role by pointing out that in cases of chronic illness and disability, the adoption of this role discourages full participation in society and encourages dependency (see chapter 7).

Similarly, the prestige and independence accorded to the medical profession might encourage the abuse of medical power and the exploitation of patients for personal gain. Functionalism tends to ignore conflict at all levels. Secondly, functionalism – like other structural theories – can be accused of playing down the degree of independence which social actors actually possess. They tend to be treated as 'pawns' in a larger game, and are assumed to be unable to alter social institutions or roles as a result of their own independent actions.

Marxism   A second structural theory within sociology is Marxism – named after its founder, Karl Marx (1818–83). If functionalism can be accused of understating the degree of conflict in society, the same cannot be said of Marxism. For Marx, the starting point for social analysis was the inherent conflicts – economic in origin – which exist between social classes. For Marx, a social class is a group of people who share a common economic position. In all forms of pre-socialist

Karl Marx
(1818–1883)

means of production
the means by which
surpluses are extracted

bourgeoisie   those who
own the means of
production

proletariat   those who
sell their labour

ideologies   system of
ideas underlying social
action

society, Marx claimed, there were essentially two classes: those who
owned the **means of production** and those who did not. Much of
Marx's analysis concentrated on Capitalist society. Under Capitalism
the two classes for Marx are the **bourgeoisie** and the **proletariat**.

Marx claimed that the relationship between the two classes was
inevitably exploitative. Wage labourers (the proletariat) generate more
wealth for their employers than they are allowed to keep: in short, the
rich get richer at the expense of the poor. For Marx, this relationship
(part of the economic *infrastructure*) was fundamental to explaining the
nature of society. For him, and his followers, the nature of the
institutions and roles which make up a society can be explained with
reference to these fundamental inequalities, and their inherently volatile
nature. Let us take the example of religion. For Marx, religious beliefs
were **ideologies** and form part of the *superstructure* of society. Religion
under Capitalism (at least the sort of nineteenth-century industrial
capitalism about which Marx wrote) stressed that social inequalities
were just and, indeed, ordained by God. Just think of the words of the
hymn 'All things bright and beautiful': 'The rich man in his castle, The
poor man at his gate, God made them, high or lowly, And ordered their
estate.' These words epitomize the ideological function of religion: it
encourages the poor to accept their condition and to tolerate,
graciously, the superior economic position of the bourgeoisie.

There have been many attempts to apply Marxist theory to the
study of health and illness. One such account is offered by McKinlay
(1984), who suggests that under modern capitalism medicine, like
any other good or service, has become commodified. In other words,
medicine has become just another product which is bought and sold,
and out of which significant profits are generated for those who own
the means of production. Although McKinlay's analysis focuses on
the United States, where health care is explicitly provided primarily by
the private sector, it may still have resonance in countries like the UK
where health care is provided principally by the State. One illustration
of this is the way in which medical practice is influenced by the
activities of the large pharmaceutical companies. It could well be
argued that drugs are developed and marketed to medical
practitioners not out of a sense of social responsibility, but primarily
as a means of making profits – and pretty huge ones at that. Thus, the
motivating factor for the development of a drug therapy is not *need*
(or, arguably, far more research would have been done to develop
drugs to combat diseases of the developing world) but the potential
to generate profit. There is simply more money to be made from
treating 'diseases' of the rich, than diseases of the poor.

Action theories

Both of the approaches considered above have in common the idea
that wider social forces exert powerful influences on individual

behaviour. Although there are stronger and weaker formulations of the idea, the essential assumption shared by structural approaches is that they seek to explain patterns of individual behaviour in terms of the location of individuals within wider social structures. It is perhaps not surprising, therefore, that some sociologists have criticized these approaches for underestimating the role of individual action in society.

One of the first sociologists to develop a critique of what he saw as the overemphasis on structural determinants of action was Max Weber. Weber's sociology is rich and complex and encompasses a recognition that human beings do not act merely in response to wider social forces, but rather for conscious reasons and towards certain purposes. At its simplest it was not enough, for Weber, to say that events occur because social structures ordain them; instead he was

Max Weber
(1864–1920)

concerned to understand how individuals come to see the world in such a way that they voluntarily choose a particular course of action. To capture the importance of this dimension, Weber used the term *verstehen*, which translates, approximately, as 'empathetic understanding'. This means, in essence, that to gain a full understanding of an individual's action, we must look at the world from their point of view and, as it were, step into their shoes. This approach is evident in Weber's analysis of the origins of capitalism (Weber, 1958). Unlike Marx, who saw capitalism as the inevitable outcome of an economically driven process, Weber insisted that it was essential to put oneself in the shoes of the early capitalist entrepreneurs and to try to understand how their view of the world differed from those which had gone before. By doing this, Weber develops a theory of how a particular interpretation of the world – that of the early Calvinist Protestants – led to patterns of behaviour which resulted, eventually, in the emergence of capitalism as an economic system.

Symbolic interactionism   Whilst Weber was responsible for sensitizing sociologists to the need to account for social action from the point of view of the actor, it was a group of philosophers and sociologists from the University of Chicago who developed a major theory of social action which became known as *symbolic interactionism*. Undoubtedly the most significant figure in the development of this approach was George Herbert Mead.

The starting point for Mead's analysis was his recognition that human beings are fundamentally different from animals, not only because their behaviour is more complex, but because it is of a fundamentally different kind. Take a simple example. If a man kicks a dog, the response of the dog is predictable. It may be that the dog's previous experiences will influence its response, and that because of this, all dogs will not react in exactly the same way. Nevertheless, the essential feature of its response is that it is predictable and, in a genuine sense, automatic. Now imagine that you are standing at a bus stop and someone walks up to you and kicks you. How will you react? Your immediate reaction might be to say you would kick them back, but a moment's reflection will reveal that the situation is more complicated than this. In fact your reaction will be influenced by a wide range of factors. Who kicked you? If it was your best friend, you might assume either that it was intended as a prank, or perhaps that you had upset them and the kick was intended maliciously. Which you choose will depend on a further set of factors: what is the expression on their face, was the kick accompanied by any words, are there any background circumstances which might explain their anger with you, etc.? If the kick was from a stranger, then a whole new set of factors will need to be considered before you can decide how to react. The point is that unlike the dog – who reacts automatically – a

George Herbert
Mead (1863–1931)

human being can, and indeed, must, *choose* how to react. And, in
making that choice, they must place themselves in the position of the
kicker and interrogate their motives. We ask the question: why did
that person kick me? Only when we have done that do we select a
course of action and, as this example illustrates, that could vary from
laughter if we decide it was a prank by a friend, to extreme fear and
panic if we decided it was an assault by a malicious stranger. This
contrasts very sharply with the reaction of the dog which is
completely oblivious to the point of view of its attacker.

Mead (1934) describes this process as *taking the role of the other*.
Human beings do not merely react to situations in automatic and
predictable ways (as both functionalists and Marxists might be
accused of assuming) but rather *interpret* situations and select courses
of action according to this interpretation. For Mead this is because we

possess a social *self*. Mead's concept of self has two parts: the *I* and the *Me*. Although this idea is rather abstract, in essence it is quite simple. Think of the *Me* as the public part of yourself, which you place on display to others, and the *I* as the private part, which is accessible only to yourself. Now think about how you choose a course of action: what you are going to wear to an interview for example. You imagine yourself in your pinstripe suit, or your floral dress, and imagine how others will react to you. In other words, your *Me* has a 'conversation' with your *I* and, on the basis of taking the role of the other, you choose a course of action which suits your goals.

Activity 1.1   **Taking the role of the other**

(a)   Describe what is meant by 'taking the role of the other'.
(b)   Is taking the role of the other important to the provision of good nursing practice? What role does it play in developing reflective practice?
(c)   How easy is it to take the role of the other when nursing children, people with mental health problems or people with learning disabilities?

What all of this means is that symbolic interactionists tend to reject theories which see human beings as passive pawns in the play of wider social forces. Rather they are concerned with understanding how people interpret situations and how these interpretations influence their future conduct. It should be obvious that this approach introduces a significant element of uncertainty in our understanding of human action: indeed, for interactionists, human conduct is to a large extent unpredictable.

In summary, sociology is often described as multi-paradigmatic; this means that there are many different competing sociological explanations. Sociological theories are generally divided into theories of social structure, such as functionalism, or theories of social action, such as symbolic interactionism. The other chapters within this book will introduce you to some other important sociological theories, and it is worth remembering that all theories are concerned with the relationship between structure and action. For example, see chapters 5 and 10 for a discussion of feminist theories, chapter 6 for theories of ageing, chapter 7, which focuses on disability theory, and chapter 9, in which you will find a theoretical discussion of 'race' and 'ethnicity'.

Activity 1.2   **Nursing: menial and mundane?**

'If nursing involves anything more complex than the most menial of tasks, and if nurses enjoy any sort of decision-making capacities independent of medicine, then they require . . . knowledge on which to base their decisions about what sort of actions they should be taking, and when they should be taking them. In other words, nurses require a theoretical grounding for their actions. This, of course, says nothing about the sort of theory that should underpin nursing practice, specifically whether or not sociology is an appropriate theoretical source . . . The point to be made at this stage of the argument is that, given that nurses deal with a myriad of different people and a multiplicity of problems, using various, often complex methods, it is inconceivable that they would be capable of making informed decisions about care if they were not in possession of some sort of overarching model of their professional activity. In short, given the nature of their job, it is axiomatic that nurses require theoretical knowledge of some sort . . . The deprecation of nursing as mundane work is often articulated by identifying it as 'women's work' . . . nothing more than a public extension of private domestic labour, which in itself is seen as requiring little thought or skill.' (Porter, 1995, p. 1131)

(a)   Do you agree with the position expressed by Porter?
(b)   Should nurses just know how to do things or should they also understand the theory behind what they are doing?
(c)   Do you think that sociology can provide nurses with the theoretical underpinnings for practice?

4   Methods of sociological research

It is important to emphasize that the theoretical debates in sociology which have just been introduced have implications for how sociologists try to explore the social world and, indeed, for the kinds of 'facts' which they assume can be discovered. Whilst we cannot directly map a particular theory onto a method of research, we can nevertheless say that different theories lead much more naturally to one method than to another. There are various ways in which we can classify methods of sociological research, but probably the most helpful is to distinguish between quantitative and qualitative approaches.

Quantitative research

As the name suggests, quantitative research methods are those which concentrate on measurement. There are many different things which sociologists can try to measure. An obvious example is 'health', and this can be approached in a variety of ways. One way is to rely on data which are routinely collected by governments, such as public records of deaths. At its simplest (and this is essentially how much research on inequalities in health is carried out) we count the number of deaths per 1000 of the population, and compare death rates between different social groups. The numerical differences between groups then become the facts for sociologists to explain. Of course, we must be careful with this, because although the data are likely to be very reliable, we might question the extent to which merely being alive is equivalent to 'health'!

We might also choose to measure such things as 'attitudes' and behaviour. Commonly, attitudes are measured using *questionnaires* or *surveys* which ask respondents to place their response to various statements on a scale ranging from one extreme to another – these are called *Lickert* scales (see box 1.1). Although this is a quick and efficient method of gathering large amounts of data, we might question the extent to which the way in which someone responds to such a statement reflects how they would actually behave.

Box 1.1   **A Lickert scale**

Lickert scales are used in surveys and usually contain between three and nine categories, although five categories is the most common.

To what extent do you agree with the following statement?

I enjoy learning about the sociology of health

Strongly agree	Agree	Undecided	Disagree	Strongly disagree
(1)	(2)	(3)	(4)	(5)

Behaviour can be measured either directly or indirectly. Direct measurement refers to actual *observations* of behaviour (see McKeganey and Barnard, 1996). For example, a researcher interested in nurse–patient interaction might simply count the number of interactions which take place between a particular group of patients and a nurse over a set period of time. The researcher may be present for this – in which case their presence may affect the behaviour of the nurse and patients – or it could be done using covert recording equipment. Although this is likely to give a more accurate picture, it does raise the ethical question of whether researchers *should* observe

Activity 1.3   **A national survey on coronary heart disease**

The table below is taken from a national survey of NHS patients who have been treated for coronary heart disease; 194 NHS Trusts and over 84,000 patients in England took part in the survey.

	% of patients at **best** Trust indicating a problem	% of patients at **worst** Trust indicating a problem	National **average**
Access to care			
Emergency admissions: waiting			
10 minutes or more for assessment	19	63	43
Waiting for a bed after admission	6	65	28
Hospital environment			
Poor food	6	45	20
Treated on a mixed sex ward	4	77	35
Toilets not clean	16	69	34
Patient involvement			
Doctors/nurses talk as if patient not there	11	41	24
Co-ordination and continuity			
Patients not told name of doctor in charge	11	50	27
Discharge and transition			
No advice given about diet, etc.	10	55	39

Source: Department of Health, 1999, p. 5.

(a)   What does the table above tell us about patients' experiences of coronary heart disease?

(b)   What do you think might be the advantages of using a survey method of data collection? What are the disadvantages of this method?

(c)   What sort of data would emerge if qualitative methods were used and how would they differ from the data presented above?

behaviour without the knowledge of those they are observing. Such observations also tell us very little about the *quality* of the interactions which take place. Health research, especially research involving NHS patients and staff, is regulated by a Research Governance Framework (2001, 2003) to ensure that research is conducted to the highest ethical standard (see box 1.2).

Behaviour may also be measured indirectly, for example by relying on accounts given by respondents through self-completed

Box 1.2   **Research governance**

- Sets standards

- Defines mechanisms to deliver standards

- Describes monitoring and assessment arrangements

- Improves research quality and safeguards the public by:
  - enhancing ethical and scientific quality
  - promoting good practice
  - reducing adverse incidents and ensuring lessons are learned
  - preventing poor performance and misconduct

- Is for all those who:
  - participate in research
  - host research in their organization
  - fund research proposals or infrastructure
  - manage research
  - undertake research

- Is for managers and staff, in all professional groups, no matter how senior or junior

- Is for those working in all health and social care research environments, including:
  - primary care
  - secondary care
  - tertiary care
  - social care
  - public health

Source: Department of Health, 2003, p. 2.

questionnaires, or structured interviews (interviews in which a limited range of possible answers is offered to the interviewee) (see Blaxter, 1990). Although such an approach would allow us to explore aspects of behaviour which are not usually directly observable – such as an individual's pattern of drinking alcohol or smoking – the reliability of such responses may need to be questioned. Merely because an individual admits to drinking between 15 and 20 units of alcohol a week, it does not follow that they actually do! It would consequently be unwise always to assume that quantitative data gathered in this way is necessarily a faithful representation of how people actually behave.

Qualitative research

An alternative approach, which has a close affinity with social action theories, is to obtain qualitative data. Here the emphasis is not upon measurement, but rather on attempting to understand the world from the point of view of social actors. Qualitative researchers use a variety of data collection techniques but are generally united by their concern to understand the meanings which underlie the behaviour of those they study. For example, a qualitative researcher interested in nurse–patient interaction would be unlikely to want to count the number of interactions which take place, but rather would be interested in discovering what the interactions mean to both parties. This is because, from a social action point of view, it is these meanings which explain the actions of those involved.

There are a number of ways in which qualitative researchers attempt to understand the points of view of social actors. First there is *interviewing*. Qualitative researchers tend to employ either semi-structured interviews, or unstructured interviews (for example, see Watson, 2000). The first of these employs a pre-determined list of questions which is asked to each respondent and the second is based more loosely on a general set of issues. In both cases, the interviewer asks open-ended questions, and allows the respondent to answer in his or her own words. In both cases, too, the interviewer can respond to the answers given and ask additional or supplementary questions as appropriate. These forms of interviewing are more akin to a guided conversation than anything else, and the object is to allow the respondent to explore an issue or topic as it affects them. The intention is to allow the respondent's own emphases to come to the surface, and for the researcher to grasp the world from the respondent's point of view. Thus, in the case of nurse–patient interaction, a researcher might ask a patient simply: 'How do you find the nurses here?', and allow the respondent to talk freely about the things that are important to them.

Qualitative researchers also sometimes employ *participant observation* (see, for example, Maxwell, 1984). This means, essentially, that the researcher participates in the activity being studied in order to grasp it from the point of view of those involved. Participant observation may be either overt – in which the researcher's identity as a researcher is made known to all concerned – or covert – in which they conceal their identity. An overt participant observer interested in nurse–patient interaction might come to work on a particular ward as a nurse, and make observations from that standpoint, but only after declaring their research activity to their colleagues and patients. A covert observer might enter a ward posing as a patient, and observe the activity from that point of view. Clearly, the former runs the risk of influencing the behaviour of those they are studying. Conversely, whilst the covert observer might obtain a more faithful view of events, the ethical issues alluded to above are once again raised.

methodological pluralism use of more than one method of data collection

◄ Some researchers use what is called **methodological pluralism**. This approach recognizes that each method of data collection has its own strengths and weaknesses, and it can be used to build a fuller picture of social life (for example, see Barker, 1984). Whether one adopts a quantitative or qualitative strategy, or both, it is important that social researchers pay attention to issues of representativeness. Most research is carried out on samples, and, on the basis of data collected from a sample, generalizations are made to a wider population. A researcher who observes interactions between Nurse Jones and Mrs Smith, Mr Jenkins and Miss Shepherd, will want to say something general about the relationship between nurses and patients, not merely these four particular individuals. It is important, therefore, that in some sense the interactions observed are shown to be typical of interactions of that kind – or if they are not, how they differ from the typical should be explained.

Activity 1.4

Nursing and sociological research methods

(a) Consider the research issues below and think about which research methods you might adopt to explore these.

Children's perceptions of going into theatre
The housing needs of people with mental health problems
Patients' views of hospital food
Student nurses' perceptions of people with learning difficulties.

(b) Think of other research issues and identify which research methods you would use to investigate them.

So, whilst there are many research methods available to social researchers, the methods chosen, and whether they are quantitative or qualitative, will depend upon the theoretical approach that has been adopted. The internet has also opened up other opportunities for social research (for example, see O'Connor and Madge, 2001 or Fox and Roberts, 1999). In the following chapter you will be able to explore the role of sociological research within nursing in more depth (see, in particular, part iv).

Summary and Resources

Summary

- Sociology is concerned with the study of human societies.

- Sociology is distinct from 'common sense' because it challenges the obvious, and assessses evidence for and against any position taken. However, there is debate concerning the role of sociology within society. That is, should sociologists simply report what they see or should they be concerned with changing the social world around them?

- Research methods are generally described as either quantitative – which include methods such as questionnaires – or qualitative – which include semi-structured or unstructured interviews and participant observation.

- The choice of sociological research methods largely depends upon the theoretical approach adopted by the researcher.

Questions for Discussion

1 Should sociologists develop neutral understandings of the social world or should they seek to influence change?

2 Next time you are on placement ask yourself, 'What is going on here?' Describe what you are doing, or seeing, and then try to explain it.

3 What do you think are the main advantages and disadvantages of adopting methodological pluralism?

Further Reading

P. Abbott and R. Sapsford: *Research Methods for Nurses and the Caring Professions.* 2nd edn. Buckingham: Open University Press, 1998.
This is a useful resource exploring how and why nurses should get involved in and understand research. It examines different methods of data collection, for example interviewing, observation and surveys, and covers data analysis and writing up.

D. L. Patrick and G. Scambler: *Sociology as Applied to Medicine.* 5th edn. London: Saunders, 2003.
This is an excellent book which is easy to read and covers a range of health-related issues.

P. Taylor, J. Richardson, A. Yeo, I. Marsh, K. Trobe, A. Pilkington, G. Hughes and K. Sharp: *Sociology in Focus.* Ormskirk: Causeway Press, 1995.

If you are really struggling with sociology then this text could be for you. It is primarily intended for an A-Level audience but covers a broad range of sociological issues in an engaging way.

References

Annandale, E. 1998: *The Sociology of Health and Medicine: A Critical Introduction*. Cambridge: Polity.

Barker, E. 1984: *The Making of a Moonie*. Oxford: Blackwell.

Blaxter, M. 1990: *Health and Lifestyles*. London: Tavistock.

Department of Health 1999: *Coronary Heart Disease 1999. National Report. Summary of Key Findings*. London: DoH.

Department of Health 2003: *Draft Research Governance Framework for Health and Social Care*, 2nd edn. London: DoH.

Durkheim, E. 1964: *The Rules of Sociological Method*. New York: Free Press.

Fox, N. and Roberts, C. 1999: 'GPs in cyberspace: the sociology of a "virtual community".' *Sociological Review*, 47(4), 643–71.

Giddens, A. 1986: *Capitalism and Modern Social Theory*. Cambridge: Cambridge University Press.

Jewkes, Y. 2003: *Dot.cons: Crime, Deviance and Identity on the Internet*. Cullompton: Willan.

Maxwell, M. 1984: *The AA Experience: A Close Up View for Professionals*. New York: McGraw-Hill.

McKeganey, N. and Barnard, M. 1996: *Sex Work on the Streets: Prostitutes and their Clients*. Buckingham: Open University Press.

McKinlay, J. B. (ed.) 1984: *Issues in the Political Economy of Healthcare*. London: Tavistock Press.

Mead, G. H. 1934: *Mind, Self, and Society: From the Standpoint of a Social Behaviourist*. London: University of Chicago Press.

O'Connor, H. and Madge, C. 2001: 'Cyber-mothers: online synchronous interviewing using conferencing software.' *Sociological Research Online*, 5(4), www.socresonline.org.uk/5/4/o'connor.html.

Porter, S. 1995: 'Sociology and the nursing curriculum: a defence.' *Journal of Advanced Nursing*, 21(6), 1130–5.

Watson, J. 2000: *Male Bodies: Health, Culture and Identity*. Buckingham: Open University Press.

Weber, M. 1958: *The Protestant Ethic and the Spirit of Capitalism*. New York: Charles Scribner's Sons.

Weeks, J. and Holland, J. 1996: *Sexual Cultures: Communities, Values and Intimacy*. London: Macmillan.

2 Why Should Nurses Study Sociology?

Barbara Green

> **Key issues within this chapter**
>
> - The difference between sociology in nursing and sociology of nursing.
> - The value of developing sociological skills.
> - Using sociological skills in nursing practice.
> - Sociological knowledge: policy, practice and change.
>
> **By the end of this chapter you should be able to . . .**
>
> - Discuss the reasons why nurses should study sociology.
> - Understand the distinction between sociology of nursing and sociology in nursing.
> - Understand the value of sociological skills.
> - Discuss the role of sociological knowledge and the future of nursing practice.

1 Introduction

As your experience in clinical practice develops you will, no doubt, come across patients with a wide range of concerns that need to be understood. The main aim of this chapter is to demonstrate the practical relevance of sociology to nursing, and to explore how sociology may provide you with exciting new ways with which to understand the needs of your patients.

The next section discusses conceptual differences between sociology in nursing and sociology of nursing. Section 3 focuses on the **cognitive** skills that an appreciation of sociology may encourage, enabling you to positively shape and influence practice. Section 4 draws on empirical studies to demonstrate

cognitive relating to thinking processes

the role of sociology in exploring social issues in health and the social worlds of patients, nurses and other health care workers. The final section addresses the role of sociological knowledge in policy, practice and the future of nursing.

2 Sociology in nursing and sociology of nursing

There are two main types of sociological knowledge relevant to nurses: one is identified as sociology in nursing and the other as the sociology of nursing. Each type of knowledge has the scope to enable the 'ordinary' day-to-day work of nurses to be seen in a different light; it is this alternative perspective which is characteristic of sociology. Sociology encourages us to view everyday **phenomena** in a different way. It is like being given a new pair of glasses. This is sometimes referred to as **problematizing**; that is, what at first sight might seen unremarkable becomes problematic. More will be said about this later but first let us turn to the distinction between sociology in and of nursing.

phenomena states or processes that can be observed

problematizing looking beyond the obvious to seek an explanation

Sociology can be defined most simply as 'the study of societies' (Giddens, 1996, p. 7) (also see chapter 1 for a further discussion of defining sociology). A sociological approach to nursing locates the work of individual nurses squarely within a social context, rather than considering it in isolation. In general terms, when a sociological analysis is applied to the essence of individual health care experience, whether it be that of patients or health care workers, this is termed 'sociology in nursing'. 'The sociology of nursing' usually refers to issues affecting the profession as a whole, such as its occupational status, or recruitment and attrition problems (see chapter 4 for further discussion of nursing as an occupation).

3 Sociology: helping develop skills

Is sociology just 'common sense'?

It is important to clarify exactly how a knowledge of sociology can be of value to practising nurses. Can sociology be described as 'just common sense'? Let us consider what sociology does have to offer nursing practice.

In her treatment of the question, Hannah Cooke (1993, p. 215) describes sociology as an 'emancipatory discipline'. By this she means that nurses need to be self-critical and to question the long-held assumptions of the profession. This may seem difficult in the light of your limited practical experiences, or an unfamiliarity with academic study. Although 'training' still has a valuable part to play in nurse education, for example in the learning of practical skills such

Activity 2.1   **Sociology *in* nursing or sociology *of* nursing?**

Read items A and B and answer the questions below.

Item A   'The majority of the sample were positive about their choice of nursing as a career option [but] . . . almost a quarter of the sample held mixed views . . .

Examples of mixed views included: . . . 'I'm a little disappointed . . . it depends on the ward you're on. If you're on a good ward, nursing can be very good . . . but in other ward situations, you think, am I nothing but a bottom wiper?' (final year pre-registration student). '. . . a few regrets . . . looking back, eighteen is very young to go into nursing . . . after being qualified for two years, I became quite disillusioned and decided to move on.' (post-registration community student) . . .

'. . . I still enjoy nursing, but, maybe with hindsight, I may have chosen another course like banking or administration . . . it's very difficult in nursing, what with promotion and the salaries' (post-registration student).' (While and Blackman, 1998, p. 223)

Item B   'Parents are characterised as confederates in the "battle" against cancer; as fund raisers; and guardians of their children's identities. Little attention is given to parents' own needs . . . parents' descriptions bear little resemblance to newspaper accounts. Rather than the cheerful uncomplaining and 'brave' newspaper reports of children, parents report that children can be distressed, anguished and difficult to manage, especially when being encouraged to submit to painful and frightening medical interventions. Parents themselves experience a range of quality of life impairments, including severe role strain, but find it difficult to voice these because they have to negotiate prevailing discourses about the duties of parenthood . . . newspapers are more likely to represent children in idealised ways and to marginalise parents as resources solely for their child's benefit.' (Dixon-Woods et al., 2003, p. 143)

(a)   Identify whether items A and B portray sociology in nursing or sociology of nursing.

(b)   Think about the significance of the research findings in items A and B both for the individuals or groups under study, and for health care planners and policy makers.

(c)   How does the media represent children with cancer? What does item B tell us about the role of nurses working with cancer patients? Does the media represent the truth of people's experiences?

as aseptic or injection techniques, it is important to distinguish between this and the acquisition of a higher education, of which the study of sociology is an example. It is argued by Ross (1981), for example, that the concept of learning in education, as opposed to training, is characterized by discovery and transformation of thought, which suggests personal growth and a radical shift in previously held beliefs and values. Ellis (1992) describes this as a 'personal education'. Arguably, any academic discipline in its authentic form is a valuable experience for students on vocational courses, but classical authors of sociology, notably Wright Mills (1959) and Berger (1963), would argue that the subject holds a unique fascination and distinctiveness.

Wright Mills (1959, p. 7) coined the term 'sociological imagination' to describe his particular view of the sociological enterprise in his classic work of the same name. What he meant by this is the ability to shift one's thinking from one perspective to another, or possession of a certain quality of mind, open to different interpretations of phenomena. This can also be applied to the difference between education and training. As previously stated, we do need elements of training in nurse education, but there is an often quoted saying that 'dogs can be trained to jump through hoops', referring to the fact that people can be trained to do tasks without having to really think very much about them. The consequences of this in nursing can be, and have been, disastrous.

Conversely, the possession of this difference in quality of mind and approach to practice, when transferred into appropriate action by nurses, will arguably ensure the evidence base for practice required by the profession. But, more than this, it represents an approach to practice underpinned by critical thinking, analytic and questioning

---

Activity 2.2	Sociology and 'common sense'

(a) Explain your understanding of the term 'common sense'. Do you think that sociology is 'just common sense'? How useful is this term when talking to patients?

(b) Imagine a patient experiencing quite severe wound pain two days post-operatively following a cholecystectomy (gall bladder removal). Leaving aside the intervention of prescribed analgesia, what kind of social influences do you think might affect this person's reaction to pain?

(c) 'It is the capacity of sociology to take nurses temporarily "out of nursing" that represents one of its strongest attributes' (Mulholland, 1997, p. 850). What do you think that Mulholland means by this statement?

skills which is crucial to achieve the 'new futures for nursing' envisioned by Cooke (1993, p. 215) and arguably supported by recent government initiatives, such as the creation of new nurse leadership roles (Department of Health, 2000a).

So, what are these new futures likely to be? Why do nurses always seem to come 'back to basics'? What are the essentials of nursing care and do you need a degree to give a bedpan? The following subsection will demonstrate how a knowledge of sociology can help you in addressing such questions.

Nursing skills and reflective practice

Arguably, the development of reflective practice can bridge the theory–practice gap and there is a wealth of literature suggesting that sociology can play an important role in the development of reflective skills within nursing (see for example Williamson, 1999).

However, all of this relates to the broader question of what nursing is and how it might be defined. This is at a time when policy changes from both the government (DoH, 2000a) and professional bodies (RCN, 2003) indicate trends which lead away from the identification of 'hands-on' care as important, in terms of both status and financial reward. It is not a new issue: Christine Hancock (1991, p. 174), then the general secretary of the Royal College of Nursing, suggested that 'If qualified nurses are content to delegate the heart of their role to others, they should not be surprised if they are supplanted in the workforce'. This reflects a legitimate concern about the future of nursing, reiterated by Castledine (1998, p. 225) who argued that nurses should 'not become the technical substitutes of physicians'.

The changes in 'core' nursing tasks are attributed to increased patient turnover, a shortage of qualified nurses, the present system of nurse training and the fact that nurses are being constantly encouraged to take on more tasks currently carried out by doctors. Contemporary policy documents (Department of Health, 2000a, pp. 83–4) appear to reflect this latter scenario (of ten future nursing roles identified, several reflect skills more usually associated with the work of doctors than with that of nurses – see box 2.1), yet it is highly questionable how far such apparent merging of traditional professional boundaries is in the best interests of future nursing practice and, ultimately, the care of patients.

It is worth considering the question of why, despite the promotion of holistic care in nurse education for decades, nurses sometimes persist in attaching more importance to those aspects of care underpinned by medical science than to those influenced by social, **paradigms** systematic ◄ cultural, psychological, spiritual and emotional **paradigms** of
and coherent bodies of knowledge (this is discussed further in chapter 4).
knowledge

Box 2.1   **Chief Nursing Officer's ten future nursing roles**

- to order diagnostic investigations such as pathology tests and X-rays

- to make and receive referrals direct, say to a therapist or pain consultant

- to admit and discharge patients for specified conditions and with agreed protocols

- to manage patient caseloads, say for diabetes or rheumatology

- to run clinics, say, for ophthalmology or dermatology

- to prescribe medicines and treatments

- to carry out a wide range of resuscitation procedures including defibrillation

- to perform minor surgery and outpatient procedures

- to triage patients using the latest IT to the most appropriate health professional

- to take a lead in the way local health services are organised and in the way that they are run.'

Source: The NHS Plan (Department of Health, 2000).

Activity 2.3   **The 'stark reality' of care?**

'Few care processes are more complex than terminal care of the distressed, incontinent elderly patient. When I and my loved ones are sick or dying, I want our nurses to be caring, patient and tolerant – and well-educated into the bargain. But perhaps most policy makers have not experienced such situations and cannot imagine why a trained intellect is crucial, even when wiping a bottom.' (Salvage, 2001, p. 21)

(a)   Can you think of other examples of what Salvage describes as the 'stark reality' of hands-on care?

(b)   Why do you think that Salvage uses this term?

(c)   Do you agree that a trained intellect is crucial, even when wiping a bottom?

4   The role of sociological knowledge

The aim of this section is to illustrate the value of sociological knowledge and the role it plays in examining the realities of nursing practice. Recognizing the significance of an evidence base within modern nursing, this section draws on a range of empirical studies, all of which have something to tell nurses about their relationships with patients, informal carers and other health professionals, or about their role in the workplace. Building on the discussion of research methodologies presented in chapter 1, the two specific themes addressed below are:

1   In what ways sociological methods can be adopted within nursing research;
2   Why an understanding of sociological research methodology will aid nurses to interpret the validity and reliability of published research.

A key feature underpinning sociological research methods is the idea that things may not be what they seem. As Berger (1963) suggests, you are 'looking behind', or 'seeing through' and generally unmasking the common façades of everyday life. As Earle (2001, p. 14) argues in her discussion of the role of sociology within the therapies, sociologists take the everyday and the taken-for-granted and try to look beyond obvious explanations to gain a deeper understanding of contemporary social issues.

Ellis (1992) attempts to integrate knowledge from various academic disciplines with the theory and practice bases of interpersonal professions. Following on from his discussion of a 'personal education', his model of 'semantic conjunction' can also be useful. In application to nursing, this term simply suggests that the subject matter of sociology is useful to nurses because sociologists and nurses share some common interests and concerns. Nowhere is this more clearly illustrated than in the piece of classic sociological research – described in Jeffery's *Normal Rubbish* (1979) – a study based on interviews with doctors and observation of three English casualty departments.

Perceptions of patients in casualty departments

Jeffery's study has as much to tell nurses, doctors and anyone working with vulnerable or health-compromised individuals about the truth of their work today as when it was published. It provides insight into perceptions of patients and demonstrates at best a lack of care, and at worst the wholesale neglect of and infliction of (further) damage on certain groups of patients. Via a process of social construction, particular patients became categorized by doctors as 'normal rubbish' (see box 2.2). This is a good example of an interactionist approach to research (see chapter 1), in which individual actions are subject to scrutiny.

social construction   the way in which social reality is constructed by individuals and groups

Box 2.2

'Normal rubbish'

Trivia

Patients who 'casually' pop into casualty with conditions neither traumatic nor urgent are described as 'normal trivia'. They trivialize the emergency services by presenting with conditions which should be taken to the GP.

Drunks

'Normal drunks' are abusive and usually appear in the middle of the night. If they are brought in unconscious, normal drunks are often kept in as it is unclear whether they are sleeping off the drink or whether they have received a blow to the head.

Overdoses

A 'normal overdose' is usually female and perceived as a self-harmer rather than as a 'genuine' suicide. She is usually a regular and 'does it for attention'.

Tramps

'Normal tramps' smell and wear layers of rotten clothing. They usually come in during the night in winter and are just trying to find a bed for the night. They often pretend to be sick in order to achieve this.

(Other patients defined as 'normal rubbish' include 'nutcases', and smelly, dirty and obese people.)

Source: Jeffery, 1979, pp. 106–7.

Significant for the sociological study of nursing is that although Jeffrey confined his interviewing to doctors, it is made clear that other staff working in the department – such as nurses and porters – were in a process of collusion with the medical staff about the way these particular patients were viewed. It is shown in the following comment made by a porter to a doctor after a person identified by the department staff as a 'tramp' was seen in the casualty department and discharged by the doctor. A short time later he collapsed and died outside on the pavement. In order to allay the worries of the doctor concerned, the porter says: 'It's alright, sir, I've turned him round so

seminal   research is seminal if it has a determining influence on sociological thought

that it looks as though he was on his way to Casualty.' This seminal piece of sociological research, which so clearly demonstrates the interface between sociology and nursing, has a tremendous amount to say to nurses.

reliability   research is reliable if it can be repeated to produce the same results

Before the results of published research can be used as evidence for practice it must be scrutinised in an informed way for reliability and validity – terms which will become more familiar and meaningful to you in the future. For now, you are strongly advised to consolidate

validity   research is valid if it measures what it has set out to measure

| Activity 2.4 | **Normal rubbish: deviant patients in casualty departments** |

In Jeffery's study (1979) 'rubbish' was a category generated by the staff themselves. It was commonly used in discussions of the work and of the patients seen within the casualty environment:

'It's a thankless task, seeing all the rubbish, as we call it, coming through.'

'I wouldn't be making the same fuss in another job – it's only because it's mostly bloody crumble like women with insect bites.'

'I think the [city centre hospital] gets more of the rubbish – the drunks and that.'

(a) It is clear from this research that nurses working in the Casualty department shared the same attitude towards some patients as the doctors. If twenty-first-century nurses are educated to underpin their practice with theory, which specific aspects of the latter do you consider that the nurses of 1979 might not have been aware of?

(b) The full title of the article appears at the top of this extract. In what sense do you think that some patients are identified by the author as 'deviant'?

(c) It is clear from Jeffrey's study that some patients are regarded as 'legitimately sick' while others are not. How do you think this impacts on the concept of 'holistic' assessment and care within contemporary nursing?

your knowledge by reading – or re-reading – chapter 1 and perhaps carrying out some further reading on research methods of your own.

The remainder of this section continues the theme of exploring the realities of nursing work by focusing on more contemporary sociological research. Some comparisons between the studies will be self-evident as the chapter progresses and it is not the remit here to focus on them, but rather to identify and emphasize the value of sociological knowledge for practising nurses.

Researching the experiences of clients with learning difficulties

Richardson (2000) explores the social context of people with learning difficulties by interviewing six people living in nurse-managed community homes over a period of 18 months (group living is discussed further in chapter 12). Drawing on the social model of disability, which is discussed at length in chapter 7, he asks three questions (p. 1384):

1   what do people with learning difficulties, living in the community, have to say about their lives and experiences?

2   what are their views about the differences between their lives and those of non-disabled people?

3   how do disablist assumptions influence the lives of people with learning difficulties and nursing practice?

The significance of this research undoubtedly lies, in part, in its inclusion of people with learning difficulties as participants, thereby reversing the stereotypical notion that 'People corralled within the frame of learning difficulties are deemed incompetent, unable to adequately speak for themselves, and thus requiring care, protection and treatment' (Richardson, 2000, p. 1384).

As well as giving nurses valuable insight into participants' views, the research also reflects current policy initiatives for people with learning difficulties which are based on the principles of rights, independence, choice and inclusion. It is a useful illustration of the way that sociological research methods can be used by nurses to explore the experiences of specific client groups, enriching the practice base of nurses and others. The concept of research validity is implicit in Richardson's work through his focus on **autobiographical voice**.

autobiographical voice methodological approach which allows participants to tell their own stories

Whereas the two articles explored so far have addressed the experiences of patients or clients, the next takes a broader perspective and explores the role of nurses in the workplace, and their relationships with other health care workers.

Relationships between nurses and health care assistants

A study by Daykin and Clarke (2000) explores the relationships between nurses and health care assistants (HCAs) in the NHS. It is based on interviews in two English hospital wards providing medical care for older adults. A sociological account of nursing is given in which various perspectives are brought to bear on aspects of the individual nursing role and the profession as a whole.

The research was carried out to evaluate a new skill-mix project which increased the number of HCAs in proportion to registered nurses and simultaneously phased out the role of primary nurses. The aim of the research was to discover what impact the project had on the staff in relation to care delivery and working conditions.

The research identified a dichotomy between professional rhetoric and professional practice (Melia, 1987; Salvage, 1992; Walby and Greenwell, 1994); that is, what nurses *should* do and what *really* happens in practice. Despite nurses heralding the concept of holistic care as reflecting best practice, the researchers found that in the context of the new skill mix described above, a hierarchical division of labour emerged between the two groups. This resulted in care

Box 2.3	Rhetoric vs reality

Perceptions of the skill–mix project

- a threat to the holistic delivery of care;

- detrimental to the quality of care;

- a threat to the ability to apply sophisticated skills of assessment and analysis.

Realities of the skill–mix project in practice

- Staff shortages and resource constraints prevented skill–mix teams;

- qualified nurses worked below their actual skill levels;

- a hierarchical division of labour emerged.

Source: Daykin and Clarke, 2000, pp. 353–4.

organization by selectivity of work and task allocation. Box 2.3 outlines some of the key findings.

The exposure of some of the realities of nursing practice necessarily suggests that the registered nurses did not want to deliver the essentials of hands-on care in keeping with the philosophy of primary nursing and holistic care delivery, but rather that when faced with the realities of financial constraints, staffing shortages, and so on, there is a clear theory–practice gap.

From these observations, the authors provide significant insights into the perceived value of nursing's professionalization project, described by the authors as an attempt by nurses to 'renegotiate their relationship with the state and secure greater recognition and professional status' (Daykin and Clarke, 2000, p. 349). A key factor in this has traditionally been the claim to a distinct knowledge base from which to develop theoretical models of holistic care, professional autonomy, the selection and ownership of higher-status technical skills, and the scope to renegotiate role boundaries between nursing and doctoring.

Taking up this issue, Daykin and Clarke suggest that given the current social context for care, where the likelihood is that nurses and HCAs will continue to do a significant proportion of the 24-hour, round-the-clock work, the profession might serve itself better by adopting an inclusive rather than a hierarchical 'outgroup' attitude towards this group of co-workers. Not only would this help to preserve the knowledge and ownership of nursing care for nurses but it would also acknowledge the crucial contribution to care made by health care assistants.

A further useful insight to emerge from this research is that although the two groups were generally united in their opposition to the skill-mix project, a range of 'multiple and apparently contradictory viewpoints' (p. 353) was expressed about respective workplace roles; health care assistants were, on the whole, far more enthusiastic than the nurses. Daykin and Clarke attribute this again to the dichotomy between ownership of a perceived appropriate theoretical stance for nursing and the social reality of the care context, steeped as it is in day-to-day issues of staff shortages, economies of scale and financial stringency. Using a structural analysis, they suggest that a possible effect of this apparent disunity of ideas and purpose (expressed in the article as 'ambivalence') is that it represents potential for exploitation by managers if perceived as a weakness of nursing systems. Likely manifestations could be (further) imposition of routinized, ritualistic, deskilled, task-based work systems onto hospital staff in direct contradiction to the concept of professional autonomy so prized by some sections of the contemporary nursing workforce.

Daykin and Clarke (2000) challenge some of the existing premises on which current nursing practice is based, and make an invaluable contribution to the sociology of nursing. For example, they explore issues that have the potential to raise awareness of professionalization among practising nurses; such awareness is a prerequisite for the necessary action to achieve future changes, which will ultimately improve the experiences of both patients and health care workers.

5   Sociological knowledge: policy, practice and change

The final section of this chapter considers the role of sociological knowledge in achieving change through policy and practice. The idea of change is perhaps daunting to those of you as yet unfamiliar with many aspects of the nursing role, yet today it is endemic to health care – the pace is relentless and the future likely to be characterized by increasing complexity and paradox (UKCC, 1999). In this chapter the significance of sociological knowledge and its unique capacity to expose areas of both nursing practice and policy where positive change might be achieved has been emphasized, but important questions remain about how far this fundamental truth is likely to be either recognized or acted upon. The issues are considered here as a critical future challenge to you as students of nursing on the threshold of dynamic and fulfilling careers.

Being a student of nursing

The role of a student nurse is often not easy, Wakefield (2000) has explored some current tensions. The 'old-school' traditional structural hierarchy of sister, staff nurse, enrolled nurse and nursing auxiliary, where student nurses at least had the security of a clearly defined role, has been replaced by an alternative system in which students and HCAs compete for authority, status and knowledge – this situation at times characterized by discord and friction (Wakefield, 2000). Qualification is not likely to herald the disappearance of these conflicts, as the anomalies between the latter group and qualified nurses described by Daykin and Clarke (2000) demonstrate.

In this context, then, what price change? As inexperienced practitioners in the nursing environment and in relation to clinical competency, you may feel relatively powerless within practice settings (Hart et al., 2003), a less than ideal situation from which to think about the possibilities for practice and policy change in relation to sociology. The fact that the issues *are* raised here, however, clearly presupposes critical thinking skills and reflects a protracted debate in nurse education about the relative merits of theory and practice in the curriculum, and how they should be organized.

The role of sociology

The problem of theory–practice integration in the nursing curriculum is particularly pertinent in relation to sociology. One reason for this is that sociology is concerned with the exposure of key issues such as health inequalities. Not only do these have a detrimental effect on individual health care but they may be constructed and maintained at an institutional level and subject to covert structural processes of which individual practitioners may be unaware. It is useful here to return to Wright Mills (1959), who argued that the sociological imagination is at its most effective in making the distinction between personal troubles and public issues, the idea that what may appear to be an individual phenomenon is actually highly determined by social structures. This is demonstrated to very good effect in chapter 7. Consequently it can be argued that the crux of the sociological enterprise for nursing should be a focused concern with the concept of power and power relations at all levels of health care practice, an area where nurses have traditionally been invisible.

All this implies that in order for nurses to use sociological knowledge effectively both in nursing and at the broader policy level, a more overtly political focus and agenda to the inclusion of sociology in the nursing curriculum is required. My guess is that this may be immediately problematic to some students in terms of their own current values and beliefs about educational requirements for nursing and it is worth thinking at this stage how comfortably (or not) these ideas about sociology sit with your own views as novice practitioners. Clifford (2000), in her discussion of international politics and nurse education, suggests that although issues of politics, power and control have been of concern to nurses, there has, to date, not been a framework in place to integrate one with the other. Important questions of direction and focus remain, as professional boundaries become blurred and traditional roles disappear.

Nursing – the future

Meeting the physical, psychological, social, cultural, emotional and spiritual needs of others, often at their times of greatest vulnerability and distress, has been misnamed the 'dirty work' of nursing. Arguably, this 'dirty work' is, in fact, a privilege, and yet it is precisely these uniquely caring aspects of nursing which seem currently to be under threat.

The structural location of nurse education in universities, its dance with academia, professionalizing agendas and new role developments coterminous with interdisciplinary working (Department of Health, 2000a) should not be allowed to detract from the core humanistic value of care on which nursing has historically been built. This in the context of increasing numbers of medical tasks being undertaken by nurses, arguably at a cost to true role *expansion* as opposed to mere extension by default. Encouragingly, there is now some evidence that the argument 'while there is much to be gained from humanizing medicine, there is nothing to be gained from medicalizing nursing' (Farmer, 1995, p. 794) is being recognized at policy level (Royal College of Nursing, 2003; Department of Health, 2002). Acknowledgement in the new NHS job evaluation scheme, **emotional labour** regulation of one's own and other people's feelings ◄ 'Agenda for Change', that 'emotional effort' – or **emotional labour** – will be assessed as one of 16 factors to determine revised pay scales is a significant step in the right direction.

Nevertheless, these are transitional times for nursing and, despite the centrality of the client within health care (Department of Health, 1999; 2000b), there are signs that the concerns voiced about the profession's future by its leaders are now shared by others, including the public.

If in the future nurses are to develop the critical awareness and analytic skill that will prepare them for action to rescind this situation, there has never been a greater need to embrace sociology as a means of illuminating their unique position for determining and influencing the overall quality of health care, practice and policy. As stated earlier, it is an issue of power relations; this is the stance taken by Clifford (2000), arguing that in an age of globalization nurses need to think politically, beyond their own boundaries of practice and towards becoming the key health policy makers of this century. Sociology has a great deal to contribute to the knowledge base for this role expansion in nursing, but it is also a truism that 'nursing as knowledge remains unrevealed to many people' (Hegyvary, 2003, p. 104) and this is where we return to the perennial issue of nursing definition. There have been many books and policy documents addressing the question of how nursing is to be defined, but it will all remain at the level of paper, policy and a superficial political correctness unless nurses are prepared to *act powerfully* to reclaim their professional role in the delivery of essential, humanistic care. It must be professional nurses who, first, identify these unique elements of best practice and, second, exert the power and influence to control the resources necessary to claim and deliver it.

Summary and Resources

Summary

- The difference between education and training is identified, as is the role of sociology in facilitating the development of reflexivity in nurses.

- The 'sociological imagination' can enable nurses to move beyond common-sense explanations to the development of a more critical approach to nursing practice.

- Sociological research and research methods are useful for nurses both in conducting their own research and in being able to evaluate research to help inform evidence-based practice.

- Nurses can use sociological knowledge as a means of empowerment and to help determine the future of the profession for the advantage of patients.

Questions for Discussion

1   In Jeffrey's (1979) study, good patients were defined in terms of their medical characteristics and whether they fulfilled at least one of the following criteria:

    (a) they allowed the doctor to practise the skills necessary for passing exams;
    (b) they allowed the doctor to practise his/her speciality;
    (c) they tested the doctor's competence and maturity.

    Reflect on this and consider the extent to which nurses and other health care workers categorize patients in this way.

2   Do you agree with Daykin and Clarke (2000), amongst others, who argue that there is a discrepancy between nursing practice and professional rhetoric?

3   Try to identify other sociological studies and explore the contribution they make to your nursing practice in particular, and to nursing as a profession, more generally.

Further Reading

There is continuous debate in the literature on whether nurses should or should not study sociology. You may be interested in reading these and might like to look at one or more of the following:
H. Cooke: 'Why teach sociology?' Nurse Education Today, 13(3), 210–17, 1993; **K. Sharp: 'Why indeed should we teach sociology? A response**

to Hannah Cooke', *Nurse Education Today*, 15, 52–5, 1995; **S. Porter: 'Why teach sociology? A contribution to the debate'**, *Nurse Education Today*, 16(3), 170–4, 1996; **D. Allen: Review article: nursing and sociology: an uneasy marriage?** *Sociology of Health and Illness*, 23(3), 386–96, 2001.

A. Williams, H. Cooke and C. May: *Sociology, Nursing and Health.* Oxford: Butterworth Heinemann, 1998.
This is a useful little book and you may find the Introduction a short but relevant summary of some of the key issues.

References

Berger, P. 1963: *Invitation to Sociology: A Humanistic Perspective.* London: Penguin.

Castledine, G. 1998: The future of specialist and advanced practice. In G. Castledine and P. McGee (eds), *Advanced and Specialist Nursing Practice*, Oxford: Blackwell, pp. 225–32.

Clifford, C. 2000: 'International politics and nursing education: power and control.' *Nurse Education Today*, 20, 4–9.

Cooke, H. 1993: 'Why teach sociology?' *Nurse Education Today*, 13, 210–16.

Daykin, N. and Clarke, B. 2000: '"They'll still get the bodily care." Discourses of care and relationships between nurses and health care assistants in the NHS.' *Sociology of Health and Illness*, 22(3), 349–63.

Dixon-Woods, M., Seale, C., Young, B., Findlay, M. and Heney, D. 2003: 'Representing childhood cancer: accounts from newspapers and parents.' *Sociology of Health and Illness*, 25(2), 143–64.

Department of Health 1999: *Making a Difference.* London: HMSO.

Department of Health 2000a: *The NHS Plan.* London: HMSO.

Department of Health 2000b: *National Service Framework for Older People.* London: HMSO.

Department of Health 2002: *Agenda for Change.* London: HMSO.

Earle, S. 2001: 'Teaching sociology within the speech and language therapy curriculum.' *Education for Health*, 14(3), 383–91.

Ellis, R. 1992: An action-focused curriculum for the interpersonal professions. In R. Barnett (ed.), *Learning to Effect*, Buckingham: Open University Press, pp. 69–86.

Farmer, E. 1995: 'Medicine and nursing: a marriage for the 21st century?' *British Journal of Nursing*, 4(14), 793–4.

Giddens, A. 1996: *Sociology.* Cambridge: Polity.

Hancock, C. 1991: 'Support workers in the UK.' *International Nursing Review*, 38(6), 172–5.

Hart, A., Hall, V. and Henwood, F. 2003: 'Helping health and social "inequalities imagination": a model for use in education and practice.' *Journal of Advanced Nursing*, 41(5), 480–9.

Hegyvary, S. T. 2003: 'Foundations of professional power.' *Journal of Nursing Scholarship*, 2, 104.

Jeffery, R. 1979: 'Normal rubbish: deviant patients in casualty departments.' *Sociology of Health and Illness*, 1(1), 90–108.

Melia, K. 1987: *Learning and Working*. London: Tavistock.

Mulholland, J. 1997: 'Assimilating sociology: critical reflections on the "Sociology in nursing" debate.' *Journal of Advanced Nursing*, 25, 844–52.

Richardson, M. 2000: 'How we live: participatory research with six people with learning difficulties.' *Journal of Advanced Nursing*, 32(6), 1383–95.

Ross, S. 1981: *Learning Discovery*. London: Gordon and Breach.

Royal College of Nursing 2003: *The Future Nurse: Interim Report*. London: RCN.

Salvage, J. 1992: *The Politics of Nursing*. London: Heinemann.

Salvage, J. 2001: 'New Year Revolution.' *Nursing Times*, 97(1), 21.

UKCC 1999: *Fitness for Practice: Report of the Commission for Education*. London: UK Central Council for Nursing, Midwifery and Health Visiting.

Wakefield, A. 2000: 'Tensions experienced by nurses in a changed NHS culture.' *Nurse Education Today*, 20(7), 571–8.

Walby, S. and Greenwell, J. (with Lesley MacKay and Keith Soothill) 1994: *Medicine and Nursing: Professions in a Changing Health Service*. London: Sage.

While, A. and Blackman, C. 1998: 'Reflections on nursing as a career choice'. *Journal of Nursing Management*, 6, 231–7.

Williamson, G. 1999: 'Teaching sociology to nurses: exploring the debate.' *Journal of Clinical Nursing*, 8, 269–74.

Wright Mills, C. 1959: *The Sociological Imagination*. London: Oxford University Press.

3 What is Health?

Sarah Earle

Key issues within this chapter

- Defining health.
- Models of health.
- Social influences on health and disease.
- Experiences of illness, sickness and disease.
- Nursing, health and holism.

By the end of this chapter you should be able to . . .

- Review official and lay definitions of health.
- Compare and contrast the biomedical and social models of health.
- Give an account of how health and disease are influenced by social factors.
- Understand illness behaviour, sickness and stigma.
- Evaluate a holistic approach to nursing practice.

---

1 Introduction

Did you know that poorer people will die sooner and suffer more ill-health than those who are wealthier? Did you know that women are more likely than men to be diagnosed with mental illness, and that older and disabled people are the two groups in society most likely to be refused life-saving treatment? Arguably, these facts are social rather than biological, and although the majority of sociologists would not deny the biological nature of disease, most would agree that our understanding, treatment and experience of health and ill-health are socially influenced. Sociologists would also agree that the production and distribution of disease are social, rather than biological, matters. The purpose of this chapter is to explore how sociology can help us to understand health better, taking as its foundation the position put forward by Turner, who argues that health and ill-health are 'fundamentally a social state of affairs' (1995, p. 37).

2   Defining health

It may seem easy, but defining health is actually quite hard. Before you read on think about what health means to you. Is your definition of health the same as that of your colleague? Kelman has argued that 'perhaps the most perplexing and ambiguous issue in the study of health since its inception centuries or millennia ago, is its definition' (1975, p. 625), but defining health is essential if we are to understand it and deliver appropriate services. It is an important issue for nurses because, to help the patient achieve health, nurses should have some understanding of the factors that contribute to 'healthiness'.

Official definitions of health

Health is often defined quite simply as an 'absence of disease'. This has been one of the most pervasive official definitions of health in the modern Western world and is one that can be frequently found within medical documentation, government reports and legislation.

Do you believe that this is a good way of defining health? How does it compare with your own definition? Health as an 'absence of disease' is also the cornerstone of the biomedical model – discussed in more detail below – which, in spite of its limits (Bowling, 1991), is the most influential model of health within modern medicine. To describe health in this way is to define it in extremely negative terms; that is, you are considered healthy only if you are not suffering from any disease. However, research suggests that it is possible to feel healthy even when suffering from severe disease (for example, see Blaxter and Patterson, 1982).

Another commonly used definition is that of the World Health Organization, which defines health as 'not merely the absence of disease, but a state of complete physical, mental, spiritual and social well-being' (WHO, 1948, p. 1). This marks a shift away from defining health solely in relation to disease and reflects an acceptance of some of the other factors that influence health. It also reflects a more positive, although idealistic, approach to health. Here, health is perceived as a goal. Lupton has suggested that this overriding concern with health has reached the proportions of a social movement which she calls **healthism**, arguing that 'the pursuit of

healthism   a personal, cultural and political health movement

health has become an end in itself, rather than a means to an end' (1995, p. 70).

More recently health has been defined as a resource:

> To reach a state of complete physical, mental and social wellbeing, an individual or group must be able to identify and to realize aspirations, to satisfy needs, and to change or cope with the environment. Health is, therefore, seen as a resource for everyday life, not the objective of living. Health is a positive concept emphasizing social and personal resources, as well as physical capacities. (WHO, 1986, p.1)

As you can see, here health is still regarded as a positive concept, but rather than being an end in itself, it is seen as a resource for living, a means to an end.

Lay definitions of health

Although sociologists are interested in unpacking official definitions of health, in the last 25 years or so sociologists have become

lay definitions of health beliefs based on individual experience or folk knowledge, as opposed to 'official' or medical definitions of health

◄ interested in understanding **lay definitions of health** and have attempted to demonstrate how an understanding of lay definitions can be useful for health professionals. This approach has been influenced by theories of social action (see chapter 1) which are concerned with the meaning that individuals give to their own experiences.

Official, or medical, definitions are thought to be based on

universal and generalizable knowledge knowledge assumed to be common

◄ **universal and generalizable knowledge** in scientific terms, whereas lay definitions are thought to be unscientific and based on individual experience. Although our own health beliefs are 'unscientific', they are essential to the way in which we make sense of health and illness and, indeed, the very subjective nature of health has led some researchers to argue that lay definitions are the only valid measure of health. Williams and Popay (1994) suggest that lay definitions of health and illness are organized in the following way:

1   they do not mimic medical views;
2   they are logical and coherent;
3   they are biographical (based on lived experience);
4   they are culturally framed within particular systems of belief.

Some researchers have also argued that whilst lay definitions of health and illness do not mimic medical views, scientific knowledge can become part of the views of lay people (Blaxter, 1990). However, other sociologists disagree and argue that subjective definitions of health can be very individual, eccentric, contradictory and just plain wrong!

One of the most comprehensive studies of lay health in the UK is the Health and Lifestyles Survey (Blaxter, 1990) involving 9,000

Activity 3.1		**Lay 'experts'?**

'It seems reasonably clear (from where we stand now) that during the latter stages of the 20th century medical practitioners have been required to be more clearly and openly accountable to lay assessment and more sensitive to patient viewpoints than had previously been the case . . . These trends are undoubtedly related to the operation of other, wider, forces that have led to a challenge on the expertise of professionals. Thus medicine – as with so many other forms of professional activity – has been confronted by something of a legitimation crisis. . . . [There has been] an increased interest in what lay people have to offer by way of knowledge of health and illness [and] there has been a tendency to argue that lay knowledge can be every bit as valuable as professional knowledge. . . . patients can have extensive knowledge of their own lives and the conditions in which they live . . . they can (and sometimes have to) turn themselves into experts in order to challenge medical hegemony. . . . [However,] for the most part, lay people are not experts . . . What is more they can often be plain wrong about the causes, course and management of common forms of disease and illness.' (Prior, 2003, pp. 42–5)

(a) Do you think that nurses are accountable to lay assessment and sensitive to patient viewpoints?

(b) Does the concept of the 'lay expert' apply equally to all groups of patients (e.g. patients with learning disabilities or mental health problems, or children). If not, try to explain why this is the case.

(c) How and why might the expertise of health professionals be challenged? Have you ever felt that your expertise has been challenged by patients? If so, how did this make you feel?

individuals. This survey asked individuals the following questions: (1) Think of someone you know who is very healthy. Who are you thinking of? How old are they? What makes you call them healthy? (2) At times people are healthier than at other times. What is it like when you are healthy? An analysis of responses to these questions revealed ten major lay concepts of health (see box 3.1).

Lay definitions of health are variable and are, generally speaking, often dependent on factors including age, gender, disability, and so on (see part II). Activity 3.2 asks you to consider children's definitions of health.

Box 3.1   **The Health and Lifestyles Survey: lay concepts of health**

Health as not ill
You are healthy when you do not have any symptoms of disease. A concept popular amongst people of all ages, but particularly older people, and most likely to be used to describe others.

Health as absence of disease/health despite disease
A definition focusing on disease and drawing on a medical model of health, most commonly used by those who described themselves as feeling healthy despite disease.

Health as a reserve
The idea that someone is healthy due to an inborn reserve of health.

Health as behaviour
A healthy person was often defined in terms of their healthy behaviour and the phrase was most likely to be used to describe the behaviour of others.

Health as physical fitness
The concept of fitness was most commonly referred to by men of all ages, although young men tended to stress strength and the ability to play sports. Young women rarely mentioned sports but often mentioned being (or feeling) slim.

Health as energy
Having energy, vitality and enthusiasm was seen by women and older men as important.

Health as a social relationship
This concept was particularly important to women who saw health in terms of having good relationships with others or the ability to help other people.

Health as function
This refers to being able to carry on with everyday tasks and was often used to describe a man. It was also used to refer to older people who could get along despite advanced age.

Health as psycho-social well-being
This category often included some of the other concepts of health, such as health as energy, or health as social relationships. However, some individuals saw health purely as a state of mind.

Negative answers
A small group of respondents were not able to define being healthy. Most of these were not interested in 'healthy behaviour' (adapted from Blaxter, 1990).

Activity 3.2   **Understanding children's perceptions of health and ill-health**

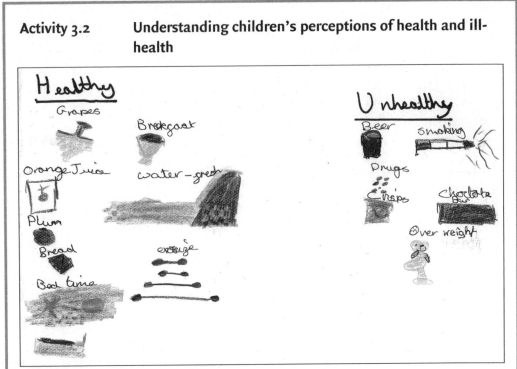

Drawing courtesy of Maria Perry, aged 9

(a)   Drawing techniques are often used as a research method when exploring children's perceptions of health and illness. What does the picture above tell us about children's views of what makes us healthy and unhealthy?

(b)   What are the implications of this for nursing children?

(c)   In what other ways could nurses encourage children to discuss their experiences of health and illness?

3   Understanding models of health

Models of health offer nurses different ways of thinking about health and how they might offer care to patients. These models differ because they identify distinct causes of illness, sickness and disease and therefore offer different suggestions for the prevention of ill-health. In this section we examine the biomedical and the social models of health.

The biomedical model

The present system of medical knowledge within modern Western societies is commonly known as the biomedical, or medical, model. This model is characterized by several features (see box 3.2).

Box 3.2   **Characteristics of the biomedical model**

- Health is the absence of disease, and disease is the absence of health;

- illness can be reduced to disordered bodily functions within the individual;

- health services treat sick and disabled people largely within specialisms (e.g. paediatrics, obstetrics, podiatry, etc.);

- health services are remedial and curative;

- each disease is thought to be caused by a specific (potentially identifiable) pathogen, often leading to an over-reliance on pharmacological intervention;

- the production of medical knowledge via the use of 'scientific' research methods is valued over the use of qualitative research methodologies;

- health professionals are the 'experts' with the power to diagnose disease and decide on treatment.

The biomedical model has been and, some would argue, still is dominant within modern Western healthcare. However, this perspective is not without its critics. Blaxter (1990), for example, argues that the medical model of health does not always focus narrowly on biomedical science and that more holistic concepts of health are also part of medical practice. Nonetheless, there are many who believe that a biomedical model is outmoded and unhelpful and that it acts as a 'strait-jacket' for thinking about nursing care (Allott and Robb, 1998).

In response to this, alternative models of health have emerged. The next model we consider here is the social model, which identifies the role of social factors in the production and distribution of disease.

The social model

The social model of health has developed largely as a critique of the biomedical model and whilst sociologists have offered various critiques of biomedicine, three characteristics are usually central (Annandale, 1998).

Firstly, the social model assumes that health and disease are socially produced; biomedicine is reductionist because it assumes that disease is natural and located in the individual. Secondly, biomedicine is characterized by the 'doctrine of specific aetiology', which refers to how the biomedical model assumes a direct relationship between pathology and disease. In contrast, the social model recognizes that other factors play a role in determining who becomes sick and why. In fact, some commentators suggest that diseases should be classified by their social causes rather than by specific aetiology.

The third critique of the biomedical model relates to the belief that medicine is neutral and scientific; this is referred to as scientific neutrality. However, the social model emphasizes the way in which health care is influenced by a range of social factors. For example, a study of the treatment of patients in accident and emergency (Jeffery, 1979) demonstrates that certain patients – 'drunks, tramps, nutcases and self-harmers' – are not treated equally (see chapter 3).

The social model cannot tell you how to nurse patients, but it can provide you with interesting insights into the causes of disease and the way in which social factors help to shape treatment. Whilst the biomedical model focuses on the diagnosis and treatment of disease, the social model focuses more on prevention and is a useful model for nurses involved in health promotion (see also chapter 10 for a discussion of a public health model) and those interested in promoting patient empowerment and partnership.

4   Social influences on health and disease

One of the most significant contributions that medical sociologists have made has been to show how health and disease are influenced by a range of social factors. In this section, we examine the relationship between changing patterns of disease and changes within society. We then explore the way in which the process of ◄ medicalization has had a significant impact on the way we define health and disease.

medicalization The process by which aspects of everyday life enter the domain of the medical profession to become medical problems requiring diagnosis, treatment and cure

Changing patterns of disease

Various writers have suggested that modern societies have passed through three distinct types of disease patterns:

1   *Disease in pre-agricultural societies* Before 10,000 BC, evidence suggests that most people died from environmental and safety hazards, for example, exposure. Infectious diseases and so-called 'lifestyle diseases' such as heart disease and cancer were uncommon.
2   *Disease in agricultural societies* A range of infectious diseases such as tuberculosis and cholera were the most common.
3   *Disease in the modern industrial era* By the mid-twentieth century infectious diseases were no longer a primary cause of death. Chronic and degenerative diseases, such as cancer, diabetes and cardiovascular disease have become more common. (Fitzpatrick, 1986)

Why do you think that disease prevalence has changed? It could be argued that advances in medicine and health care provision have had a significant impact on the prevalence of certain diseases. This may be true in some instances, but sociologists would suggest that if we examine the changing patterns of disease, we can see that they are closely related to social and economic factors. If, for example, we take the case of tuberculosis (TB), official records show that death rates began to fall quite rapidly in the first half of the nineteenth century, well before the introduction of chemotherapy treatments in the 1940s and the BCG vaccination in the 1950s, and even before the identification in 1882 of the tubercle bacillus (Department of Health, 1998). It is worth noting, however, that reported cases of TB in England and Wales have risen by 27 per cent in the last 10 years (www.doh.gov.uk), particularly amongst migrants from Africa and the Indian subcontinent and refugees. Again, this reinforces the view that social and economic factors can have a significant influence on patterns of disease.

The medicalization of everyday life

Zola (1973, p. 261) argues that 'if anything can be shown in some way to affect the workings of the body and to a lesser extent the mind, then it can be labelled . . . "a medical problem"'. Sociologists have shown that healthy physical processes, such as menstruation, pregnancy and the menopause have become medicalized (see, for example, Martin, 1989 and Oakley, 1984). Sociologists also suggest that what comes to be defined as a disease is dependent upon a range of political and economic factors. For example, Hunt (1994) and Lee (1998) point out that the construction of the menopause as an 'oestrogen-deficiency' disease developed in the 1960s and was strongly associated with the development and availability of hormone replacement therapies. Gambling (Rossol, 2001), alcoholism (May, 2001) and sexuality (Hart and Wellings, 2002) have been similarly medicalized.

However, just as some healthy processes become medicalized, others become demedicalized. A good example of this is the demedicalization of homosexuality, which until 1973 was listed in the Diagnostic and Statistical Manual of Mental Disorders as a pathological psychiatric disorder. This demonstrates how the labelling of a process or behaviour as a disease is only tangentially related to a distinct physiological or psychological occurrence.

Medicalization has been widely criticized by sociologists. For example, Ivan Illich (1976) developed a theory of **iatrogenesis** in which he identifies three types:

iatrogenesis 'doctor-caused illness'

clinical *iatrogenesis*: where individuals are directly harmed by medicine through treatment itself or through the ineffectiveness or the uncertainty of treatment. This also includes the actions taken by

---

Activity 3.3   **Medical 'problems'?**

BALDNESS	FRECKLES	UGLINESS
JET LAG	GAP TEETH	SMOKING
SHORTNESS	NAIL-BITING	BAD BREATH
SHYNESS	INSOMNIA	HAIRINESS

(a)   Think about the list of 'problems' identified above. Are these medical problems?

(b)   Who decides what becomes a medical problem and why?

(c)   What are the implications of medicalizing such problems, for individuals, for health professionals and for society as a whole?

---

doctors to avoid litigation, for example: an increase in the caesarean section rate.

social iatrogenesis: where individuals become dependent upon medicine for their understanding of natural processes and become consumers of health care.

structural iatrogenesis: where the nature of society renders people unable to care for themselves and each other without recourse to medical attention and medical concepts of health. It also refers to the way that individuals strive to achieve better health.

surveillance
observation of
individuals/populations

The rise of health **surveillance** is becoming an increasingly normal part of everyday life for those living in the modern Western world and is another example of how people's lives have become medicalized. For example, most women will, at some time in their life, be asked when they had their last cervical smear (Howson, 1998), and men are now under increasing surveillance for diseases such as prostate and testicular cancers.

There is a great deal of evidence to suggest that surveillance serves to create tension and anxiety (for example, see Press, Fishman and Koenig, 2000). However, some commentators have argued that the process of medicalization is not so widespread, and despite the expectation that individuals will comply with various aspects of medicalization and surveillance, there is a great deal of 'non-compliance' in participation and treatment (Stevenson et al., 2002).

5   Experiences of illness, sickness and disease

Whilst some sociologists have focused on the social factors influencing health and disease, others are more interested in the experiences of ill-health, recognizing that responses to illness are influenced by our own experiences as much as by the biological symptoms of disease (see chapter 2 for a discussion of the role of sociology in nursing).

Illness behaviour

Everybody feels ill at some point in their lives but, as we all know from our own experiences, when we feel ill we don't always go to the doctor. Research suggests that most of the illness in society goes unreported as health professionals only get to see a very small proportion of all illness; this is known as the clinical iceberg.

illness behaviour
actions of people when
they feel unwell

Sociologists are interested in **illness behaviour** because, as Robinson argues, 'a person's readiness to consider himself, or another, ill cannot adequately be explained by reference to the severity of the symptomatic person's condition' (1971, p. 7). In other words, it would appear that the nature of disease has little relation to the likelihood of someone consulting their doctor. In a classic study carried out by Mechanic (1968) a wide range of factors were seen to contribute to seeking help (see box 3.3).

Box 3.3 **Factors influencing help-seeking behaviour**

- The extent to which symptoms are visible and recognizable.

- Their perceived seriousness and consequent levels of anxiety.

- The extent to which they impact on the sufferer's life.

- Their perceived frequency and persistence.

- The degree to which an individual can tolerate them.

- Knowledge about what symptoms may mean.

- Competing needs.

- Competing explanations for the symptoms.

- Availability of treatment and assistance.

In this context, we can see that individuals respond not just to a symptom, but to the meaning of the symptom and the effect that it has on their lives. Zola (1973) suggests that there are triggers which lead individuals to seek medical attention:

1 *The occurrence of an interpersonal crisis* This refers to the presence of an event of some kind which calls attention to the symptoms, forcing the individual to do something about them.
2 *The perceived interference with social or personal relations* The extent to which symptoms seem to interfere, at any given time, with daily life.
3 *Sanctioning* This refers to when the decision to seek medical attention lies with another person, who sanctions that decision.
4 *The perceived interference with vocational or physical activity* This usually refers to the extent to which symptoms seem to interfere with work.

5   *The temporalizing of symptomatology* The setting of external time criteria, after which treatment will be sought.

The sick role

sick role   the sanctioning of illness within society

deviance   behaviour considered unacceptable within a society or culture

As we have seen above, not everyone that is ill will receive treatment for their illness, but sociologists have argued that those who do, achieve the status 'sick'. The concept of the **sick role** was developed by the sociologist Talcott Parsons who believed that illness is 'partly biologically and partly socially defined' (1991, p. 431). Parsons argued that ill-health was a form of **deviance** and disruptive to the normal functioning of society (also see chapter 1). He also suggested that the role of medicine was to ensure that only those who are truly ill are permitted to adopt the sick role. Those who claim to be sick without being truly ill are perceived as skivers and malingerers. Entering the sick role, therefore, requires that certain conditions be met; these are best understood in terms of expectations placed on the patient and on the doctor (see box 3.4).

Box 3.4 **On being sick: roles and responsibilities**

The patient

• is exempted from normal social role responsibilities, e.g. going to work;

• is not responsible for his or her illness and cannot get well on his or her own, cannot, for example, just 'pull himself together';

• must want to get better; and

• must seek technically competent help and comply with treatment.

The doctor

• must act in a professional and objective manner;

• must do everything possible to help the patient recover;

• must be well trained and competent;

• must be able to examine the patient.

The concept of the sick role is perceived to be a good explanation for temporary bouts of ill-health to which any of us could reasonably become susceptible, for example, influenza or a broken leg. However, there have been many criticisms of the concept of a sick role especially in relation to its inability to explain the experiences of specific groups, for example those with chronic illness (see chapter 7).

Stigma and disease

stigma social disgrace attached to any condition

The sociology of **stigma** and disease has been particularly influenced by the work of Erving Goffman (1963) who argued that stigma is a powerful discrediting label that can change, and 'spoil', the way in which the person is viewed. Goffman's work is influenced by theories of social action (see chapter 1) and the view that individuals are active agents within the social world.

Goffman argues that there are two types of condition: discrediting conditions, which are conditions that are clearly visible to others, for example eczema, psoriasis, physical impairments, or stammering, and discreditable conditions, those that are usually not visible to others, or can be easily concealed, for example epilepsy, HIV, depression, or diabetes. The attention given to people with Down's Syndrome provides us with a good example of the distinction between discrediting and discreditable conditions. Generally speaking, Down's Syndrome is a discrediting condition as the facial features of the individual are distinct from those of other people, thus immediately stigmatizing that person. Media reports have highlighted cases of parents who are seeking cosmetic surgery for their children with Down's Syndrome arguing that it is the visibility of this condition which leads to stigma, rather than the condition itself. Arguably, by changing the visible aspects of Down's Syndrome parents are turning a discrediting condition into a discreditable one. The ethics of this type of surgery on children are strongly disputed by organizations such as the Down's Syndrome Association (downs-syndrome.org.uk).

Some conditions lead to stigma because of the moral attributes associated with a particular condition. HIV and AIDS are commonly associated with sexual promiscuity, drug use and homosexuality (Rhodes and Cusick, 2000) so individuals who are HIV-positive often experience what is known as 'enacted' stigma (Scambler, 1989); this is the type of stigma that leads to actual discrimination. People with other types of condition may experience 'felt' stigma which refers more to feelings of shame rather than to an actual experience of discrimination. This is often relevant to people with rectal cancer (Macdonald and Anderson, 1984), epilepsy (Scambler, 1989) and prostatic problems (Pateman and Johnson, 2000).

Lastly, it is worth considering the concept of 'courtesy stigma', which has been defined as a 'tendency for stigma to spread from the stigmatised individual to his close connections' (Goffman, 1963, p. 30). There is evidence, for example, that the family and carers of those with Alzheimer's disease often experience considerable embarrassment and shame (Blum, 1991; MacRae, 1999). Courtesy stigma is also relevant to others, including the family and friends of those with mental health problems and learning disabilities.

Activity 3.4   **Autism and stigma**

The extract below presents data from a study of stigma among parents of children with high functioning autism living in the Brisbane metropolitan region of Australia. The data were collected using in-depth semi-structured interviews with 53 parents whose children were aged between five and 26 years (Gray, 2002, pp. 739–41).

'As a mother, when a child sort of acts up . . . you don't want him to do it, because it's a bit embarrassing. And you feel like it reflects on you a little bit. I mean I'm intelligent enough to know that that's not the case, but it's very difficult to take yourself away from the situation.' [mother]

'I have always taken my boys shopping, always . . . Oh it's a disaster initially. [My son] threw a jar of vegemite at an elderly old lady who smiled at him, you know . . . they look at me as though I'm a mother who obviously isn't very good at being a mother.' [mother]

'Occasionally we'd ask [some] family down and we'd have a drink or whatever, but we never got invited [back] . . . we never seem to be reciprocated. They don't say, "Well, come over". So, yes, you do feel like they've sort of judged and thought, "Give them a miss".' [father]

'We went on . . . camp and we were pretty apprehensive about going . . . We were the only ones with an autistic child and . . . he performed in front of all those people there and had to take charge. And he called me an idiot in front of all those people, and swearing started to come out, and everybody just freezes. Everybody is just embarrassed.' [mother]

(a)   What kinds of stigma are being experienced by these parents of autistic children?

(b)   Why might mothers be more likely than fathers to experience stigma?

(c)   Do you think that nurses contribute to the stigma experienced by patients and their relatives or carers? Can you think of any examples from practice?

(d)   What role can nurses play in enabling patients and their carers to live with stigma?

6 Health, holism and nursing

Sociology can provide nurses with a great deal of insight into the social factors that contribute to health and illness, but it is not surprising that some nurses and other health professionals feel that this is nothing to do with them. However, although nursing is still predominantly situated within a biomedical model of health, it is widely acknowledged that contemporary nursing is also influenced by the notion of holistic care. However, the exact nature of this term is not always clear and it can be subject to numerous interpretations.

What is holistic care?

In very general terms, holistic care has been equated with the biopsychosocial model, or as Wynne et al. (1997, p. 471) have argued, a holistic approach is underpinned by an 'acceptance that health is determined and defined by inter-related social, psychological and biological factors'. Other commentators have defined **holism** in nursing as an understanding that 'the whole is greater than the sum of its parts'; this is known as whole-person holism (Kolcaba, 1997). Other definitions of holism also exist; for example, Patterson argues that holism 'implies mind, body and spirit' (1998, p. 289).

holism an approach which seeks to move away from a biomedical model

Holistic care: rhetoric or reality?

However holism is defined, the question of whether nurses do, in fact, deliver holistic care has also been widely discussed in the literature (for example, Wynne et al., 1997). Whilst the provision of nursing care within a holistic framework provides an idealistic picture of the role of the nurse, it must be acknowledged that nursing work is both 'messy and contingent' (Williams et al., 1998, p. 122). For example, a lack of resources can limit the amount of time that nurses devote to each individual patient, which interferes with the provision of holistic care. Some sociologists argue that for the vast majority of nursing work, it is the pathological and dysfunctional body that remains the primary focus. However, it is important to consider why the concept of holistic care has become so popular within nursing. May (1992) suggests that it is a way of defining what nursing is and what nurses do, adding emotional and intellectual value to nursing work. Indeed, Radwin (1996) claims that knowing the patient is fundamental and marks expertise in nursing. Other sociologists are more sceptical and suggest that the concept of holism is simply another way in which medicine attempts to gain control over people's lives (Armstrong, 1986). However, if nurses continue to adopt a holistic model of patient care then this clearly demonstrates the role of sociology in understanding the social world.

Summary and Resources

Summary

- Official definitions of health have changed over time but the most pervasive is that of health as an absence of disease.

- The biomedical model is dominant within Western health care and is characterized by the belief that illness can be reduced to the existence of a specific pathogen.

- The social model developed as a critique of the biomedical model and highlights the importance of social factors in understanding health and illness. The types of disease prevalent within any society are related to social, political and economic factors.

- There are many reasons to explain why people who feel ill do not go to the doctor, including the stigma associated with some conditions.

- Holistic care is characterized by the emphasis on the physical, social, psychological and spiritual needs of the person. Holism is widely accepted within nursing but questioned by sociologists.

Questions for Discussion

1. In what ways does specialization within nursing reinforce a medical model of health and illness?

2. Think about Illich's theory of iatrogenesis and consider it in relation to (a) breast enhancement, and (b) sadness.

3. How far do you think that Parsons's concept of the sick role can be used to explain ill-health amongst the following groups: older people who care for ageing spouses; fat children; and people with myalgic encephalomyelitis (ME)?

4. Do you agree that a holistic approach makes nursing more emotionally and intellectually rewarding?

Further Reading

E. Annandale: *The Sociology of Health and Medicine: A Critical Introduction.* Cambridge: Polity, 1998.
This book explores issues in much more depth but may be useful once you have mastered the material presented here.

M. Blaxter: *Health and Lifestyles.* London: Routledge. 1990.
Health and Lifestyles provides an excellent and comprehensive discussion of lay definitions of health.

S. Nettleton: *The Sociology of Health and Illness.* Cambridge: Polity, 1995.
This text will enable you to follow up on some of the themes identified within this chapter. Chapter 2 ('The social construction of medical knowledge') and chapter 3 ('Lay health beliefs, lifestyles and risk') are particularly useful.

References

Allott, M. and Robb, M. 1998: *Understanding Health and Social Care: An Introductory Reader.* London: Sage.

Annandale, E. 1998: *The Sociology of Health and Medicine: A Critical Introduction.* Cambridge: Polity.

Armstrong, D. 1986: 'The problem of the whole-person in holistic medicine.' *Holistic Medicine,* 1, 27–36.

Blaxter, M. 1990: *Health and Lifestyles.* London: Routledge.

Blaxter, M. and Patterson, E. 1982: *Mothers and Daughters: A Three-Generational Study of Health Attitudes and Behaviour.* London: Heinemann.

Blum, N. S. 1991: 'The management of stigma by Alzheimer family caregivers.' *Journal of Contemporary Ethnography,* 20, 263–84.

Bowling, A. 1991: *Measuring Health – A Review of Quality of Life Measurement Scales.* Buckingham: Open University Press.

Department of Health 1998: *The Interdepartmental Working Group on Tuberculosis. The Prevention and Control of Tuberculosis in the United Kingdom.* London: DoH.

Fitzpatrick, R. M. 1986: Society and changing patterns of disease. In D. L. Patrick and G. Scambler (eds), *Sociology as Applied to Medicine,* 2nd edn, London: Ballière Tindall, pp. 16–39.

Goffman, E. 1963: *Stigma: Notes on the Management of a Spoiled Identity.* Englewood Cliffs, NJ: Prentice-Hall.

Gray, D. E. 2002: '"Everybody just freezes. Everybody is just embarrassed": felt and enacted stigma among parents of children with high functioning autism.' *Sociology of Health and Illness,* 24(6), 734–49.

Hart, G. and Wellings, K. 2002: 'Sexual behaviour and its medicalisation: in sickness and in health'. *British Medical Journal,* April, 324, 896–900.

Howson, A. 1998: Embodied obligation: the female body and health surveillance. In S. Nettleton and J. Watson (eds), *The Body in Everyday Life,* London: Routledge, pp. 218–40.

Hunt, K. 1994: A 'cure for all ills?' Constructions of the menopause and the chequered fortunes of hormone replacement therapy. In S. Wilkinson and C. Kitzinger (eds), *Women and Health: Feminist Perspectives,* London: Taylor and Francis, pp. 141–65.

Illich, I. 1976: *The Limits to Medicine.* London: Penguin.

Jeffery, R. 1979: 'Normal rubbish: deviant patients in casualty departments.' *Sociology of Health and Illness*, 1(1), 90–108.

Kelman, S. 1975: 'The social nature of the definition problem in health.' *International Journal of Health Services*, 5(4), 625–42.

Kolcaba, R. 1997: 'The primary holism in nursing.' *Journal of Advanced Nursing*, 25, 290–6.

Lee, C. 1998: *Women's Health: Psychological and Social Perspectives.* London: Sage.

Lupton, D. 1995: *The Imperative of Health.* London: Sage.

Macdonald, L. and Anderson, H. 1984: 'Stigma in patients with rectal cancer: a community study.' *Journal of Epidemiology and Community Health*, 38, 284–90.

MacRae, H. 1999: 'Managing courtesy stigma: the case of Alzheimer's Disease.' *Sociology of Health and Illness*, 21(1), 54–70.

Martin, E. 1989: *The Woman in the Body: A Cultural Analysis of Reproduction.* Buckingham: Open University Press.

May, C. 1992: 'Nursing work, nursing knowledge and the subjectification of the patient.' *Sociology of Health and Illness*, 14, 307–15.

May, C. 2001: 'Pathology, identity and the social construction of alcohol dependence.' *Sociology*, 35(2), 385–401.

Mechanic, D. 1968: *Medical Sociology.* New York: Free Press.

Oakley, A. 1984: *The Captured Womb: A History of the Medical Care of Pregnant Women.* Oxford: Blackwell.

Parsons, T. 1991: *The Social System.* London: Routledge.

Pateman, B. and Johnson, M. 2000: 'Men's lived experiences following transurethral prostatectomy for benign prostatic hypertrophy.' *Journal of Advanced Nursing*, 31(1), 51–8.

Patterson, E. F. 1998: 'The philosophy and physics of holistic health care: spiritual healing as workable interpretation.' *Journal of Advanced Nursing*, 27, 287–93.

Press, N., Fishman, J. R. and Koenig, B. A. 2000: 'Collective fear, individualized risk: the social and cultural context of genetic testing for breast cancer.' *Nursing Ethics*, 7(3), 237–49.

Prior, L. 2003: 'Belief, knowledge and expertise: the emergence of the lay expert in medical sociology.' *Sociology of Health and Illness*, 25, silver anniversary issue.

Radwin, L. E. 1996: 'Knowing the patient: a review of research on an emerging concept.' *Journal of Advanced Nursing*, 23, 1142–6.

Rhodes, T. and Cusick, L. 2000: 'Love and intimacy in relationship risk management: HIV positive people and their sexual partners.' *Sociology of Health and Illness*, 22(1), 1–26.

Robinson, D. 1971: *The Process of Becoming Ill.* London: Routledge.

Rossol, J. 2001: 'The medicalization of deviance as an interactive achievement: the construction of compulsive gambling.' *Symbolic Interaction*, 24(3), 315–41.

Scambler, G. 1989: *Epilepsy.* London: Routledge.

Stevenson, F., Britten, N., Barry, C. A., Bradley, C. P. and Barber, N. 2002: 'Perceptions of legitimacy: the influence on medicine taking and prescribing.' *Health*, 6(1), 85–104.

Turner, B. S. 1995: *Medical Power and Social Knowledge*, 2nd edn. London: Sage.

Williams, A., Cooke, H. and May, C. 1998: *Sociology, Nursing and Health*. Oxford: Butterworth Heinemann.

Willliams, G. and Popay, J. 1994: Lay knowledge and the privilege of experience. In J. Gabe, D. Kelleher and G. Williams (eds), *Challenging Medicine*, London: Routledge, pp. 118–39.

WHO 1948: Preamble to the constitution of the World Health Organization as adopted by the International Health Conference, New York, 19–22 June 1946 by the representatives of 61 states (Official Records of the World Health Organization, no. 2, p. 100) and entered into force on 7 April 1948. Geneva: World Health Organization.

WHO 1986: Ottawa Charter for Health Promotion First International Conference, Ottawa, 21 November 1986 – who/hpr/hep/95.1. Charter adopted at an international conference on health promotion – The Move Towards a New Public Health, November 17–21, 1986. Ottawa, Ontario: World Health Organization.

Wynne, N., Brand, S. and Smith, R. 1997: 'Incomplete holism in pre-registration nurse education: the position of the biological sciences.' *Journal of Advanced Nursing*, 26, 470–4.

Zola, I. K. 1973: 'Pathways to the doctor – from person to patient.' *Social Science and Medicine*, 7, 766–89.

4 Nursing as an Occupation

Elaine Denny

Key issues within this chapter

- The origins of nursing.
- Nursing and gender.
- Socialization into nursing.
- Nursing within the health division of labour.
- Nurse education.

By the end of this chapter you should be able to . . .

- Understand the link between the history of nursing and its present construction.
- Discuss the effects of gender stereotypes on nursing.
- Identify the mechanisms by which nurses internalize the values of the occupation.
- Discuss nursing's place within the health division of labour.
- Understand the role played by education in the production of nurses.

---

1   Introduction

When you decided to become a nurse your decision was probably based on an idea of what you thought that nursing was. This in turn is likely to involve the work that nurses do, or nursing tasks. As you progress through your nurse education your ideas about the role of nursing may change, as the reality of the job begins to influence your thinking. You may become less certain that you really know what nursing is.

This is not surprising, as nurses and academics have debated for many years the question 'What is nursing?' Is it an art or a science? Does it possess a discrete body of knowledge? The debates continue, and to date no one has devised a universally agreed definition of nursing.

If we begin by considering nursing's origins and the influences on its development, we can begin to see why 'nursing' is such a problematic concept. The chapter will continue the theme raised in chapter 2, which highlighted the concept of a sociology of nursing, that is, it will examine the occupation of nursing and the structural influences on it, particularly gender, socialization and the division of labour.

2   The origins of nursing

Nursing in a form that would be recognizable to us today began in the nineteenth century, but has been in existence since ancient times. Before the dissolution of the monasteries in England and Wales in the sixteenth century monks would care for people in need, and the care of military casualties was until the mid-nineteenth century carried out by men.

The majority of care of the elderly, the sick, and women during and after childbirth was, however, undertaken by a variety of healers, mainly female, such as handy women and midwives, and by other women as part of their domestic role. In hospitals nurses were mainly concerned with domestic duties, and although they had the reputation of being drunken, dishonest and promiscuous, there is evidence that many hospitals strove to employ respectable working women (Dingwall et al., 1988). More skilled roles were undertaken by male apothecaries, dressers and medical students. Within the 'madhouses' and asylums, which housed those we would today describe as having mental health problems or learning disability, men dominated, as control and constraint were the main duties, so a gender division of labour was apparent within institutions, based on the type of work carried out.

During the nineteenth century as the UK industrialized and became a more urban society, care became institutionalized and medicine developed into a unified and collegiate profession. A different type of worker was needed on hospital wards to observe the patient's condition and to report it accurately, and to be trustworthy in carrying out the doctor's instructions when he was not present. Within Victorian patriarchal society it was considered that female nurses who conformed to the ideal of acquiescent and subservient femininity could carry out this role, yet would not threaten the doctor's authority as male workers might (Rafferty, 1995). Nursing has always been defined and constructed by its relationship to medicine (Denny, 2003) and changes in the medical profession acted as a catalyst for developments in nursing.

This shift in the nursing role could not have occurred without another change within Victorian society. From 1851 the census showed an excess of women over men. The middle-class woman, who was brought up to manage the domestic sphere, did not have the skills necessary to support herself financially. University education and entry into the emerging professions was barred to women until the end of the century, so the only occupations available to them were those of companion or governess.

To attract middle-class women into nursing with the aim of transforming it into a professional occupation, the hygiene and

The author's mother, a trained psychiatric nurse c.1944. Notice the uniform, which was adopted from the traditional general nurse uniform

domestic elements of the nursing role were redefined as scientific (Rafferty, 1996), and training schemes modelled on medical training were introduced. Initially this was confined to the voluntary hospitals, but the ethos spread to other forms of institution (see photograph). Asylums and children's hospitals began to regard a training in general nursing as superior to a specialist training, and by the early twentieth century had made it a requirement for promotion above staff nurse level.

Nurse registration, with its separate registers for children's nurses, asylum nurses and male nurses amongst others, served to reinforce these hierarchical divisions within nursing.

The call for nurse registration was made by those who wanted to develop nursing as a profession, and opposed by those who perceived nursing as a vocation, with 'character' as the primary requirement. Witz (1992) called the campaign for registration a female **professional project** in that pro-registrationists were attempting to create an autonomous occupation for women, on a par with medicine, aiming for **occupational closure**. Although registration was introduced in 1919 nursing failed to gain autonomy or control of entry to the occupation. The General Nursing Council (GNC) set up to certify nurses was a body with few powers.

professional project an attempt by an occupation to become a profession, using strategies aimed at enhancing power and status

occupational closure the monopoly of work to maintain power and status over other occupational groups

In summary, nursing evolved over the course of the nineteenth century from the female domestic role of caring, in a subservient position to medicine, to a more skilled occupation which was attempting to professionalize. A hierarchy of nursing specialisms developed, with the values originally associated with general nursing being adopted by other areas of nursing.

3 Men in nursing

If nursing has traditionally been viewed as 'women's work', what does this mean for men who take up nursing as a career? In the past men mainly worked in areas such as psychiatry or the military, which were not associated with the feminine caring roles of female nurses. As men have moved into other areas of nursing (moves often resisted by female nurse leaders) certain suspicions have been raised about their motives. Evans (1997) states that, within patriarchal society, men in nursing, although in a minority, are given a special and privileged status. They gain power disproportionate to their numbers, and dominate in elite specialisms and administrative positions, which are considered more reflective of masculine values. Williams (1995) notes that male nurses in her American study felt that physicians treated them better than their female colleagues. For example, they would call an assertive male nurse 'strong' but an assertive female nurse 'a bitch'. She also found that stereotypes of men as possessing leadership qualities, technical prowess and physical strength gave them an advantage in recruitment and promotion. This advantage was furthered by the view that married status led to permanence in men's careers, but not in women's.

In the UK men constitute around 10 per cent of the nursing workforce (a percentage that has remained more or less unchanged over the past 20 years) yet hold over 40 per cent of senior management and education posts (Miers, 2000). Williams (1995) argues that men view nursing differently from women, and move into management as a way of reinforcing their masculinity. She further states that as well as advantage men also encounter discriminatory treatment based on gender stereotypes. Williams (1994) has summed up the stereotype of male nurses as lazy, on the glass escalator, or gay. Evans (2002) adds that the stereotype of male nurses as gay is compounded by the stereotype of gay men as deviant and sexually predatory. This is particularly difficult when men are working with vulnerable groups such as children or people with learning disabilities.

In a small qualitative study by Evans (2002) on the experience of men in nursing, touch was identified as central to the practice of nursing, yet problematic for male nurses. The participants in the study had to learn to feel comfortable with expressions of caring not previously practised, but this exposed them to the risk of misinterpretation and accusations of inappropriate behaviour. 'Unlike women's touch which is considered a natural extension of women's traditional caregiver role, men's touch is surrounded by suspicion that implies that men nurses' motives for touching are not care oriented, but sexual in nature' (Evans 2002, p. 446). Men may therefore gravitate to areas that require less intimate touching of patients, and in so doing avoid having to confront the stereotypes.

The view of nursing as a female occupation has proved problematic for men entering nursing, as stereotypes of masculine and feminine qualities can lead to the motivation of men in nursing being questioned. On the other hand those same stereotypes can lead to men experiencing advantage in recruitment and promotion.

4 Socialization into nursing

The first time you went on placement and someone called you 'nurse' it probably felt rather strange; you may even have felt an impostor. By the end of your education you will feel quite comfortable with the term, not only because you will have more knowledge and be confident in carrying out the work, but also because you will have internalized the values and attitudes of nursing.

The way that this occurs has been demonstrated by two sociological studies.

Davis in 1975 described the way in which over the course of training students are socialized into nursing. Davis states that the socialization of student nurses is 'the process by which the student passes from identification with a "lay" to a "professional" culture' (Davis 1975, p. 116).

He argues that the socialization process comprises six stages during which the nurse passes from 'lay innocence', when his or her imagery of nursing is that shaped by previous perceptions, to 'stable internalization' where the self-image of students is that of a professional nurse.

More recently, Melia (1987) studied student nurses' experiences of education and training, and found a division existed between the way that nursing was represented in college and the way it was practised on the wards. This is often referred to as the 'theory–practice gap', examples of which were given in chapter 2. Students learned to manage this tension by adopting strategies which allowed them to fit in on the wards. Melia identifies five categories by which students achieve this (see box 4.1).

In describing the way in which student nurses internalize the values of nursing and begin to identify themselves as members of the occupation, Davis and Melia show how this is not just the result of increasing nursing knowledge, but also a social process in which the student learns the shared norms of nursing.

Box 4.1 **Strategies adopted by student nurses**

- 'Learning the rules' is concerned with the way in which students pass as workers to the satisfaction of permanent workers on the ward.

- 'Getting the work done' describes how nursing work is organized and achieved on hospital wards. Clarke (1978) found that student nurses feel they are judged by their success in 'learning the ropes' and 'getting through the work', in other words by how soon they can function effectively within the ward routine.

- Student nurses have to achieve the above within the constraints of the dual role of the third category, 'learning and working', although the situation has changed somewhat with student nurses achieving supernumerary status.

- 'Just passing through' reflects on the student's transient status, with the consequent relearning of the first and second categories on each new placement.

- Another consequence of the transient experience is the fifth category of 'nursing in the dark' where students find that they are not always given the information about patients that the permanent staff possess.

Source: Adapted from Melia, 1987.

Activity 4.1 **Socialization into nursing**

(Melia's study was carried out before nursing moved into higher education, and nurses became supernumerary.)
Think about a placement that you have done.

(a) How well does each of Melia's categories apply to your experience?

(b) Do different types of placement (e.g. hospital, community, group home) have different rules and different ways of 'getting the work done'?

(c) Discuss your experience with someone from a different branch of nursing.

5 Nursing within the health division of labour

Profession and professionalization

Although the image of nursing as women's work described in section 2 persists, and 90 per cent of the nursing workforce is female, the position of nursing within the health division of labour today is more complex than that described above.

In order to examine nursing's place within the health division of labour, it is useful to review the concept of profession as it has traditionally been defined within sociology, and to consider whether we need a new way of looking at occupations in order to explain the development of nursing practice.

Sociological definitions have tended to view professions as particular types of occupation which possess specific traits or attributes that distinguish them, and give them a higher status within society. Typically these include public service, an ethical code, and some form of training in higher education (see, for example, Millerson, 1964). This Functionalist approach is criticized as being ahistorical, that is, it does not question how or why these occupations were able to achieve these attributes and become dominant in an area of work. Neither does it take a critical approach to the motives for professional development, but stresses the important role professions play within society, the altruistic role of medicine being a prime example.

Freidson (1970), adopting a neo-Weberian stance (see chapter 1) defines a profession as possessing certain characteristics (see box 4.2).

So a profession has a large amount of control over its working practices. The power that professions possess within Western societies has enabled them to lay claim to areas of work, and to dominate and constrain subordinate occupations within the same

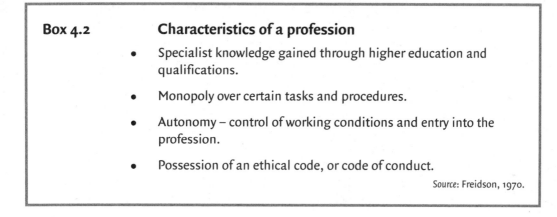

Box 4.2 **Characteristics of a profession**

- Specialist knowledge gained through higher education and qualifications.

- Monopoly over certain tasks and procedures.

- Autonomy – control of working conditions and entry into the profession.

- Possession of an ethical code, or code of conduct.

Source: Freidson, 1970.

social closure the means by which one social group maintains power and status in society by closing entry to other groups. In occupational closure control of entry into the occupation and monopoly over an area of work are the means usually adopted

expanded roles roles that include activities formerly carried out within other occupations, which expands the range of tasks that nurses carry out

sphere. This is **social closure** (Parkin, 1979), and can be used to explain the actions of both dominant and subservient occupations. Exclusionary tactics include the use of entry qualifications, legislation or other means to restrict access to the occupation, and demarcation describes the placing of boundaries around the work of a subordinate occupation. For example, the medical profession fought against the introduction of nurse prescribing for several years, as it would erode the monopoly power they enjoyed.

Subordinate occupations may attempt to adopt the same values and characteristics as the dominant one – what are known as inclusionary tactics. **Expanded roles** in nursing, where nurses take on tasks traditionally undertaken by doctors, may be defined as inclusionary strategies. Subordinate occupations may also use exclusionary tactics in order to maintain boundaries between themselves and occupations that they consider subordinate, for example the division between the roles of qualified nurses and health care assistants (HCAs). The latter are restricted in the tasks they may carry out, with some roles being reserved for qualified nurses.

If medicine is viewed as the archetypal profession within the health care system, nursing has been described as a semi-profession (Etzioni, 1969), because of its perceived limited knowledge base and lack of autonomy. This concept is somewhat deterministic as it implies that there is no opportunity for nursing to develop professionally. In order to counter such definitions of nursing some feminist writers (notably Davies, 1995; Witz, 1992) have criticized traditional notions of profession for emphasizing power and an esoteric knowledge base which separates the practitioner from the client. Davies (1995) argues that this form of power, which relies on denying knowledge to others, is a very masculinist interpretation of profession. Within this model nursing can never be accepted as a profession, as it seeks to share expertise and to encourage empowerment and participation by patients and families through strategies such as negotiated care. Davies advocates a new model of professionalism in which partnership and reflective practice constitute the basis of professional expertise, and where nursing roles and values are acknowledged and given credibility. This is

enhanced roles   roles that allow nurses to use their expert knowledge to make autonomous decisions

consistent with the notion of **enhanced roles** in nursing, in which the carative elements of health care are viewed as part of the specialist skills of nursing, and as an area of autonomous nursing practice.

Elitism in nursing

elite   A small group that has power and influence by virtue of its social position

The idea of an **elite** in nursing would seem to be paradoxical, as nurses are not viewed as a powerful group (Mowforth, 1999). They are often marginalized when decisions are made, which in theory should preclude them from power. However, both horizontal and vertical elites exist within nursing.

Vertical elitism exists between nurses of different grades. The higher the position within the organization, the greater is the prestige. In nursing, status is gained by moving away from clinical work with patients/clients into management or education. So in order to gain promotion nurses must cease to do the work they came into nursing for. What Davies (1995) has called the polo mint problem is created, a hole caused by a skills shortage at the bedside and in clinical teaching, as experienced nurses no longer undertake this work. As Daykin and Clarke (2000) demonstrate, this has raised questions about the relationship of nursing to basic health care, with nurses in their study demonstrating ambivalence to the changing role of the nurse. Many nurses expressed concern at the perceived threat to nurses' claim to a distinct contribution to health care if HCAs carry out much of the bedside care, albeit in a subservient position. At the same time they recognized the reality of workplace imperatives, most crucially the shortage of qualified nurses to carry out care (see also chapter 2 for a longer discussion of this research).

Horizontal elitism is influenced by the medical model, and the value this places on science and technology. Medicine, along with other professions, uses its possession of expert knowledge to maintain its high status. The gap between the knowledge of the doctor and that of the patient creates a mystique about medical knowledge. This is said to depersonalize, or deny the experience of, the patient, privileging the scientific over other forms of knowledge. It is those within nursing who are seen to have some insight into this scientific knowledge, such as those in intensive therapy units (ITU), special care baby units or accident and emergency departments (A & E) who are perceived as elite by themselves and by the public. Each nursing discipline has its elite roles, but those within the high-technology areas associated with adult and children's nursing have the highest status within wider society.

New technologies which require extra monitoring and interpretation are associated with clean as opposed to dirty work.

Wolf (1996) has argued that those who perform dirty work are soiled by association. Being involved with bodily functions has little status, and Clarke (1999) states that many nurses believe that an increase in nursing status is not compatible with these tasks. So care of the elderly or chronically ill does not carry the same prestige as more high-technology specialisms, even though it could be argued that the art of nursing (the skills that make nursing unique) is more apparent in the former. Nursing work associated with caring is seen as 'natural' and therefore not requiring intellect or education (Miers, 1999). Nurses within highly technologized areas do carry out 'dirty work', such as continence care; however, they are characterized not by this, but by their work with the technology.

Within mental health nursing, status is aligned to the clean work of psychotherapy with short-term patients, rather than to what is often regarded as the menial work of care of long-term patients (Godin, 2003).

The concept of expanded roles within nursing, such as nurse prescribing or acting as a surgeon's assistant, adds status by taking nurses further away from the caring role of nursing, and towards cure, which is a feature of clinical medicine. These roles remove the nurse from the 'dirty work' of nursing and into the 'clean' world of medicine. A consideration of the roles that nurses have taken on shows most to be fairly routine, repetitive tasks, which doctors themselves do not find as rewarding as other parts of their job. Paradoxically these new roles also bring nursing further under the control of medicine, as the medical profession defines the terms of nursing involvement, and circumscribes and supervises the work that the nurse takes over (Denny, 2003).

Activity 4.2   **Elitism in nursing**

Make a list of nursing tasks or roles within your branch that are generally considered to be high-status, and another list of low-status tasks and roles.

(a)   What do you think makes them high- or low-status?
(b)   Who usually carries out the high- and low-status work?
(c)   Discuss your lists with someone from another branch of nursing. Are there similarities and differences in the lists?

Working with doctors

Earlier in the chapter we considered the nineteenth-century image of doctors as powerful and nurses as obedient and subservient. This emanated from the relative position of men and women in Victorian society, which is now obsolete. Relationships are less monolithic; for example, mental-health nurses tend to see their role as complementary to that of psychiatrists, and learning-disability nurses view themselves as the expert workers in an area where the closure of institutions has seen the decline of the medical specialist (Denny, 2003).

Porter (1999) summarizes research that has looked at the doctor/nurse relationship. The first to consider this issue was Stein (1967) who viewed matters as more complex than the traditional power relationship, and described them as a game. Doctors are trained in a manner that creates certainty (in diagnosis, and in treatment), and for nurses to question or comment on their decisions would undermine this. Stein showed how nurses often had more knowledge of patients and their treatments than doctors who rotated through the specialisms, but they would never openly contradict them. Instead the nurse would put forward suggestions which the doctor could present as his or her own idea. The subservient nurse would not risk disagreement with the more powerful doctor. As Stein (1967, p. 699) states: 'The nurse is to be bold, have initiative, and be responsible for making significant recommendations, while at the same time she must appear passive. This must be done in such a manner so as to make her recommendations appear to be initiated by the physician.' For example, nurses often complete forms for diagnostic tests for a doctor to sign, or tell the doctor that a patient cannot sleep and suggest that a particular drug has helped in the past. The doctor then makes the decision to do the test or to prescribe the drug as if it was his or her decision. The notion of the doctor/nurse game as a process of negotiation is taken up in chapter 14.

More recently other writers have reviewed the doctor/nurse game and found that it has evolved as roles have developed, and Stein et al. noted in 1990 that in many hospital settings nurses were challenging medical decisions.

Hughes (1988) found that, given the right circumstances, nurses have the power to contribute to decision making. These can relate to the turnover of medical staff, the degree of post-registration nurse training, or the closeness of the working relationship. It most often occurs in areas such as accident and emergency departments or ITU. However, structural power relationships mean that doctors can always overrule nurses if they wish.

Porter (1999) also states that nurses themselves have the authority to identify and solve problems. Nurses have formally sanctioned decision-making processes that are independent of medical power. Central to this is the concept of the nursing process and care planning, which is nurse-led and outside the control of medicine.

Porter (1995) found that in different circumstances all of these processes are involved. He argues that the above relationships still apply and are played out differently according to the specific circumstances of the clinical area, and were more apparent within informal decision-making processes than in formal ones. He found that in areas where most nurses had specialist qualifications, such as accident and emergency departments, they were more likely to have some autonomy and be involved in decision making, although this was still constrained by professional boundaries. Expanding roles within nursing are likely to make these relationships more complex, as some nurses gain in autonomy, but others gain skills that bring them more under the control of medicine.

Activity 4.3

Relationship with doctors

The following are examples of interactions between nurses and doctors taken from Porter's (1995) observational research on nursing's relationship with medicine.

A
Doctor: Everything OK?
Nurse: [The patient's] pain isn't well controlled.
Doctor: Yes, I think he could do with another 2 ml per hour of morphine.
Nurse: Fine.

B
Doctor: Could you take Mrs _____'s morphine pump down please? She's been on it long enough now.
Nurse: I don't think she's ready for that yet. We've been trying to reduce it today, but every time we do you can see the pain breaking through.
Doctor: If you can try and reduce it over the next 24 hours, we'll think about it again tomorrow.

C
Nurse: Did I tell you that we stopped his morphine at midnight?
Doctor: No, I don't think so.
Nurse: He was too doped.
Doctor: That's grand. We'll keep it down unless he gets sore again.

(a) Which of the categories below do you think that each example falls into?
   The doctor–nurse game
   Nurses contributing to decision making
(b) Think about a situation where you have witnessed an interaction between a nurse and a doctor.
   Who did most of the talking?
   Who made the decisions?
   Who carried them out?

These studies support Wicks's (1998) findings that structural factors, such as power relationships, may be overcome by individual agency in certain circumstances, most usually when nurses have expertise derived from experience and specialist education.

This section has examined nursing's place within the health division of labour. It has pointed to a changing power relationship between medicine and nursing as nursing develops, and also to the complex situation within nursing specialisms brought about by the expansion of nursing roles and the greater autonomy achieved by some nurses.

6   Nurse education

One of the factors that have facilitated changing roles within nursing has been the shift from an apprentice style of training to an education system based on a university model. This can be explained as an inclusionary strategy, based on traditional professional training, and Witz (1994) describes the model of nurse education introduced by Project 2000 (P2K) as a credentialist tactic, giving nurses greater control over the educational curriculum and entry onto nursing courses. Despite this these moves have not been uncritically accepted.

Miers (2002) points to cultural factors inhibiting the entry of nursing into higher education. Attitudes within higher education concerning the status of practice-based professions, particularly care professions, have seen many nursing departments viewed as less than academic. Within nursing there exists an anti-intellectualism, where nursing research is viewed as 'ivory tower', removed from the real work of nursing. So nurses themselves are often hostile to diplomas and degrees in nursing, and have used sanctions against those who expressed individuality, questioned or challenged existing practices. Miers argues that this has been a consequence of an education system where practical caring courses more often undertaken by students from lower social classes have the lowest status in the educational hierarchy. The anti-intellectualism within nursing may be viewed as a defensive reaction against a culture that values abstract thinking more highly than practical activity.

Nurses with degrees have been particularly affected by this anti-intellectualism, as was discussed by Green in chapter 2.

Davies et al. (2000) state that there was an expectation that changes in nurse education introduced by P2K would result in diplomates receiving faster promotion and making more effective managers than those who were traditionally trained. From a random sample of nurses entered on the UKCC register between 1992 and 1995, both P2K and traditionally trained, it was found that there was no significant difference in the type of nurse recruited by employers, or in career grade. However, P2K nurses felt more prepared to work in rehabilitation, ITU or terminal care, and more willing to work in primary care. Degree nurses considered themselves able to work in management, research and education. Traditionally trained nurses felt more prepared to work in learning disability, paediatrics and mental health, and this group were most likely to be considering leaving nursing. The study was carried out with nurses who had been qualified between one and four years, and so was a restricted sample.

Activity 4.4	**Nurse education**

'The ability to care for a patient in its most basic sense means being able to wash, feed, and dress them. These are tasks which appear to be regarded as too menial or unimportant to the new breed of "nurse practitioner", who is now too busy writing "care plans", "learning contracts" or "evidence based practice protocols". . . . Despite the intellectualisation of the nursing profession and the move to degree courses, it is still the rule to find wards where none of the trained staff know when 'Mrs Smith' last had her bowels open, let alone can administer intravenous drugs, or know how to measure the central venous pressure. . . . Nursing has been perverted into an academically demanding occupation by a small band of frustrated doctors, but finds that the reality on the wards can neither interest, pay, or keep the calibre of recruit. If you want to send men to Mars, look for rocket scientists; if you want to nurse the sick, look for people who like to look after others.' (Extract from a letter from I. McKenzie to the *British Medical Journal*, 25 November 1998)

(a) Does the nurse of the twenty-first century need a degree or diploma to carry out his or her role? Why or why not?

(b) Is nursing the ability to 'wash, feed and dress' patients? If not, what else is it?

(c) How can academic knowledge from sociology, psychology and physiology aid a nurse in managing Mrs Smith's bowel function?

In summary, nursing has shifted from an apprenticeship model of training to an academic professional education. This has not been uncritically accepted, either by the higher-education sector, or by nurses themselves.

Summary and Resources

Summary

- The present occupation of nursing developed from the domestic role of women in caring for the sick in institutions and the community.

- The idea of nursing as 'women's work' has led to advantages for men in nursing, as they are deemed to possess qualities required for leadership, but they may also be treated with suspicion, particularly when working with vulnerable groups.

- Nurses have attempted social closure strategies in order to raise the status of nursing, and to lay claim to a distinct contribution to health care.

- Although nursing has traditionally been constrained in its development by a powerful medical profession, recent nursing developments have made occupational relationships more complex.

- Nurse education has shifted from an apprenticeship model of nursing training in health care institutions, to an academic professional education, with the award of degrees and diplomas.

Questions for Discussion

1. Historically nursing was considered as 'women's work' because of the association between women and caring work. Does this have any relevance for nursing today? Do men and women have different expectations from a career in nursing?

2. 'In all branches of nursing status is gained by moving away from direct care, creating the "polo mint problem"' (Davies, 1995). What can nurses do to raise the value of caring roles within society?

3. Debates continue over whether the move of nurse education into higher education better prepares nurses for present and future roles than the old apprenticeship training. What are the benefits to nursing of a combination of an academic education and learning in practice?

Further Reading

G. Wilkinson and M. Miers (eds): *Power and Nursing Practice.*
Basingstoke: Palgrave, 1999.
This edited text examines sociological concepts of power, and applies
them to nursing work. It is particularly useful in that separate
chapters explore power issues for each branch of nursing.

A. M. Rafferty: *The Politics of Nursing Knowledge.* London:
Routledge, 1996.
This book considers the historical influences that have shaped the way
in which nursing has developed from the Nightingale era. In particular
it analyses nurse education, and the extent to which nursing fulfils the
definition of both profession and academic discipline.

D. Wicks: *Nurses and Doctors at Work.* Buckingham: Open
University Press, 1998.
Wicks uses empirical research to examine the relationship between
nursing and medicine. She moves beyond traditional descriptions of
a powerful medical profession and subservient nurses to an analysis
of the tension between structure and agency in nursing work.

References

Clarke, J. 1999: 'The diminishing role of nurses in hands on care.'
    Nursing Times, 95(27), 48–9.
Clarke, M. 1978: Getting through the work. In R. Dingwall and J.
    Macintosh (eds), *Readings in the Sociology of Nursing*, Edinburgh:
    Churchill Livingstone, pp. 67–86.
Davies, C. 1995: *Gender and the Professional Predicament in Nursing.*
    Buckingham: Open University Press.
Davies, C., Stillwell, J., Wilson, R., Carlisle, C. and Luker, K. 2000:
    'Did Project 2000 training change recruitment patterns or career
    expectations?' *Nurse Education Today*, 20, 408–17.
Davis, F. 1975: Professional socialisation as subjective experience: the
    process of doctrinal conversion among student nurses. In C. Cox
    and A. Meade (eds), *The Sociology of Medical Practice*, London:
    Collier-Macmillan, pp. 116–31.
Daykin, N. and Clarke B. 2000: '"They'll still get the bodily care."
    Discourse of care and relationships between nurses and health
    care assistants in the NHS.' *Sociology of Health and Illness*, 22(3),
    349–63.
Denny, E. 2003: The class context of nursing. In M. Miers (ed.) *Class,
    Inequalities and Nursing Practice*, Basingstoke: Palgrave, pp. 77–97.
Dingwall, R., Rafferty, A. M. and Webster, C. 1988: *An Introduction to
    the Social History of Medicine.* London: Routledge.
Etzioni, A. 1969: *The Semi-professions and their Organization.* New York:
    Free Press.

Evans, J. A. 1997: 'Men in nursing: issues of gender segregation and hidden advantage.' *Journal of Advanced Nursing*, 26, 226–31.

Evans, J. A. 2002: 'Cautious caregivers: gender stereotypes and the sexualisation of men nurses' touch.' *Journal of Advanced Nursing*, 40(4), 441–8.

Freidson, E. 1970: *The Profession of Medicine: A Study in the Sociology of Applied Knowledge.* New York: Dodd Mead.

Godin, P. 2003: Class inequalities in mental health nursing. In M. Miers (ed.), *Class, Inequalities and Nursing Practice.* Basingstoke: Palgrave, pp. 125–43.

Hughes, D. 1988: 'When nurse knows best: some aspects of nurse/doctor interaction in a casualty department.' *Sociology of Health and Illness*, 10(1), 1–22.

Melia, K. 1987: *Learning and Working: The Occupational Socialisation of Nurses.* London: Tavistock.

Miers, M. 1999: Nursing teams and hierarchies: nurses working with nurses. In G. Wilkinson and M. Miers (eds), *Power and Nursing Practice*, Basingstoke: Palgrave, pp. 64–79.

Miers, M. 2000: *Gender Issues and Nursing Practice.* Basingstoke: Macmillan.

Miers, M. 2002: 'Nurse education in higher education: understanding cultural barriers to progress.' *Nurse Education Today*, 22(21), 2–9.

Millerson, G. L. 1964: *The Qualifying Association.* London: Routledge and Kegan Paul.

Mowforth, G. 1999: Elitism in nursing. In G. Wilkinson and M. Miers, *Power and Nursing Practice*, Basingstoke: Palgrave, pp. 51–63.

Parkin, F. 1979: *Marxism and Class Theory: A Bourgeois Critique.* London: Tavistock.

Porter, S. 1995: *Nursing's Relationship with Medicine.* Aldershot: Avebury.

Porter, S. 1999: Working with doctors. In G. Wilkinson and M. Miers, *Power and Nursing Practice*, Basingstoke: Palgrave, pp. 97–110.

Rafferty, A. M. 1995: 'The anomaly of autonomy: space and status in early nursing reform.' *International History of Nursing Journal*, 1, 43–56.

Rafferty, A. M. 1996: *The Politics of Nursing Knowledge.* London, Routledge.

Stein, L. 1967: 'The doctor/nurse game.' *Archives of General Psychiatry*, 16, 699–703.

Stein, L., Watts, D. T., Howell, T. 1990: 'The doctor–nurse game revisited.' *New England Journal of Medicine*, 322(8), 546–9.

Wicks, D. 1998: *Nurses and Doctors at Work.* Buckingham: Open University Press.

Williams, C. 1994: 'Nurses' voices – men in nursing: lazy? On the glass escalator? Or gay?' Paper presented at the British Sociological Association Annual Conference, Preston.

Williams, C. 1995: 'Hidden advantages for men in nursing.' *Nursing Administration Quarterly*, 19(2), 63–70.

Witz, A. 1992: *Professions and Patriarchy*. London: Routledge.
Witz, A. 1994: The challenge of nursing. In J. Gabe, D. Kelleher and G. Williams (eds), *Challenging Medicine* London: Sage, pp. 23–45.
Wolf, Z. R. 1996: 'Bowel management and nursing's hidden work.' *Nursing Times*, 92(21), 26–8.

Part II

Inequalities and Diversities in Health and Health Care

It is important to be aware of diversity amongst patient/client groups and the impact of this on health and health care. This part examines health inequality and diversity, focusing specifically on gender, age, disability, class, and race and ethnicity.

In chapter 5, 'Gendered Concerns', the emphasis is on the significance of sex and gender for health and illness. The chapter provides a definition of sex and gender and a historical overview of some key gendered concerns, emphasizing how 'gender issues' do not relate just to women and girls, but also to men and boys. Whilst it is often the case than 'men get sick and women die', the picture is much more complex than this, and this chapter unpacks some of the key issues. The concepts of masculinity and femininity are explored and the question 'What makes women and men sick?' is addressed. The chapter concludes by arguing that just as sexism affects perceptions of what makes women and men sick, it also affects service provision. You are encouraged to think about how gender and sexism influence the treatment and care you offer to patients.

Chapter 6, 'Contemporary Perspectives on Ageing', suggests that whilst we may think about 'ageing' solely in relation to older people, the study of age and ageing is relevant to all nurses. Nurses work with patients of all ages, and assumptions are made about health care in relation to age. Drawing on a life-course perspective, this chapter challenges some of these assumptions and explores the social construction of ageing. The chapter explores definitions of 'age' and examines the changing structure of the population. You will be introduced to both traditional and more contemporary theories of ageing and will examine the impact of ageism on health. The chapter encourages you to explore your own stereotypes about 'age', to reflect on anti-ageist policies and to consider how these might affect your nursing practice.

Diversity and inequality in relation to disability are dealt with in chapter 7, 'Chronic Illness, Disabling Barriers, Discrimination and Prejudice'. The classification and definition of disability and impairment are considered and you are introduced to some of the sociological theorizing on disability. The chapter discusses the social model, which has been very influential within sociological thinking on disability; the social model makes a distinction between 'impairment' and 'disability' and suggests that disability is socially constructed. You are encouraged to reflect on the challenges posed by the social model and the disabled people's movement to a largely biomedical model of nursing care and to reflect on how nurses can avoid the disabling barriers, discrimination and prejudice that affect disabled people.

In chapter 8, 'Social Class and Health', we explain the traditional sociological concept of class and discuss the more contemporary measurement of socio-economic differences. The chapter maps the history of the relationship between class and health and considers the widening gap in inequalities between the richest and poorest. The chapter then turns to a discussion of the evidence relating to class inequalities in health. Some of the policies used to tackle health inequalities in the twenty-first century are discussed and the explanations for such inequalities are evaluated. Chapter 8 encourages you to investigate and understand the significance of class and health for nursing practice.

Chapter 9, 'Race and Ethnicity', draws the distinction between the concepts of 'race' and 'ethnicity'. Although ethnicity relates to both individual identity and structural or cultural differences, this chapter highlights that it is important for nurses to recognize the considerable individual and social diversity within and between ethnic groups. This chapter provides a brief history of immigration in Britain, which now boasts over 4.5 million people who describe themselves as belonging to a minority ethnic group. The relationship between ethnicity and health and health care is examined and there is some discussion of the methodological issues involved in measuring the relationship between health and ethnicity. This chapter encourages you to reflect on the implications of ethnic diversity for nursing practice.

All of the chapters within this section share certain features. First, they each explore the significance of definition and classification, demonstrating not just how this has changed over time, but also how the definition of difference and diversity can affect treatment and care. Second, they also share methodological concerns and highlight the fact that we cannot separate what we know to be true from the way in which that 'truth' has emerged. Although there is consensus on the existence of inequalities in health, there is considerable debate on the extent and nature of these inequalities and how they should be measured. Finally, all of the chapters within this section encourage you to reflect on the way in which diversity affects your practice and how inequalities in health may influence treatment and care.

5 Gendered Concerns

Gayle Letherby

Key issues in this chapter

- Definitional and historical issues.
- The significance of sex and gender in relation to health and illness.
- The gendered experience of health care.
- The relationship between gender and other 'measures' of stratification.

By the end of this chapter you should be able to . . .

- Explain how historical definitions and expectations of men and women affect contemporary definitions and experiences.
- Explain how historical views on the relationship between gender and health affect contemporary views and experiences.
- Understand the significance of sex and gender for patterns of health and illness.
- Explain the relationship between gender roles, masculinity and femininity, and health and illness.
- Recognize the need to take a gendered perspective, whilst acknowledging that other differences are also relevant.

1 Introduction

To begin this chapter on the gendered concerns of health and illness it is important to establish some definitions. When considering issues of gender in relation to health and illness (or in relation to family life, work and leisure, crime and deviance, in fact in relation to anything) it is important to understand what taking a gendered perspective means. The word gender does not (as some people mistakenly think) refer only to the experiences and perspectives of women but to the significance of similarities and differences between female and male experiences. Furthermore, it is also important to remember that gender is a concept distinct from the concept of sex: **sex** is a term referring to biological differences between men and women and **gender** a term referring to cultural differences (Oakley, 1972). Gender, then, refers to culturally prescribed expectations of women and men and differs over time and place.

sex the biological differences between males and females

gender cultural differences between males and females

In this chapter the relationship between sex and gender, and health, illness and caring is considered. The chapter is divided into four main sections: 2, 'The importance of gender: historical definitions and contemporary concerns'; 3, 'Challenging gender and health myths: the relationship between gender roles: masculinity, femininity and health and illness'; 4, 'Gender, health, illness and caring: the gendered experience of health care'; and 5, 'The importance of gender revisited: diversity and difference'. This is followed by a brief summary of the main issues.

2   The importance of gender: historical definitions and contemporary concerns

A particularly significant time affecting current understanding of the relationship between gender and health in the Western world was the sixteenth and seventeenth centuries. The scientific knowledge which emerged at this time was argued to be objective knowledge. As Gunew (1990) and Wajcman (1991) note, historically (and to date) men are believed to be capable of objectivity and women are not.

The dominant message then was that women were not just different from but physically, psychologically and socially inferior to men (Doyal, 1995, p. 2) and characterized as 'sensitive, intuitive, incapable of objectivity and emotional detachment and . . . immersed in the business of making and maintaining personal relationships' (Oakley, 1981, p. 38). Thus, women were considered naturally weak and easy to exploit and their psychological characteristics implied subordination, for example, submission, passivity, dependency and so on. From this perspective women are more like children than adults in that they are immature, weak and helpless (Oakley, 1981; Evans, 1997). If women adopt these characteristics they are considered well adjusted (Miller, 1976; Oakley, 1981), but being considered well adjusted clearly comes with a price; in the eighteenth and nineteenth centuries defining women as weak justified their exclusion from the world of work and education.

However, although women have historically been constructed as weak and hysterical, they have always performed large amounts of physical labour both in the home and outside of it, and on top of this have been, and still are, held responsible for the dominant share of domestic and **emotion work** (Coppock et al., 1995; Evans, 1997; Frith and Kitzinger, 1998) (see chapter 2). Despite this, the image of women as inferior both physically and emotionally is still significant in defining women's lives (for example, Evans, 1997; Coppock et al., 1995; and Doyal, 1995).

emotion work   the regulation, management and care of one's own and others' feelings and emotions

Of course, all of this has implications for women in terms of their health and of general perceptions of women as healthy or not. In the nineteenth century, middle-class women were thought to be particularly weak and susceptible to illness: menstruation was thought to be an 'indisposition' or illness which sapped women's energy, making it necessary for them to rest; childbirth was termed 'confinement' and a long period of bed rest was thought to be necessary after the birth of a baby; and the menopause was considered a disease which marked the beginning of senility (Webb, 1986).

Oddly, working-class women were not seen as being susceptible to the same problems. They were seen as physically stronger and emotionally less sensitive and well able to work 14 hours a day outside of the home and still be able to 'cook, clean and service their husbands, and bear children without such suffering' (Webb, 1986, p. 6). Furthermore, working-class women were seen as potentially polluting through their work in the kitchen, the nursery and the brothel (Abbott and Wallace, 1997). The harshest reading of this is that working-class women were not viewed as women at all, and the most generous that whereas middle-class women were 'sickly', working-class women were 'sickening'.

Current lay and medical definitions of the gendered significance of health seem to continue the sexist view of women as 'sickly'. When asked to think of someone they think of as healthy both men and women are likely to choose a man (Blaxter, 1990). Psychologists and clinicians are more likely to define women's than men's health problems as psychological and definitions of mental health are often related to traditional notions of **masculinity and femininity**: healthy men are thought to be independent, logical and adventurous and healthy women less aggressive, more emotional and easily hurt (Miers, 2000; Webb, 1986).

masculinity and femininity   the ways in which men and women are expected to behave, think and feel

Evidence from research also suggests that women make more use of health services and appear to feel less healthy than men (Annandale and Clark, 1996). However, in some interpretations of data where comparisons are made between males and females, male

Activity 5.1   **Gendered definitions: the case of hysteria**

'The word hysteria is usually used to describe a woman as though she were simply behaving according to expectations . . . Hysteria now refers to a specific psychoneurosis that may affect anyone, male or female. In popular usage it is a state of excessive fear or other emotion in individuals or masses of people, but in this sense men – whether individually or in groups – are seldom said to be hysterical. After a series of rapes at a large college in 1974, news stories repeatedly described a "mood of hysteria" among women students on the campus. The description, according to the dean of women, was totally false. "The mood of the women is one of concern and anger," she told reporters. "When men feel concern and anger, it is called concern and anger, never hysteria."' (Mills, 1991, p. 127)

(a)   Can you think of some more examples of women being described as hysterical?

(b)   Do you think that the association of hysteria with womanhood affects the ways we popularly define women and men's, and girls' and boys', mental health and well-being? If so, what are the implications for the treatment and care of women and men with mental health problems?

health status is glossed over or informed by simplistic, stereotypical approaches (Miers, 2000; Watson, 2000). This construction of women's health as poor has consequences for men too in that there is an implicit assumption that men's health is 'good' (Annandale and Clark, 1996; Watson, 2000). The result of this is that men's poor health remains invisible.

Research suggests that men are reluctant both to listen to health promotion messages and to go to the doctor for 'minor' complaints. Despite this, a popular view among many women is that: '[t]o the average man, a bad cold has five-act potential and he will use it to extract every last drop of sympathy' (Bradford, 1995, cited by Watson, 2000, p. 18). Relevant here too is the fact that women are often blamed when their family members are seen as unhealthy:

They [women] are seen as responsible for bringing up healthy children and maintaining the health of their men for the nation. Health visitors, social workers and other professional state employees 'police' the family to ensure that women are carrying out their task adequately. (Abbott and Wallace, 1997, p. 198)

Activity 5.2   **Gender and socialization: learning to be different?**

'When I grow up
I'm going to be
a carer'

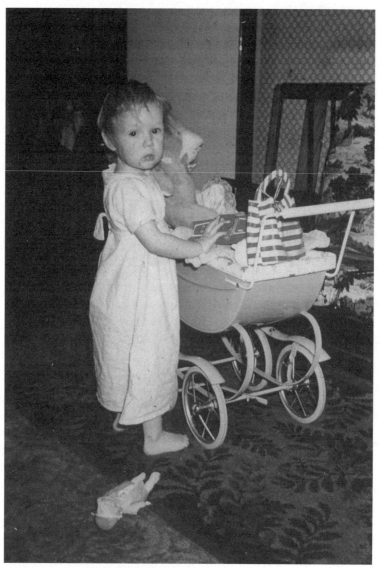

Photograph courtesy Gayle Letherby

(a)   Why are women still expected to be mainly responsible for the
care of children – in the home and in the nursery, the school and
the hospital? How does our childhood socialization perpetuate
this view?

(b)   Can you think of examples from your own childhood were gender
stereotypes were reinforced?

(c)   What are the positives and negatives of encouraging more men to
care for children (in both the private and public spheres)?

So, historically and to date, lay and medical perceptions of the relationship between sex, gender, health and illness are based on sexist assumptions of what women and men are like.

3   Challenging gender and health myths: the relationship between gender roles: masculinity, femininity and health and illness

The phrase 'women get sick and men die', which has been at the heart of research findings in the area of gender inequalities in health, still has some truth in it but it oversimplifies the complex relationship between gender and health (Annandale, 1998; Miers, 2000). Male life expectancy is less than that of women in all but a few Asian countries but, even in Western countries, the male mortality disadvantage has slipped and is relatively small at the beginning of the twenty-first century (Miers, 2000). Furthermore, writers in this area argue that there is a need to reflect critically on the reasons for the differences that do exist. For example, when considering apparent differences in morbidity it is necessary to critically reflect on the reasons why women are higher users of health services than men. Women live longer, and their use of health services increases with age; higher consultation rates over a lifetime would therefore be expected, especially when we take into account the visits related to menstruation, pregnancy, childbirth, postnatal care and menopause. Furthermore, women appear to find it easier and more socially acceptable to discuss their own health (Miers, 2000). There may also be important psychosocial factors such as how men and women evaluate symptoms (Watson, 2000).

The main causes of lower life expectancy for men lie in higher death rates from coronary heart disease, lung cancer and chronic obstructive airways disease, accidents, homicides, suicides and AIDS (Miers, 2000). Men are more likely to die of occupationally related illnesses, men engage in more physical risk taking than women, and accidents and homicides have always been a feature of masculine rather than feminine experience. Cigarette smoking has, hitherto, been a major cause of male death (although in the 1990s male and female smoking rates in the UK began to even out), men drink more than women, and are more likely to suffer alcohol-related deaths (including those in motor vehicle accidents). Furthermore, suicide among men has increased in recent years, particularly young men. However, men's higher level of exercise participation may counteract some of the health disadvantages apparently resulting from their less healthy lifestyles (Miers, 2000).

Writers in the area suggest that prevailing explanations for such differences in both medical and lay discourse are that men's poor health results from their trying to live up to a macho image and lifestyle which is itself dangerous to health. From this perspective, much ill-health among men is a consequence of lifestyle, which nurses and other health professionals can address in their role as health educators, helping men to recognize that stereotypical male gender role behaviour is a risk to health and could and should be changed. However, as Watson (2000) notes, the challenge to change male behaviour and resist stereotypical masculinity is problematic because it presumes that masculinity is a unitary construct and that all men benefit equally from being male in a patriarchal society.

In common with stereotypical views, just as men's dangerous lives are thought to be detrimental to their health, women's mental and physical weaknesses are thought to be of major significance to women's ill-health. Statistics suggest that about twice as many women as men suffer from a mental disorder. However, yet again, in reality things are more complex as there are distinctive gender patterns associated with different mental phenomena. For example, anorexia nervosa is a predominantly female condition and women

---

Activity 5.3	**Reproductive health**

'Women with disabilities often do not receive adequate and necessary health care services important for all women. Reasons given by women with disabilities for not having regular pelvic exams include not being aware of the need to have one, difficulty getting onto the exam table, being too busy, and the inability to find a doctor who suited them or who was knowledgeable about their disability.

In addition, health care providers may mistakenly assume that women with disabilities are not sexually active, especially if their disability is severe or disfiguring. They may neglect to screen these women for sexually transmitted diseases (STDs) or even perform a gynaecological examination. Unfortunately, some health care providers recommend that women with disabilities abstain from sex and not bear children, even if they have the capacity to conceive children.

Women with disabilities need the same level of access to reproductive health information, including information about safe sex practices, STDs, and planning a healthy pregnancy, as their non-disabled counterparts. It also is important for women with disabilities to receive the same preventive health care, such as pap smears and clinical breast exams.' (National Women's Health Information Centre, www.4woman.gov)

- Go to the website of the National Women's Health Information Centre. What other information can you find about the reproductive and other health needs of women and men with disabilities, including learning disabilities?

report anxiety, phobias and depression twice as often as men. However, substance-use disorders are more common among men than women and diagnoses of schizophrenia, paranoia or mania do not show a gender preference (Doyal, 1995; Busfield, 1996). Despite this, the labelling of an illness or a condition as 'women's business' has serious medical, social and emotional consequences for women.

However, our critique of this must include reference to the fact that women's roles and responsibilities have consequences for their health just as men's do. As noted earlier, despite enduring stereotypical views of women as weak and helpless, work, both paid and unpaid, is a significant aspect of women's lives. However, most research into the relationship between paid work and ill-health has focused on male-dominated occupations. It is widely believed that female jobs are neither physically hazardous nor stressful but recent research into nursing and clerical work demonstrates otherwise (Doyal, 1995). On your next placement, it is worth considering the extent to which you find nursing work hazardous or stressful. This sexist bias in occupational health research is further extended by traditional assumptions of women's weaknesses, for example: 'Researchers have been concerned for some time to determine whether or not menstruation interferes with women's capacity to work. They have been much less interested in how women's work affects their experiences of menstruation' (Doyal, 1995, p. 169). The hazards of domestic work are even more hidden although we know that being a 'good' wife and mother can make women sick. Evidence suggests that women prioritize the needs of other family members, allocating them more resources and caring for them to the detriment of their own health – not least because, as argued earlier, this is expected of them (for example, Doyal, 1995; Abbott and Wallace, 1997).

Furthermore, many women and children live in danger of ill-health, even death, as the result of men's emotional, psychological, sexual and physical violence (Stanko, 1985; 1990; 1995). Kelly (1988) and Daly and Wilson's (1988) careful examination of homicide reveals men's use of violence to control their female partners across industrial and non-industrial societies. While they argue that the killing of women is relatively rare, the use of violence is not. While men's violence to women is usually characterized as 'losing control' or flying into a 'blind rage', all the evidence suggests that both battered women and the men who batter tell the same story, that men's behaviour is used as a means of control. On the other hand, although men do experience violent attacks by women this constitutes the smallest proportion of assaults on men, and men are much more likely to be victims of physical and sexual violence from other men (Newburn and Stanko, 1994).

Overall then, although differences between male and female patterns of health and illness do have some basis in biology (for example, the protective effects of oestrogen in pre-menopausal women), these patterns are more complicated than biology alone (Doyal, 1995). As noted in chapter 3, whilst sociologists accept the significance of biology, they look for social explanations of health and illness that do not rely on sexist stereotypes of 'male' and 'female' illnesses and problems.

4   Gender, health, illness and caring: the gendered experience of health care

Just as sexism affects the dominant views on what makes men and women sick, it also affects the treatment and care individuals receive. As Doyal (1998) argues, although waiting lists have an impact on both men and women there is evidence that women are disproportionately affected in particular areas. For example, family-planning services have been significantly reduced in many parts of the UK, and their longer life expectancy means that older women are more likely than older men to be affected by the withdrawal of the NHS from the provision of continuing-care beds. Domestic responsibilities, lack of transport and cultural or linguistic barriers may also affect women more (Doyal, 1998).

It has long been argued that diseases and illnesses that proportionately affect men in greater numbers receive more resources than those that more often affect women. Writers now argue that it is not just that 'men's diseases' are taken more seriously but that male patients are too. For example, in the US men on dialysis are significantly more likely than women with the same symptoms to obtain a kidney transplant and men with cardiac symptoms are more likely than women to be given diagnostic catheterization. The continuing failure to include women in sufficient numbers either in epidemiological research or in clinical trials has also made it difficult to investigate gender differences or to assess the overall significance of gender in the delivery of effective care (Doyal, 1998).

paternalism/paternalistic
the sexist treatment of
women

Webb (1986) suggests that **paternalism** is the hallmark of much present-day health care. Although men sometimes appear to find it difficult to communicate with health professionals, women seem to find it even harder, because of both their socialization and the stereotypical views that others have of them (Doyal, 1998). One example of sexist treatment is provided by Wilkinson and Kitzinger (1994) in their writing about women's experience of breast cancer. They argue that the cultural emphasis on breasts as objects of male sexual interest and male sexual pleasure is relevant within treatment. They suggest that a 'page 3' mentality is reproduced in the medical and psychological literature, as well as in the material produced by major cancer charities. Thus, the implicit assumption throughout is that women's breasts are there for men's sexual pleasure, with the woman who has a mastectomy described as mutilated or disfigured.

When dissatisfaction with treatment is an issue, complaining can be difficult. Patients who resist may be labelled a nuisance and become unpopular with medical staff (for example, Coyle, 1999; Playle and Keeley, 1998), which could in turn affect their experience of treatment. The 'gratitude factor' (Coyle, 1999, p. 98) has also been identified as a barrier to patients complaining or expressing dissatisfaction. Given assumptions of and socialization into 'appropriate' feminine behaviour it would be easy to think that women are more likely to find it difficult to resist and complain than men. However, it is important not to view patients – male or female – as passive victims. Research suggests that both patients and doctors attempt to control and direct the consultation along their own desired line, to persuade the other to their preferred solution (Stimson and Webb, 1975; Annandale and Hunt, 1998). In her article on patient dissatisfaction Coyle (1999) suggests that the involvement of the men and women in her study could be regarded as challenge and resistance to medical dominance.

A response to sexism in health care has been the production of books with the aim of informing individuals about their own bodies and their own health. A number of them hit the bookstores in the 1970s (perhaps the most well-known being *Our Bodies Our Selves*, first published by the Boston Women's Health Book Collective in 1973, but now celebrating its 25th anniversary!). These were written by women and were grounded in women's experiences. However, as Hockey (1997) notes, these early texts were relevant mostly for white middle-class audiences. It was not until the 1980s that books aimed at black, lesbian, working-class and older women began to appear. There are fewer books even today specifically concerned with men's health although, during the 1990s, men's health was an increasing concern within the media with reports on increasing stress and incidences of cancer, declining fertility and reluctance to visit the doctor (Watson, 2000). In turn all of this has led to further debate on the state of men's health and what to do about it. A recent attempt in the UK to encourage men to pay more attention to their health has been the production of a men's health manual modelled on the car manuals produced by Haynes.

With their emphasis on empowerment, many of the personal health texts stress the fact that individuals should take control of their own bodies and minds and be active rather than passive. Empowerment from this perspective then often suggests resistance to the dominant medical model and supports 'alternative' health care. Yet there is a problem here, as the dominant message from many alternative health care self-help books and tapes is that we become ill because of unhealthy attitudes and that we can cure ourselves.

Activity 5.4   **Gender, health and media**

The following extract is taken from a popular UK women's magazine, *Take a Break* (9 October 2003, p. 23):

'Everyone knows that men and women are different. Everyone, it seems, but the people who make and test our medicines.

For the best part of 50 years, the drugs industry has assumed that despite our distinctively different external features, men and women are pretty much the same on the inside.

But that's a dangerous assumption to make.

Vivienne Parry carried out research into the way that drugs work for One Man's Medicine, a programme broadcast by BBC Radio 4.

She says: "Out of ten recent recalls in the US, four have been related solely to adverse effects in women. But given that men and women differ fundamentally in almost every system of their bodies, it shouldn't be a surprise that they have such different responses to drugs. Many are well known."

She says that women:

- come out of anaesthesia faster than men
- have a greater response to some painkillers
- have more side effects with antihistamines, antibiotics, antidepressants and steroids.
- And drugs which prevent fatal alternations to the heartbeat in men can cause them in women.'

(a)   Consider some of the implications of these findings for women's and men's health.

(b)   What are the implications of popular magazines reporting regularly on health issues?

(c)   Find some other examples of women's and men's magazines that have articles on health. Can you identify any differences in the articles aimed at men from those aimed at women?

One of the most important attractions of the alternative health movement is that it offers us the illusion of 'stepping out of the victim role', but it deflects attention from the state's failure to provide health services for all society's members (Wilkinson and Kitzinger, 1994). Wilkinson and Kitzinger (1994) note that, by contrast, a **feminist** analysis of health and illness begins by acknowledging that women are victims of a patriarchal world and a heterosexist health system. Furthermore, they advocate campaigns and community action to change current medical, social and political attitudes. Theories of social structure are relevant here in that the structure of society is seen to perpetuate gendered inequalities in health (see also chapter 1).

feminist   relating to the political theory and practice that challenges the oppression of women

Obviously, it is not only women who are disempowered by the health service. Male members of economically and ethnically marginalized or disadvantaged groups are likely to find it hard too. Such groups are increasingly being brought within the policy gaze (Watson, 2000). However, as noted earlier, because of their reluctance to access services, men from apparently privileged groups also need attention: 'Ironically, white heterosexual middle-aged men are visible in the public health literature but relatively invisible in practice' (Watson, 2000, p. 41). Sexist assumptions then affect the treatment and care available both for women and for men.

5   The importance of gender revisited: diversity and difference

As Doyal (1995, p. 1) notes: 'All societies continue to be divided along the "fault line" of gender and this too has a profound effect on the well-being of both men and women.' In 1998 she adds:

> Men and women will be exposed to different health risks, both physical and psychological. They have access to different amounts and types of resources for maintaining or promoting their own health and may also have different levels of responsibility for the care of others. If they become ill they may have very different strategies for coping. They may define their symptoms in very different ways, will probably seek help from different sources and may respond very differently to treatment. (Doyal, 1998, p. 9)

So, as Di Stephano (1990, p. 78) argues, gender functions as 'a difference that makes a difference'. On the other hand when we do consider differences between men and women we need to remember that 'Much of what it is to be human and live in societies is the same for men and women' (Carpenter, 1998, p. 48).

Also, as you will become aware from the other chapters in this part, gender is not the only 'difference' that we need to take seriously. Differences of age, class, sexuality, ethnicity, and physical and learning disability are also relevant to our experience of health, illness and health care. Taking ethnicity as an example, we know that 'race' adversely affects black women's and men's experiences in relation to health (and indeed all other areas of social life). Yet 'race' is not a coherent category and the lives of those usually classified together under the label 'black' can be very different. Thus, culture, class, religion, nationality, sexuality, age and so on in addition to gender can all have an impact on women's and men's lives and it is necessary to challenge the homogeneity of experience previously ascribed to women by virtue of being 'black'. For example, as Douglas (1998) notes, the health status of black and ethnic-minority women in the

UK reflects the interaction between their experiences of race, gender, class and culture (see also chapter 9). So health and well-being are determined in these groups of women by a complex mixture of social and psychological influences and biological and genetic factors. Ethnic-minority women are not a homogeneous group with uniform needs: 'They may be South Asian, Asian, Chinese, Vietnamese, African or African-Caribbean. They may have been born in the UK, may have migrated recently and may be refugees. They may have disabilities, be older, be lesbian . . .' (Douglas, 1998, p. 70). Further, as Maynard (1994) points out, individuals do not have to be black to experience racism, as attention to the historical and contemporary experience of Jewish and Irish people demonstrates.

Thus, it is important that, in addition to taking gender seriously, we take other aspects of difference equally seriously and consider when and how gender intersects and overlaps with other aspects of difference.

Summary and Resources

Summary

- The historical definition of women as weaker – both physically and emotionally – affects contemporary definitions, and when asked to think of a healthy person most people choose a man.

- The view that men die but women are more likely to get sick simplifies the complex relationship between gender and health. Women's and men's roles and responsibilities do have consequences for health so patterns of health and illness relate to more than biological differences. Having said this it is important not to rely on sexist stereotypes of 'male' and 'female' illnesses and problems.

- Dominant views on what makes men and women sick also affect the treatment and care individuals receive and there is some evidence to suggest that 'men's diseases' and male patients are taken more seriously. However, both men and women are able to challenge and resist medical dominance.

- It is clear that gender is significant to the health and well-being of men and women, and boys and girls, but it is also important to consider how gender intersects with other aspects of difference such as age, class, sexuality, ethnicity, and physical and learning dis/ability.

Questions for Discussion

1 Why and how is gender significant when we consider issues of health and illness?

2 Why and how is gender significant when we consider the care of the sick? To what extent have you been aware of this significance during your placements?

3 Why is it important to consider the relationship between gender and other aspects of difference and diversity when considering health and illness and the care of the sick?

Further Reading

E. Annandale and K. Hunt (eds): *Gender Inequalities in Health*. Buckingham: Open University Press, 2000; J. M. Ussher (ed.): *Women's Health: Contemporary International Perspectives*. Leicester: The British Psychological Society, 2000; J. Watson: *Male Bodies: Health, Culture and Identity*. Buckingham: Open University Press, 2000.

For gender-specific books have a look at one of the above. A useful book that focuses on both male *and* female experience is the text by Annandale and Hunt, which not only provides detailed insight into gender differences but considers the relationship between sex and gender and other differences. Thus, attention is given to (amongst other things) social class, age and cross-cultural issues.

S. Earle and G. Letherby (eds): *Gender, Identity and Reproduction: Social Perspectives.* London: Palgrave, 2003.
Difference and diversity are also a key theme within this text as are agency and resistance in relation to health care.

M. Miers: *Gender Issues and Nursing Practice.* Basingstoke: Macmillan, 2000.
This provides a very useful discussion of the relationship between gender and nursing practices.

References

Abbott, P. and Wallace, C. 1997: *An Introduction to Sociology: Feminist Perspectives*, 2nd edn. London: Routledge.

Annandale, E. 1998: *The Sociology of Health and Medicine: A Critical Introduction.* Cambridge: Polity.

Annandale, E. and Clark, J. 1996: 'What is gender? Feminist theory and the sociology of human reproduction.' *Sociology of Health and Illness*, 18(1), 17–44.

Annandale, E. and Hunt, K. 1998: 'Accounts of disagreements with doctors.' *Social Science and Medicine*, 46(1), 119–29.

Annandale, E. and Hunt, K. (eds) 2000: *Gender Inequalities in Health.* Buckingham: Open University Press.

Blaxter, M. 1990: *Health and Lifestyles.* London: Tavistock Routledge.

Boston Women's Health Book Collective, 1998: *Our Bodies Our Selves* (25th anniversary edn). New York: Touchstone.

Bradford, N. 1995: 'Is this a sick joke?' *Good Housekeeping*, May.

Busfield, J. 1996: *Men and Madness.* Basingstoke: Macmillan.

Carpenter, M. 1998: Reinforcing the pillars: rethinking gender, social divisions and health. In E. Annandale and K. Hunt (eds), *Gender Inequalities and Health*, Buckingham: Open University Press, pp. 36–63.

Coppock, V., Haydon, D. and Richter, I. 1995: *The Illusions of 'Post-Feminism': New Women, Old Myths.* London: Taylor and Francis.

Coyle, J. 1999: 'Exploring the meaning of "dissatisfaction" with health care: the importance of "personal identity threat".' *Sociology of Health and Illness*, 18(1), 17–44.

Daly, M. and Wilson, M. 1988: *Homicide: Foundations of Human Behaviour.* New York: Aldine de Gruyter.

Di Stephano, C. 1990: Dilemmas of difference: feminism, modernity and postmodernism. In L. Nicholson (ed.), *Feminism/Postmodernism*, London: Routledge, pp. 63–82.

Douglas, J. 1998: Meeting the health needs of women from black and minority ethnic communities. In L. Doyal (ed.), *Women and Health Care Services*, Buckingham: Open University Press, pp. 69–82.

Doyal, L. 1995: *What Makes Women Sick: Gender and the Political Economy of Health.* Basingstoke: Macmillan.

Doyal, L. (ed.) 1998: *Women and Health Services: An Agenda for Change.* Buckingham: Open University Press.

Evans, M. 1997: *Introducing Contemporary Feminist Thought.* Cambridge: Polity.

Frith, H. and Kitzinger, C. 1998: '"Emotion Work" as a participant resource: a feminist analysis of young women's talk-in-interaction.' *Sociology*, 32(2), 299–320.

Gunew, S. (ed.) 1990: *Feminist Knowledge: Critique and Construct.* London: Routledge.

Hockey, J. 1997: Women and health. In D. Richardson and V. Robinson (eds), *Introducing Women's Studies*, 2nd edn, London: Macmillan, pp. 250–71.

Kelly, L. 1988: *Surviving Sexual Violence.* Cambridge: Polity.

Loverstone, S. and Fahy, T. 1991: 'Psychological factors in breast cancer.' *British Medical Journal*, 302, 25 May, 1219–20.

Maynard, M. 1994: 'Race', gender and the concept of 'difference' in feminist thought. In H. Afshar and M. Maynard (eds), *The Dynamics of 'Race' and Gender: Some Feminist Interventions*, London: Taylor and Francis, pp. 9–25.

Miers, M. 2000: *Gender Issues and Nursing Practices.* Basingstoke: Macmillan.

Miller, J. Baker 1976: *Towards a New Psychology of Women.* Boston: Beacon.

Mills, J. 1991: *Womanwords.* London: Virago.

Newburn, T. and Stanko, E. A. 1994: When men are victims: the failure of victimology. In T. Newburn and E. A. Stanko (eds), *Just Boys Doing Business? Men, Masculinities and Crime*, London: Routledge, pp. 153–65.

Oakley, A. 1972: *Sex, Gender and Society.* London: Temple Smith.

Oakley, A. 1981: *Subject Women.* Oxford: Martin Robinson.

Playle, J. F. and Keeley, P. 1998: 'Non-compliance and professional power.' *Journal of Advanced Nursing*, 27, 304–11.

Stanko, E. A. 1985: *Intimate Intrusions.* London: Unwin Hyman.

Stanko, E. A. 1990: *Everyday Violence: How Women and Men Experience Sexual and Physical Danger.* London: Pandora.

Stanko, E. A. 1995: Challenging the problem of men's individual violence. In T. Newburn and A. E. Stanko (eds), *Just Boys Doing Business? Men, Masculinity and Crime*, London: Routledge, pp. 32–45.

Stimson, G. and Webb, B. 1975: *Going to See the Doctor.* London: Routledge and Kegan Paul.

van Balen, F. and Inhorn, M. C. 2002: Interpreting infertility: a view from the social sciences. In M. C. Inhorn and F. van Balen (eds), *Infertility Around The Globe: New Thinking on Childlessness, Gender and Reproductive Technologies*. Berkeley and Los Angeles: University of California Press, pp. 3–32.

Wajcman, J. 1991: *Feminism Confronts Technology*. Cambridge: Polity.

Watson, J. 2000: *Male Bodies: Health, Culture and Identity*. Buckingham: Open University Press.

Webb, C. 1986: *Feminist Practice in Women's Health Care*. Chichester: John Wiley and Sons.

Wilkinson, S. and Kitzinger, C. 1994: Towards a feminist approach to breast cancer. In S. Wilkinson and C. Kitzinger (eds), *Women and Health: Feminist Perspectives*, London: Taylor and Francis, pp. 124–40.

6 Contemporary Perspectives on Ageing

Pat Chambers

Key issues within this chapter

- The relevance of 'age' and 'ageing' to all nurses.
- Defining age.
- The social construction of age.
- Theoretical perspectives of age and ageing.
- Ageism, diversity, discrimination and best nursing practice.

By the end of this chapter you should be able to . . .

- Explore your own stereotypes of 'age'.
- Consider the ways in which 'age' is structured in contemporary Western societies.
- Consider the impact of 'ageism' on nursing practice.
- Develop your own guidelines for anti-ageist practice.
- Reconsider the relevance of 'age' for nurses.

1   Introduction

It is a truism to say that nurses work with patients of all ages, from prenatal to very old. Indeed, pathways within nursing programmes are often delineated by 'age' either explicitly or implicitly. However, 'age' is often assumed to be 'neutral', an undeniable 'fact' on which we all agree. Sociologists often refer to this as making use of taken-for-granted knowledge. Surely 'age' is simply a useful way of summarizing the number of years we have been alive, and is manifested and celebrated via ceremonies such as birthdays, and symbols such as birthday cards and presents. And yet, as this chapter seeks to demonstrate, chronological age is only one aspect of 'age'.

social gerontology the critical study of ageing

Rather, as the study of **social gerontology** demonstrates, the way in which 'age' is constructed and understood in any society is extremely complex, and has implications for practice. The image of working with older people created by well-worn phrases such as 'no previous experience needed' only serves to reinforce the 'age' hierarchy.

The first part of this chapter seeks to challenge some of these assumptions. A discussion follows of the way in which the age structure of societies is changing and how this has given rise to what might be described as a **moral panic** amongst policy makers and some professional groups. Sociological theories of ageing, and their relevance to 'age' across the life course will be explored, and a **life-course perspective** on 'age' that draws on current social gerontological thinking will be developed. In the final section of the chapter, we will consider the potential impact of 'ageism' on nursing practice. An opportunity will be provided to develop personal guidelines for anti-ageist practice in nursing.

moral panic media-inspired overreaction to a certain group or to a type of behaviour that is taken as a sign of impending social disorder

life-course perspective a view of a person's whole life, taken in order to better comprehend their present experiences and beliefs

2 Definitions of age

Activity 6.1

What is 'age'?

Individually list five characteristics which you associate with the following age groups: 65+; 18–64; 12–17; 0–11.

Compare your answers with a colleague's and note similarities and differences in your lists. Are there differences between the ways in which you characterize the different age groups?

If yes, why do you think this is? Do you think there would be further differences if you were to consider the issue of learning disability in relation to these age groups?

Sociologists have found that more positive characteristics are often noted for under-65s than for over-65s. 'Growth and development', 'good health' and 'happiness', for example, are more likely to be listed as characteristics of the under-65s, whereas 'decline', 'ill-health' and 'loneliness' are likely to be listed for the over-65s. Indeed, Victor (1989) reports that there are a number of commonly held negative stereotypes about old age. These include:

- Older people are all alike.
- Most older people are in poor health.

- Most older people are isolated from their families and ignored by them.
- Older people cannot learn.
- Older people are not interested in, or capable of, an active sex life.
- Older people are unproductive and are a drain on NHS resources.
- Older people are dependent.
- Older people are the principal victims of crime.

Each of these stereotypes has been refuted by research findings and yet they persist, even in nursing practice (Bernard, 1998), as will be explored later in this chapter.

Given that 'age' is clearly more than the sum total of a person's birthdays, we must beware of making assumptions or engaging with stereotypes based purely on chronology. Kirkwood (1999) concurs and argues that although physiology, linked to chronology, is popularly (and sometimes professionally) assumed to be the most important component in defining 'age', it is only one among many. For example, evidence suggests that we do not all 'age' physiologically at the same rate: social, economic and cultural factors have a profound effect on this process (Fennell et al., 1989). Poverty, low educational attainment, poor diet, unhealthy social behaviours, such as smoking, and low levels of exercise all contribute to our physiological status.

Let us consider two phenomena of the twentieth century and their relationship to the changes in economics and social policy during that time in order to understand the way in which society conceptualizes and organizes, sometimes through social policy, an age grouping to meet its perceived values, ideas or needs. Firstly, 'pensioner', a term which did not exist in the earlier part of the last century but one which is now applied collectively to all those who on reaching 'retirement age' (which itself is fluid and dependent on the economy of a society) are forced to retire from employment in order to create jobs for younger members of society. For some, this is a sentence to living on a vastly reduced income whereas for others it is a time of choice and opportunity. Secondly, 'teenager', a term applied to those between the ages of thirteen and eighteen. Although originally conceived in the 1950s as a descriptor for the time between childhood and adulthood, a time of rebellion against adult values, and certainly during the 1960s encompassing young workers with disposable incomes, the term 'teenager' is now increasingly synonymous with extended full-time education and economic dependency on parents or the state.

History, that is the period of time in which we live, and the cultural values of the society at that time in relation to normality and difference, also have a place in the construction of 'age'. Let us consider this briefly in relation firstly to childhood and then to adulthood.

Childhood

Interestingly, one dictionary definition of 'child' offers a physiological explanation: 'young human being below the age of puberty' (*Concise Oxford Dictionary*, 1996, p. 227). Such a definition, however, takes no account of more complex ideas of 'age'. Social history accounts (see, for example, Pinchbeck and Hewitt, 1973) remind us that childhood, like old age, has been constructed and defined differently across history and cultures. In nineteenth-century Britain, child labour was the norm (and remains so within some cultures), with education and health care only available for the privileged few; indeed what we would now consider to be 'childhood' was a relatively short period prior to adulthood. 'Extended' childhood and state provision for children – financial support, education, health care – are all products of the post-war Welfare State, and reflect specific 'historical' values towards an 'age group'. The emergence of the child as 'dependent' on adults until achieving adult status was a phenomenon of the twentieth century, a process which Lee (2001, p. xiii) describes as 'child human becomings' moving through to 'adult human beings', with 'adulthood' as the desired state of stability and completion that constituted arrival at the 'journey's end' (p. 7). He goes on to argue that this image of the 'journey's end' has been crucial in maintaining the authority that adults have had over children and the right and duty to make decisions for them (p. 9). The international conferment of rights on 'children' in the United Nations Convention on the Rights of the Child (1989) has begun to shift this relationship and at the beginning of the twenty-first century the status of children as beings in their own right ('child human beings') is emerging. Childhood, then, although it has always existed, has been redefined and restructured and will continue to be so (see Hockey, 1993). Our understanding of what constitutes the 'age of childhood' is both culturally and historically bound and is in a state of continual flux.

Adulthood

Let us now turn to 'adulthood', using a dictionary definition again as our starting point: 'adult: mature, grown-up; a person who has reached the age of majority' (*Concise Oxford Dictionary*, 1996, p. 19). A definition such as this one is, however, static and takes no account of the way in which adulthood, like childhood and old age, has been subject to redefinition and restructure. Even the term 'age of majority' is fluid and dependent on social policy and law. In the nineteenth century, 'adulthood', when construed in policy terms, encompassed what we now perceive to be adolescence and old age, although it must be acknowledged that chronologically 'old age' differed from today. Boys and girls born in 1901 could only expect to live to 45 years and 49 years respectively. Results from the 2001 census tell us that these figures have changed dramatically in the course of one hundred years: boys born in 2000 can expect to live for 75 years and girls for 80 years.

3   The changing age structure of the population

Just as childhood and middle age have been redefined and restructured historically so, too, has old age. In the 1980s fears about the ageing of the population, sometimes described as the 'greying' of the population, both contributed to and were a part of the negative stereotyping of older people, and have reinforced our notions of age structures. **Demography** can tell us the age structure of a particular population at a particular point in time. For example, numbers of over-60s have increased by 8.3% over the last 20 years and, more recently, the proportion of over-60s in England and Wales increased from 20.7% in the 1991 census (ONS, 1991) to 20.9% in the 2001 census (ONS, 2001). By contrast, children under 16 made up 20% of the population in 2001, compared with 23% in 1961. Projections suggest that the proportion of the population who are children will continue to fall to around 18% of the total by 2011. Figure 6.1 shows that by 2014 there will be more people over 65 than under 16, and by 2025 there will be more 1.6 million more people over the age of 65 than people under 16.

Why is the population ageing? The age structure is dependent on three variables: fertility, mortality and migration. Let us focus on the first two.

demography   the study of populations

Figure 6.1 Age structure of the population

Source: Summerfield and Babb, 2003.

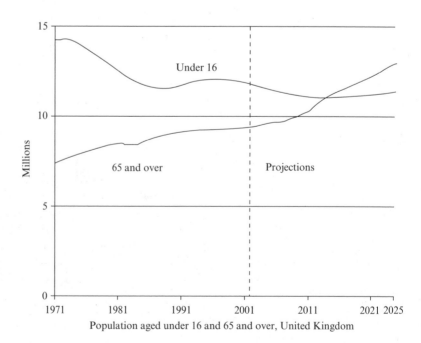

Population aged under 16 and 65 and over, United Kingdom

Fertility and mortality

Before the end of the nineteenth century, fertility rates were high but life expectancy was low. High rates of infant mortality, epidemics and infections, poor working conditions, and deaths in childbirth meant that those who survived to old age were in the minority. At the beginning of the twenty-first century in the UK, as elsewhere, fertility rates have decreased as a result of education, access to contraception, government policies, and so on. At the same time, we have seen improved mortality rates as a result of the massive public health measures undertaken in the nineteenth and twentieth centuries. At a local level, migration can accelerate the greying of the population, by either an exodus (for employment) or an influx (for retirement) of one age group. This changing demography has caused alarm in some quarters and, in the last part of the twentieth century, 'old age' became the source of a moral panic, and the ensuing debate only served to reinforce the ageist structure of British society. Rather than old age being celebrated and the prospect of a longer life span and a potentially fitter old age being welcomed, the ageing of the population was thought instead to be burdensome, and claims were made that younger adults would have to work for longer and pay higher taxes in order to support 'hordes' of frail, dependent older people. Gerontologists (such as Phillipson, 1998) have challenged this perspective, pointing to the diversity of the ageing population, which includes older adults who contribute to the overall economy as volunteers and as family carers (of children and other adults), as well as those who continue in paid employment beyond the 'state' retirement age. Like all other 'age groups', old age is certainly not a homogeneous state; some older people will find themselves in need of more health and social care services than others, but for most older people 'old age' itself is not problematic.

4   Theories of ageing

Traditional theories

structured ageing the social construction of ageing

Traditional theories of human development and decline have also served to reinforce age difference and contribute to notions of ◄ **structured ageing**. Until the 1980s old age was theorized as a life stage, separate from childhood and adulthood. Cumming and Henry (1961) put forward a theory, disengagement theory, which suggested that in their sixties older people 'disengage' from society: they do this willingly and with the approval of successive generations who benefit via the enhanced employment opportunities which then become available. By contrast, activity theorists argued that the only way to resist disengagement was to maintain a 'middle age' life style (Fennell et al., 1989). Disengagement theory has been challenged as a convenient rationale for supporting the exclusion of older people from public life and activity theory as taking no account of diversity. Critics argued that although many older people do withdraw from the public sphere, there is little evidence to suggest that they do so voluntarily; rather, ageist policies and practices (low retirement income and dependency-creating services) restrict their capacity to remain active citizens.

Contemporary theories

Contemporary theories have sought to challenge such rigid, and uncritical, perspectives on ageing, highlighting societal, rather than individual, responsibility for structuring ageing. Firstly, the political economy perspective highlights the impact of an individual's location within the social and economic structure during the earlier part of their life course, on their financial status, their social location and the life choices available in old age (Phillipson, 1998). This perspective, in particular, acknowledges the way in which advantages and disadvantages accrued earlier in the life course impact on an individual in old age. An example of this is the way in which many older women find themselves with reduced access to financial resources in later life as a result of working in part-time, low-paid and low-status employment or a lifetime's financial dependence on a spouse (Arber and Ginn, 1991). A political economy perspective on ageing also points to increasing polarity of the ageing experience, ranging from the social exclusion of those older people living in areas of extreme economic deprivation (Scharf et al., 2002) to those 'young-at-heart', fit and wealthy older people, who are the new 'niche' markets of the tourism and travel industry (Warnes et al., 1999; Ylanne-McEwen, 1999).

Secondly, social gerontologists are increasingly acknowledging the importance of the subjective experience of ageing, as encapsulated in biographical studies, and the impact of this on ageing identities (Birren, 1996; Chambers, 2002). This cannot be understood in isolation from historical location or political economy. Ruth and Oberg (1996, p. 171), for example, in a quest to understand the experience of old age for Finns from the generation of 'the Wars and the Depression', argue that knowledge based solely on current circumstances is inadequate: 'Ageing must be seen as a continuation of an integrated process, starting with an earlier life, where the life lived gives meaning to old age.' In chapter 1 we argued that sociology is multi-paradigmatic; thus experiences of ageing must be understood from the perspective of social structure as well as that of social action.

Age throughout the life course is characterized by and perhaps best understood in terms of 'diversity' of gender, ethnicity, social class, disability, geographical location, and so on. Talking about 'age groups' is only useful as a marker, a shorthand term to describe those people who share a chronological age, and to provide some information relating to physiology. We would do better to try to understand an individual's experience of the life course, wherever she or he happens to be located at a particular point in time.

Activity 6.2 **Biography and ageing**

(a) Note down the major events or 'milestones' in your own life so far, in relation to your early years, family, relationships, school, work and so on.

(b) Interview a person who is much older than you, but the same gender, about the major milestones in their life. Note the differences and similarities.

(c) What does this exercise tell you about individual (personal) and collective (cohort, sharing the same historical time) ageing and the way in which 'age', at different points in the life course, has been differentially structured over time?

(d) How might this understanding help you in your nursing practice?

---

5 Ageism

ageism discrimination on the basis of age

According to Bytheway (1995) **ageism** exists throughout the life course. For example, a survey on ageism in 2003 found that in some industries, particularly those 'young' areas such as information technology or the media, workers were 'too old' at 35 (BBC News Online, 10 June 2003). One in 10 of the workers who told researchers they had been victims of ageism were between 35 and 40 years old and 3 per cent of those who felt their employers were discriminating against them for being too old were under 35. By contrast, school leavers and graduates feel themselves to be less favoured than older workers doing similar jobs, according to a report by the Department for Work and Pensions' Age Positive team (Department for Work and Pensions, 2001). Anecdotal evidence pointed to ageism working against young employees, who felt they had unfairly missed out on job vacancies, promotions and pay rises. Some young people felt they were stereotyped as being unreliable. The report suggested that while those in their teens and twenties felt they were less discriminated against than workers in their fifties, sixties and beyond, they were nonetheless concerned.

It would seem therefore that stereotypes of all ages abound in the world of employment. However, the term 'ageism' is usually used in relation to later life and is rooted in the 'social construction' of ageing highlighted earlier (see chapter 2 for a definition of ageism). According to Bytheway and Johnson (1990, pp. 25–6):

> Ageism is a set of beliefs originating in the biological variation
> between people and relating to the ageing process. It is in the
> actions of corporate bodies, what is said and done by their
> representatives, and the resulting views that are held by
> ordinary ageing people that ageism is made manifest.

Bytheway (1995) goes on to say:

> Ageism generates and reinforces a fear and denigration of the
> ageing process, and the stereotyping assumptions regarding
> competence and need for protection. In particular ageism
> *legitimates* the use of chronological age to mark out classes of
> people who are systematically denied resources and
> opportunities that others enjoy, and who suffer the
> consequences of such denigration – ranging from well-
> meaning patronage to unambiguous vilification.
>
> Ageism therefore is not simply a matter of personal
> prejudice but has its roots in the way society is organised and
> unlike many other 'isms', will potentially be experienced by us
> all to some degree. It is manifested in the following ways:
>
> • marginalization;
> • the use of dismissive and demeaning language;
> • humour and mockery;
> • physical, sexual, emotional and financial abuse;
> • economic disadvantage;
> • and, restricted opportunities or life chances.

As a result of living in an ageist society, many older people internalize
ageist views, become ageist towards their peers, and try to distance
themselves from other 'old people'. Furthermore, ageing women in
particular feel coerced into 'passing' for middle-aged via strategies
such as colouring their hair, dressing in 'younger' clothes and, more
recently, cosmetic surgery. However, they have to tread a fine line if
they are not to be accused of being 'mutton dressed as lamb': it is not
easy being an older woman in an ageist and sexist world!

According to Thompson (1995) ageism occurs on a number of
fronts, including: personal (individual experience); cultural
(language, images, media); and structural (differential access to
services and opportunities). He goes on to demonstrate that the
impact of ageism on health and social care practice with older people
includes: dehumanization; ageist language; elder abuse;
infantilization (treating older people as if they were children); denial
of citizenship; welfarism; and medicalization. Unlike some other
forms of discrimination, ageism is not illegal and, in 2000, Age
Concern England conducted a survey which reported evidence of
ageism within the NHS (Age Concern England, 2000). In addition, a
small body of literature has highlighted evidence of ageism within
nursing practice (Bernard, 1998; Koch and Webb, 1996). However, in

Activity 6.3   **Nurses and ageism**

'There is now a certain amount of evidence to support the contention that ageism is not only rife amongst the population at large, but also amongst many of those who care for older people in a professional capacity. Given that many of these professionals are women caring for other women . . . this should at the very least give us serious cause for concern. . . . Negative attitudes though are merely one facet of that particular form of social oppression which we now recognise as "ageism". One feature of the operation of ageism is that it can generate and reinforce a fear and denigration of the process of ageing. Nurses, like everyone else, work and live against this societal backdrop and are therefore not totally immune to the impact of these pressures on their own practice. Perhaps more worrying though is the evidence that many professionals, nurses included, in actual fact hold more ageist attitudes than do the population at large. . . . [Previous] research showed that nurses responded quite differently according to whether their patients were male or female: women patients were far more likely to be depersonalised; the nurses knew a lot less about them than they did about their male patients; they were cared for in quite different ways; and they tended to be labelled as more 'difficult' than the men culprits. . . . there are various reasons for these observed differences in professional attitudes and behaviours. First, there is a suggestion that looking after men, was less problematic for female nurses because this was more closely related to what many of them did anyway. . . . Second, the men too tended to be 'in role' and were much more accepting of being looked after. In other words, being a patient was often simply an extension of their conventional relationship to women in their families. Third, . . . for many of the older women, who had themselves been experts in caring work, for their own families in their own homes – being in a situation of dependency on other women was extremely difficult . . . many of the nurses actually found caring for older women threatening . . . both groups see themselves as "expert carers" and this can set up tensions. [And they were daily confronted with images of what they themselves might become in the future, and so would operate strategies which enabled them to distance themselves to a degree from their female patients.]' (Bernard, 1998)

Read the extract above (or, better, the whole article – see References).

(a)   To what does the author attribute nurses' ageism?
(b)   What can you learn from this about guiding your own practice?

2002 the Labour government made a commitment to rooting out ageism in health and social care services and Standard One of the National Service Framework for Older People (DoH, 2001) states that health services will be provided, regardless of age, on the basis of clinical need alone.

6   Anti-ageist practice

In working with older people we must recognize that our starting point is one of disadvantage and discrimination rather than equality. According to Hughes (1997), **anti-ageist practice** embodies the following three values:

Personhood: ascribes to all people of all ages the authenticity and worth of being alive and of having lived.
Citizenship: relationship between the individual and society and how that relationship is defined; emphasizes rights of individual and reciprocal responsibilities of individual and society; validates membership of society; and is different from 'consumer'.
Celebration: age to be celebrated as an achievement and as a period to be valued in its own right.

Although specifically addressing 'old age', these values should underpin practice with all age groups. Furthermore, such practice should be underpinned by the key principles set out in box 6.1.

anti-ageist practice
health and social care practice which does not discriminate on the basis of age

---

Box 6.1

The principles of anti-ageist practice

Empowerment: ensuring that the person has or acquires control over their own life and all that goes with power and control (freedom, autonomy, dignity and feelings of self-worth).

Participation: meaningful sharing and involvement.

Choice: important means of personal validation as well as a right in terms of personhood and citizenship.

Integration: into mainstream of life at every level.

Normalization: making available whatever is necessary to enable all people to live in the same way, with the same quality of life as other people in society.

Anti-ageist practice then requires that we do not discriminate on the basis of 'age'. This means for example that we do not assume that the early years of life are a period of development and the later years a period of decline. Nor do we assume that the 'voice' of a child is less important, or less believable, than that of an adult. Rather, for all

those for whom we care, we should seek to maximize qua
and build in potential development, regardless of age. This
now be explored further in relation to three areas of practice:
conceptualizing and responding to falls; understanding the patie
subjective experience; and working with grief and loss.

Falls and our response to them

Firstly, let us consider the way in which we 'conceptualize' and
respond to falls. Young children regularly fall over when they are
learning to walk. The common response is to encourage the child to
get back on its feet and try again. Imagine then another scenario, this
time with an older person. She has already fallen a couple of times
and has been deemed by family and professionals to be 'at risk of
falling'. Nonetheless, the older person wishes to maintain her
independence. However, in going to the toilet, a very private sphere of
life and one in which she does not wish for support, she falls, and is
told off for taking risks. Why the difference? According to Kingston
(1998), falls are socially constructed on the basis of age, and risk-
assessment tools are a manifestation of such a construction. Older
people are not allowed to take risks, and if they do, they are chastised
and considered to be 'reckless' and 'selfish'. Young children who fall,
by contrast, are considered to be 'bold'. It would seem that 'age' is the
determining factor.

An anti-ageist approach to practice ensures that a nurse using a
risk-assessment tool with an older person does not use it
mechanistically but rather takes into account the key values of
'personhood', 'citizenship' and 'celebration' discussed above.

Patients' subjective experiences

Increasingly, the literature on childhood, learning disability, mental
ill-health and old age points to the importance of the subjective
experiences: 'how it feels' from the inside (patients' perspective)
rather than 'how it is' from the outside (professionals' perspective).
Fundamental to this approach is 'personhood' and listening to the
'voice' of patients rather than jumping to 'age-based assumptions'.
Lee (2001) reminds us that until fairly recently, children's voices were
silent. Even today, although the failings of individual adults and adult
institutions are acknowledged, there is still a tension between the
need for children to speak and the traditional view that only adults are
worth listening to (p. 91). He goes on to stress the importance of
recognizing that policies and practices devised for children have often
rested on assumptions that children are vulnerable 'becomings',
'investments to be cultivated and protected' (p. 100). Anti-ageist
practice challenges this, and enables the nurse to work in partnership
with the child or young adult and to value the patient's subjective

experience, that is, 'what it feels like'. One way of accomplishing this is through the use of 'life story' books, in which the patient is encouraged to share their understanding of their illness, in pictures or words, or both, in the context of personal autobiography. This is particularly helpful with children with chronic illness, or learning disability, and can enable the nurse to gain an 'insider' perspective. It can provide a useful counterbalance to so-called objective, often age-based, accounts of illness.

Depression, grief and loss

Finally, let us consider the way in which anti-ageist practice can be used in relation to depression, grief and loss in work with older people and young children. Old age is commonly construed as 'a time of loss', and it therefore follows that depression in old age is an automatic consequence of the ageing process and does not need to be treated. The reality is that many older people adjust perfectly well to loss; after all, they expect to experience loss at that point in their life (Chambers, 2000; 2002). However, they may need support and acknowledgement of their loss and must be allowed the time and space to give expression to their feelings. Some older people, will suffer from depression; it may or may not be associated with loss, but without treatment they may not recover. Nurses who follow anti-ageist practices will be vigilant and will not assume that depression is an automatic consequence of the ageing process. Instead, they will seek appropriate interventions to enable the older person to return to maximum health (see, for example, Department of Health, 2001, Standard 7). Nor will they ignore the older person who needs time and space to grieve in order to adjust to loss.

In a similar vein, the social construction of 'early childhood' often militates against the needs of very young children who experience loss being adequately addressed. Nurses who have an understanding of, and follow, anti-ageist practice are well placed to support children who are bereaved.

Activity 6.4	**Anti-ageist practice**

Using the guidelines offered by Hughes (1997) and with reference to one of the three values listed in section 6, draw up a list of your own do's and don'ts for anti-ageist practice in relation to working with one of the following groups:

(a) children;
(b) young adults with learning difficulties;
(c) adults with mental ill-health;
(d) older people.

There is now general agreement, resulting primarily from the pioneering work of Stroebe et al., (1996), that the bereaved person, young or old, has to confront both the loss and the changes that result from that loss; this has come to be known as the dual-orientation approach, that is, to both loss and restoration.

Summary and Resources

Summary

- 'Age' is a complex process and state of being which is more than the sum total of birthdays a person has notched up. In addition to chronology, it encompasses physiology, psychology, law, social policy, culture and sociology.

- A society constructs its own meanings of 'childhood', 'adulthood' and 'old age', and these are constantly changing according to the social and economic needs of that society.

- Stereotypical assumptions are made on the basis of age, and nurses are no more or less immune to such ageist assumptions than other members of society.

- A life-course perspective, rather than an 'age-based' perspective, is advocated.

- An understanding of ageism and anti-ageist practice is essential for nurses in all branches of nursing.

Questions for Discussion

1 What, in relation to 'age', informed your choice of nursing route? Consider the values and attitudes underpinning this choice.

2 How can an understanding of the social construction of 'age' inform best practice? Discuss this in relation to your chosen branch of nursing.

3 Look at the way in which birthday cards and road signs depict different ages. What do you notice? What does it tell us about the way age is constructed in contemporary British society?

4 Why might the next generation of older people – 'the baby boomers' – challenge notions of ageism?

Further Reading

B. Bytheway: *Ageism*. Buckingham: Open University Press, 1995.
This engaging book explores the way in which 'age' is constructed in contemporary British society. Numerous examples are provided in the text which seek to challenge dominant stereotypes.

J. Hockey and A. James: *Growing Up and Growing Old: Ageing and Dependency across the Life Course*. London: Sage, 1993.
This book employs a life-course perspective to explore the diversity of the experience of growing up and growing older, from childhood

through adulthood to old age. The inclusion of 'disability' across the life course is a particularly useful aspect of this text.

N. Lee: *Childhood and Society: Growing Up in a Age of Uncertainty.*
Buckingham: Open University Press, 2001.
From a sociological perspective, Nick Lee examines what it means to be a child and critically evaluates the way in which our understanding of 'childhood' is ever changing.

References

Age Concern England 2000: Age Concern / NOP, May 2000, at www.ace.org.uk/ageconcern/media/Policy_Paper_1400.pdf.

Arber, S. and Ginn, J. 1991: *Gender and Later Life*. London: Sage.

Bernard, M. 1998: 'Backs to the future? Reflections on women, ageing and nursing.' *Journal of Advanced Nursing*, 27, 633–40.

Birren, J. E. 1996: Autobiography. In J. E. Birren, G. M. Kenyon, J. C. Ruth, J. J. F. Schroots and T. Svensson (eds), *Explorations in Adult Development*, New York: Springer, pp. 283–99.

Bytheway, B. 1995: *Ageism*. Buckingham: Open University Press.

Bytheway, B. and Johnson, J. 1990: 'On defining ageism.' *Critical Social Policy*, 27, 27–9.

Chambers, P. 1994: 'A biographical approach to later life widowhood.' *Generations Review*, 4(3), 8–12.

Chambers, P. 2000: Widowhood in later life. In M. Bernard, J. Phillips, L. Machin and V. Davies (eds), *Women Ageing: Changing Identities, Challenging Myths*. London: Routledge, pp. 127–47.

Chambers, P. 2002: The life stories of older widows: situating later life widowhood within the life course. In C. Horrocks, K. Milnes, B. Roberts and D. Robinson (eds), *Narrative, Memory and Life Transitions*. Huddersfield: Huddersfield University Press, pp. 23–41.

Concise Oxford Dictionary 1996. London: Oxford University Press.

Cumming, E. and Henry, W. E. 1961: *Growing Old: The Process of Disengagement*. New York: Basic Books.

Currer, C. 2002: Dying and bereavement. In R. Adams, L. Dominelli and M. Payne (eds), *Critical Practice in Social Work*, Basingstoke: Palgrave, pp. 210–20.

Department for Work and Pensions 2001: *Ageism: Attitudes and Experiences of Young People*. Nottingham: DWP.

Department of Health 2001: *National Service Framework for Older People*. London: DoH.

Dilley, R. 2003: Ageism hits generation X? BBC News Online, 10 June, at http://news.bbc.co.uk/1/hi/uk/2975754.stm.

Fennell, G., Phillipson, C. and Evers, H. (eds) 1989: *The Sociology of Old Age*. Milton Keynes: Open University Press.

Giele, J. Z. and Elder, G. H. 1998: *Methods of Life Course Research: Qualitative and Quantitative Approaches*. Thousand Oaks, CA: Sage.

Hockey, J. 1993: Constructing personhood: changing categories of the child. In J. Hockey and A. James (eds), *Growing Up and Growing Old*, London: Sage, pp. 45–72.

Hughes, B. 1997: *Older People and Community Care*. Buckingham: Open University Press.

Kingston, P. 1998: 'Older people and falls: a randomised control trial of Health Visitor intervention – a study of 108 older women who attended an Accident and Emergency Department after a fall.' PhD thesis, Keele University.

Kirkwood, T. 1999: *Time of Our Lives: The Science of Human Ageing*. London: Weidenfeld and Nicolson.

Koch, T. and Webb, C. 1996: 'The biomedical construction of ageing: implications for nursing care of older people.' *Journal of Advanced Nursing*, 23, 954–9.

Lee, N. 2001: *Childhood and Society*. Buckingham: Open University Press.

Office for National Statistics 1991: Census, etc., at www.statistics.gov.uk.

Office for National Statistics 2001: Census, etc., at www.statistics.gov.uk/census2001.

Phillipson, C. 1998: *Reconstructing Old Age*. London: Sage.

Pinchbeck, I. and Hewitt, M. 1973: *Children in English Society, volumes 1 and 2*. London: Routledge and Kegan Paul.

Riley, M., Johnson, M. and Foner, A. 1972: *Ageing and Society, vol. 3: A Sociology of Age Stratification*. New York: Russell State Foundation.

Ruth, J.-E. and Oberg, P. 1996: Ways of life: old age in a life history perspective. In J. E. Birren et al. (eds), *Explorations in Adult Development*. New York: Springer, pp. 167–86.

Scharf, T., Phillipson, C., Smith, A. E. and Kingston, P. 2002: *Growing Older in Socially Deprived Areas: Social Exclusion in Later Life*. London: Help the Aged.

Stroebe, M., Gergen, M. Gergen, K. and Stroebe, W. 1996: Broken hearts or broken bonds. In D. Klass, P. R. Silverman and S. L. Nickman (eds), *Continuing Bonds: New Understandings of Grief*, Washington, D. C. and London: Taylor and Francis, pp. 31–44.

Summerfield, C. and Babb, P. (eds) 2003: *Social Trends*, 33. London: HMSO.

Thompson, N. 1995: *Age and Dignity*. Aldershot: Arena.

United Nations Convention on the Rights of the Child, 1989, at www.unicef.org.

Victor, C. 1989: *Health and Health Care in Later Life*. London: Edward Arnold.

Warnes, A. M., King, R., Williams, A. M. and Patterson, G. 1999: 'The well-being of British expatriate retirees in southern Europe.' *Ageing and Society*, 19(6), 717–40.

Ylanne-McEwen, V. 1999: 'Young at heart: discourses of age identity in travel agency interaction.' *Ageing and Society*, 19(4), 417–40.

7 Chronic Illness, Disabling Barriers, Discrimination and Prejudice

Nick Watson

Key issues within this chapter

- Definitions of disability.
- Sociological theories of disability and chronic illness.
- The social model of disability, barriers and discrimination
- The sociology of the body.
- Disability and the role of nurses.

By the end of this chapter you should be able to . . .

- Understand differences between definitions and classifications of disability.
- Explore different sociological theories of disability and chronic illness.
- Recognize the role of the disability movement and the significance of the social model of disability.
- Discuss disabling barriers.
- Examine the role of nursing in relationship to removing disabling barriers.

---

1 Introduction

It is estimated that there are around 500 million disabled people worldwide, the largest number of whom are to be found ◄ in the **majority world**. There is, moreover, a higher prevalence of disabled people in wealthier nations relative to population. Advances in medical science and medical interventions which

majority world also referred to as the 'developing world'

prolong life, coupled with demographic changes in the age of the population, suggest that these numbers will increase in the future. The implications of this in terms of social and economic policy will be far-reaching. This chapter introduces you to sociological perspectives on disability. It draws on a discussion of the classification and definition of disability and explores different models of disability. It will also examine how organizations of disabled people have demanded, and to some extent achieved, a rethinking of what it means to be a disabled person. They have argued that disabled people should be seen as a minority group, as a group that faces discrimination, prejudice and oppression, and that this is the result of the way that society is organized and not a consequence of their impairment. The chapter also focuses on disabling barriers and encourages you to think about what nurses can do to dismantle these.

The meaning of disability and the personal consequences for individual lives of being a disabled person have changed considerably in the last 35 years. Beore the 1970s the majority of disabled people, in most of the Western world at least, would have been found in large, isolated, residential establishments. Employment opportunities for many were restricted to special 'training centres' or sheltered employment with an emphasis on work as rehabilitation. These centres typically offered poor training, little opportunity for advancement and low wage levels. Disabled children were segregated from their non-disabled peers and, under the guise of rehabilitation, denied access to a full curriculum, spending much of their time in physiotherapy. This in turn served to deny them future opportunities. Disabled people were also denied sexual rights, the right to form relationships, reproductive rights and the right to lead independent lives. Whilst these conditions still exist for many disabled people, increasing numbers have been able to access mainstream employment and mainstream schooling, live independently in the community, form relationships and have children. The fact that some can do it suggests that all should be able to do it and that they are held back by social, economic and political factors rather than their impairment.

discrimination may occur as the consequence of prejudice which disadvantages certain social groups

Further evidence for the **discrimination** experienced by disabled people is provided by an overview of disability in Scotland by Riddell and Banks (2001) (see box 7.1).

Box 7.1	**Disability and discrimination**

- Disabled people are less likely to be in employment than non-disabled people and the unemployment rate for disabled people is almost double that for non-disabled people.

- Disabled people are around eight times as likely as non-disabled people to be out of work and claiming benefits.

- Disabled people are twice as likely as non-disabled people to have no qualifications.

- Disabled people have difficulty in finding suitable housing and are less likely to be owner-occupiers than non-disabled people.

- There are approximately 20,000 households in Scotland where a household member uses a wheelchair, but only 5,000 dwellings of full wheelchair standard.

- Only 12 per cent of buses in operation in Scotland have a lowered floor and over 50 per cent of bus providers do not intend to operate low-floor buses in the next three years.

- In Scotland in 2000 disabled people were more likely to be living in poverty than the rest of the population. Thirty-three per cent of households have an income of less than £6,000 per annum compared with 26 per cent of households without a disabled person. Only 6 per cent of households with a disabled person have an income of more than £20,000, in contrast to 24 per cent without a disabled person.

Source: Riddell and Banks, 2001.

2   The classification and definition of disability

The traditional way to view disablement is to see it simply as a medical problem. Disability, in this approach, and the problems faced by disabled people, arise as a result of impairment. For example, people would say, 'She is disabled because she has epilepsy' (Thomas, 1999). This is called the medical or individual model of disability. It is the basis for most current social policy aimed at resolving the problems faced by disabled people and it is also the approach that lies at the centre of much medical treatment aimed at disabled people. It is the basis of the World Health Organization's (WHO) *International Classification of Impairments, Disabilities and Handicaps* (ICIDH), produced in 1980. Put simply, this approach suggests that impairments are the result of a biological or psychological abnormality, that disabilities are the resulting restrictions in activity and that handicaps are the disadvantages faced by disabled people that arise as a result of impairments or disabilities. Impairment is therefore seen as the cause of the disadvantages faced by disabled people.

Box 7.2   **International classification of impairments, disabilities and handicaps**

Impairments (I) Abnormalities of the body structure and appearance and of organ system function, resulting from any cause; in principle 'impairments' means impairments at the organ level.

Disabilities (D) The consequences of impairment in terms of the functional performance and activity of the individual; disabilities thus represent disturbances at the level of the person.

Handicap (H) The disadvantages experienced by the individuals as a result of impairments and disabilities; handicaps reflect interaction with and adaptation to the individual's surroundings.

Source: Wood, 1980, p. 14

Activity 7.1   **Representations of disability in soap operas**

Think about how disabled people are represented in popular soap operas.

(a)   How many disabled people are there in soap operas?
(b)   What are the main impairment groups covered?
(c)   How is disability handled, as an issue, in soap operas? What does this tell you about how disabled people are perceived in popular culture?

The intention in the development of this model was to move from a disease-based classification system to a more socio-medical approach. Unlike impairment and disability, handicap is not classified in terms of the individual, but in the terms of the situations in which individuals find themselves. The medical sociologist Michael Bury (1979; 1996; 1997) argues that this model, whilst not without its problems, has been a useful tool in assessing the social needs of disabled people. The emphasis placed on material and social needs and their articulation with health needs, he suggests, has enabled, a more nuanced understanding of the problems faced by disabled people to emerge.

However, many disabled activists and organizations of disabled people have been very critical of the WHO's model. The individual disabled person becomes the centre of attention and the focus is on changing the individual, usually through the modification of their impairment. Emphasis is placed on cure and rehabilitative medical intervention. Through this reification of impairment, control over the lives of disabled people moves to the medical profession. If disablement can only be cured through medical intervention, it follows that the fortunes of disabled people lie in the hands of the medical profession (regardless of whether or not it can treat a particular impairment). The medical 'expert' defines what it is that an individual needs, how these needs should be met and how the negative consequences of an individual's disability can be minimized (Barnes et al., 1999). Autonomy is removed and the picture of a disabled person as one who is a victim of their impairment emerges, what Oliver (1990, p. 1) has called 'the personal tragedy theory of disability'.

In addition, as Barnes and his colleagues (1999) point out, the medical model, by linking impairment with disability, presents the environment as 'neutral' and stable. The possibility of changing environments and thus removing barriers is ignored. These authors also suggest that in the medical model the onus is on the individual to adapt, to adopt coping strategies and to limit their own hopes and ambitions.

These criticisms of the ICIDH have led the WHO to produce what is termed the International Classification of Functioning and Disability (ICF) (World Health Organization, 1997; 2002). In this model, disability arises through the interaction between the health condition (the disease or the disorder) and contextual factors, such as environmental factors (which are external to the individual and include disabling attitudes and architectural barriers) and personal factors (such as the individual's gender, age and social background). There are three levels of human functioning in this model: functioning at the level of the body or body part, of the whole person, and of the whole person in a social context. Disability arises when there are problems at one or more of these levels. The definitions of the components of the ICF are given in box 7.3.

Whilst this model removes the causal link between impairment and disablement and allows for a socio-medical analysis, much emphasis is still placed on health classified within a medical domain and its approach is still individualistic (Hurst, 2000). It is also expert-led; that is, health service professionals are, through this model, able to judge and make decisions about the quality of life of people who are disabled (Pfeiffer, 2000).

This, however, is the domain in which much mainstream medical sociology operates when it writes about disability. It ignores, in the main, the socio-political aspects to life as a disabled person, focusing instead on the impacts that an impairment can have on an individual. Sections 3 and 4 examine two main ways in which disability has been theorized in medical sociology.

Box 7.3   **International classification of functioning and disability**

Part 1 Functioning and disability
Body functions   The physiological functions of body systems (including psychological functions).

Impairments   Problems in body function or structure such as a significant deviation or loss.

Activity   The execution of a task or action by an individual.

Participation   Involvement in a life situation.

Activity limitations   Difficulties an individual may have in executing activities.

Participation restrictions   Problems an individual may experience in involvement in life situations.

PART 2 Contextual factors
Environmental factors   The physical, social and attitudinal environment in which people live their lives.

---

3   Sociological theorizing on disability

Disability and the 'sick role'

As discussed in chapter 3, the sick role was first proposed by the American sociologist Talcott Parsons (also see the discussion of functionalism in chapter 1). According to Parsons, illness results in physical disability or incapacity, which acts to prevent an individual from fulfilling his or her role in society. People who have an impairment or illness are seen as **involuntarily deviant**, but regardless of the involuntary nature of the condition they must fulfil certain roles if they are to escape censure from society. They must try to get well and put themselves in the hands of their doctor or other medical professional, fulfilling their sick role. By doing this they are absolved from societal obligations and culpability for their condition is removed (Parsons, 1951).

However, when it is applied to disabled people there are problems with Parsons's analysis. For many people with stable impairments such as cerebral palsy, the impairment can cease to be a medical problem. Albrecht (1993) points out that impairments which are short-lived lend themselves better to Parsons's sick role whilst those which are chronic, and from which recovery is unlikely, do not allow a return to the full pre-illness role; thus, Parsons's analysis is unworkable. This applies whatever the impairment, be it physical,

involuntarily deviant enacting the unwilled transgression of prescribed norms sensory, intellectual or mental. So it could be argued that a discussion of the sick role has no place in a chapter on the sociology of disability!

Exploring disability through individual accounts of chronic illness

In two of the most influential reviews of the sociological literature on chronic illness and impairment, Michael Bury (1991; 1997) has identified three main themes which have emerged within a body of literature that has been strongly influenced by sociological theories of social action (see chapter 1).

Firstly, *biographical disruption*, as described by Bury (1982; 1991; 1997), is a term used to explain the impact that a chronic condition can have on an individual's expectations and achievements. The presence of a chronic condition and its effect on activity and independence, Bury contends, shatter and disrupt that person's life, altering their life situation and social relationships (1997, p. 124). However, this changes over time.

At the onset of the condition, it is the *consequences* and *significance* of that condition that are paramount. That is, it is the impact that it has on a person's everyday roles and relationships and the **symbolic and cultural meanings** which surround different sorts of illnesses and impairments. Over time, biographical disruption can be overcome through individuals constructing explanations for their conditions and establishing their **legitimacy**. Through the twin processes of legitimization and explanation people with a chronic condition are able to create a meaningful story about their condition.

The impact of treatment on everyday life refers to the way in which individuals come 'to grips with treatment regimes and medical interventions, and with the bureaucracies from which they emanate' (Bury, 1997, p. 126). It involves the person gaining an understanding of the official diagnosis and labelling, searching for information on their condition, making sense of this and incorporating it into their restructured social world. It is about learning how to manage health requirements and discriminating between 'helpful' and 'unhelpful' sources of knowledge, advice and expertise (Dingwall, 1976). As discussed in chapter 3 (see, in particular, Activity 3.1), people living with chronic illness are increasingly regarded as 'lay experts' on their own health and health care needs.

Adaptation and management of illness and disability describes how individuals cope with an impairment, how they develop a strategy and a style to achieve 'the best quality of life possible' (Bury, 1997, p. 129). It is the way that individuals achieve a 'normal' life, despite the presence of an impairment. The term *coping*, as Bury (1991, 1997) acknowledges, implies a moral framework against which an individual's ability to cope is judged. However, he argues that coping should be seen as a means of determining the ways in which

symbolic and cultural meanings the way in which concepts and ideas are expressed through culture

legitimacy is achieved when an individual acknowledges that their lifestyle has changed as a consequence of acquiring a chronic condition and incorporates these changes into social interactions individuals maintain or recover a sense of self-worth. It is about the emotional and cognitive mechanisms that people with impairment employ in adaptation to their new life situation; it involves 'maintaining a sense of value and meaning in life, in spite of symptoms and their effects' (Bury, 1991, p. 461).

Despite claims by Bury and others that the notion of 'coping' is not judgemental, the very nature of the approach implies that there is something wrong with the individual in the first place. Disabled people or people with a chronic condition are presented as essentially different from their non-disabled peers in that they have lost their sense of worth or that this is challenged because of the presence of impairment. Their sense of worth has to be worked on and they have to learn how to cope with this and, further, this ability to cope is judged against a moral backdrop of success or non-success. Success and non-success are themselves, of course,

normative describes expected or preferred social behaviours ◄ **normative** constructions.

The *strategies* that disabled people adopt are the second element of what Bury (1991; 1997) describes as the adaptation process. They are to the actions or practices people adopt in the face of chronic illness or impairment rather than to meanings or attitudes. Through successful actions the individual learns how to maintain hope and a sense of the future. *Style* is the way in which people respond to and manage their condition, the performance that people living with impairments undertake (Bury, 1997, p. 132). It is about finding an appropriate style of living so as to minimize the impact of the condition and maximize participation in society (Radley, 1994).

Whilst this approach has provided useful avenues of research within sociology, the analysis does raise a number of issues, and it is to these that this chapter now turns. Bury, and others, have allowed an exploration of the consequences of being a disabled person in practical situations. The position of disabled people is taken seriously and credence is given to the views of disabled people so that they can themselves become the best guide to their own position. However, whilst, by definition, research and theory that emerge from this paradigm place disability as social in origin, the analysis raises many problems. In spite of the acknowledgement of conditions of inequality, powerlessness and violence (see, for example, Bury, 1997, pp. 118–19), they are rarely placed at the centre of the research or analysis (Williams, 1996). Even in work that claims to incorporate or acknowledge wider social issues the focus is still very much on the individual. This work, by focusing on the impact of treatment and care, presents an image of disabled people as being in need of care. This serves to reinforce the dominant view of disability as a medical rather than social problem, with the emphasis on individual adaptation to impairment. Having an impairment, it appears, separates the individual from the rest of society and their impairment becomes their defining characteristic. It also fails to analyse how people who are born with an impairment perceive that impairment and the impact it has on their lives.

Much of the analysis seems voyeuristic; that is, the disabled person is objectified, as is their life. Simon Williams (1996) writes about the ups and downs of chronic illness, but seems to ignore these in daily life. We all face change throughout our lives: leaving school, getting a job, ending a relationship, buying a house, having children and so on, and they all challenge an individual's sense of worth and identity. All result in biographical disruption – impact on one's sense of self – and require coping, strategy and style as one adapts to their consequences. Yet these are seen as normal; they are rarely used as defining characteristics of an individual. Disability or impairment are presented as a *master status*, one that limits an individual's ability to access social roles, so that they are reduced to adopting a range of subsidiary roles (Gerhardt, 1989).

For these reasons, and others, the disabled people's movement have not endorsed this approach to disability. This chapter now examines how disabled people and their organizations have focused on disability.

4   The social model of disability

In the late 1960s and 1970s disabled people throughout the world began to organize, to challenge their isolation and to demand equal rights. In doing so they also challenged the individual medical model of disability. Organizations such as the Union of the Physically Impaired Against Segregation (UPIAS) in the United Kingdom, the Independent Living Movement in America and the Handicappenförbundens Centralkommitté in Sweden all called for an alternative approach to disability. The UPIAS document, *The Fundamental Principles of Disability*, published in 1976, laid the foundations for what Oliver (1990) later called the social model of disability. Put simply, this approach argues that it is society which disables people with impairment by its failure to include them. Society, it is argued, is responsible for the creation of disability through social, cultural and environmental barriers.

The rejection of any link between impairment and disability, in contrast to the view of the ICIDH above, has been adopted by the majority of organizations of disabled people throughout the world. Disabled People International has adopted the definition of disability shown in box 7.4.

The disabled writer Jenny Morris eloquently explains the difference between impairment and disability:

> An inability to walk is an impairment, whereas an inability to enter a building because the entrance is up a flight of stairs is a disability. An inability to speak is an impairment but an

Box 7.4	The social model of disability

Impairment   The functional limitation within the individual caused by physical, mental or sensory impairment.

Disability   The loss or limitation of opportunities to take part in the normal life of the community on an equal level with others owing to physical and social barriers.

> inability to communicate because appropriate technical aids are not made available is a disability. An inability to move one's body is an impairment but an inability to get out of bed because appropriate physical help is not available is a disability. (1993, p. x)

The social model moves the attention from an individual's impairment to the external environment in which they are situated and the obstacles imposed on disabled people, thus drawing predominantly on sociological theories of social structure (see chapter 1). Disablement has nothing to do with an individual's impairment, but is the result of social oppression (Oliver, 1996). Implicit in this approach to disability, in contrast to that of the ICF, is the idea that disabled people are the best experts on their own lives. This last point has also laid the foundation for a new approach to the study of disability, termed by Oliver (1992) *emancipatory research*. Oliver contends that oppression cannot be addressed in an objective or scientific manner; it warrants an openly partisan and politically committed approach. The approach also seeks to involve disabled people in the design of research, in the analysis of data and in the dissemination of findings. It is an attempt to break the divide that exists between disabled people (the researched) and those who research disabled people (Barnes and Mercer, 1997). Emancipatory research seeks to address the social oppression faced by disabled people or to establish an alternative social policy that may bring about an improvement in the lives of disabled people. It is firmly wedded to the social model of disability.

Michael Oliver, in his influential monograph, *The Politics of Disablement* (1990), gives a clear description of the social model. His work is materialist, in that he emphasizes the role of social structures and political, economic and environmental factors as the cause of disability (see chapter 1 for an introduction to materialist approaches within sociology). These are factors beyond the control of the individual and his approach contrasts sharply with that of Bury and others described above where the emphasis rests on the individual and his or her experience of a chronic condition. He argues that disability is a consequence of the individualizing nature of capitalism and also, importantly, the rise of medicalization in everyday life. Through increased control he contends that medicine determined who, for example, was able to work, who had the right to go to school, who could get married and who could have children. Medicine created the notion of 'able-bodiedness' against which normality could be judged and it is this ideology that permeates society and impacts on the way that disabled people are treated.

This political shift in the definition of disability has led to an upsurge in the consciousness of disabled people, the formation of new self-organized groups, and campaigns for anti-discrimination legislation and independent living. The Disability Discrimination Act (1995) arose as a consequence of the adoption of the social model by organizations of disabled people. New techniques, such as direct action, and new forms of cultural expression, such as disability arts, have accompanied new ways of identifying and organizing.

Kristi Zontini, who has diabetes, uses the instruments and equipment needed to treat diabetes to create wearable jewellery and charms. Her charms convey a personal message such as 'prisoner'

'Prisoner' sterling (7.5 × 5 × 0.3 cm) © 1994 Kristi Zontini; image provided courtesy of VSA arts, www.vsarts.org

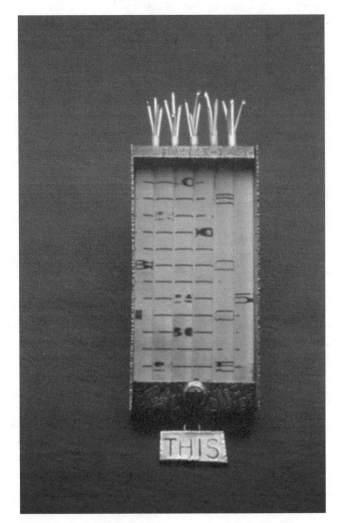

Activity 7.2 **Impairment groups**

(a)　Think about the various impairment groups: people with learning difficulties, people with mental health problems, people with visual impairments, people with hearing impairments and people with mobility impairments. Make a list of the main problems and barriers these groups face in their day-to-day lives.

(b)　Which of these problems are due to barriers and which are due to their impairment?

(c)　Is the social model of disability equally applicable to all these groups?

5　What are the barriers?

The barriers that disabled people face can be divided into two broad categories: those arising from discrimination and those arising from prejudice. Discriminatory **barriers** include those that physically exclude disabled people, such as stairs rather than lifts, the absence of disabled toilets, heavy doors, poor lighting or high counters. These barriers also include those of a more structural nature. For example, Barnes et al. (1999) document how educational attainment for the many disabled children who are educated in segregated schools is below that of their non-disabled peers and they experience a narrower curriculum. Consequently they leave school with fewer academic skills and qualifications than their peers, which limits their opportunities in later life.

barriers　barriers which prevent disabled people from participating fully within society

Employment, as the same authors show, is another area where disabled people face exclusion. In the UK the unemployment rate for disabled people in 1995 was nearly three times that of non-disabled people. Similarly, a poll in the USA found the employment rate for people with disabilities was 57 per cent, compared to 63.9 per cent for non-disabled people. Among those with severe disabilities, the employment rate is about 30 per cent (US Census Bureau, 2002). Furthermore, the majority of jobs open to disabled people tend to be low-paid, low-skilled jobs. Disabled men earn about a quarter less than their non-disabled counterparts.

Structural discrimination also exists in housing, in the provision of public transport, and in welfare and other social services. Oliver and Barnes (1998) argue that the systemic nature of the inequalities faced by disabled people has not been addressed by social policy initiatives that, they suggest, have tended to focus on the individual as the problem rather than address the social and economic causes of the problem. At best these policy initiatives will simply fail to solve the problem they seek to address, at worst they will add to the problems faced by disabled people as, for example, in the case of special education.

prejudice the negative feelings of an individual towards a particular social group

Prejudice also presents barriers to the full participation in society of disabled people. Disabled people are subjected to stares, are made the centre of unwanted attention, are denied anonymity as they go about their day-to-day lives and are patronized (Morris, 1991). Disabled people have an identity imposed upon them. It does not matter what they do, what their job is or what they say, what is important in the eyes of many is the fact that they are disabled. As a consequence non-disabled people feel free to stare at them, to make comments about their physical condition and deny them the respect they would accord to others (Watson, 2003).

Lois Keith (2001) provides a graphic description of how society's attitudes about disability and disabled people are produced in her analysis of disability in classic fiction for girls. In books such as *Heidi* or *The Secret Garden* disabled characters are displayed as suffering and unhappy. By the end of the books they are all miraculously cured and running about. Similarly Barnes (1992) in his exploration of disabled imagery in the media shows how disabled people are presented as pitiable and pathetic, as objects of violence, as sinister and evil, as a 'super cripple', as an object of ridicule, as their own worst and only enemy, as a burden, as sexually abnormal, as a person incapable of participating fully in community life, or as normal.

When such identities are fostered onto disabled people not only can these, as Morris (1991) argues, impact on the way that people think about themselves, they also constrain opportunities for disabled people. For example, Davis et al. (2000) illustrate how the closed

---

Activity 7.3 · **Disability and charity**

This activity asks you to consider the representation of disabled people within society.

(a) Go to the websites of various charities and organizations of and for disabled people, for example:
   Scope (www.scope.org.uk/)
   Capability (www.capability-scotland.org.uk/)
   People First (www.peoplefirst.org.uk)
   Spinal Injuries Association (www.spinal.co.uk/)
   Multiple Sclerosis Society (www.mssociety.org.uk/)
   Christopher Reeve Paralysis Foundation (www.apacure.com/)
   Children in Need (www.bbc.co.uk/pudsey/index.shtml)

(b) What models of disability are these various organizations using?

(c) Why are these models being used and what message do these groups send out about disability?

minds of some people working with severely disabled children limit not only their expectations of the child, but also what the child is willing to do. They show how, through employing what they term reflexivity when working with the children, that is, self-analysis and political awareness, they encourage the children to show much more ability and are more willing to co-operate and communicate. They argue that the key to meeting the challenge of working with these children is to examine your own feelings and prejudices and how these impact on practice. The problems, they suggest, lie not with the child, but with the way that the child is treated. It is worth thinking about this in relation to your own practice.

6   Critiques of the social model of disability – sociology of the body

While the social model has provided an invaluable model for explaining disability, it is not without its critics, from within the ranks of disabled people as well as without. Some of their critiques focus on the body, a relatively new concept for sociological investigation, which, as chapter 1 has explained, has been traditionally concerned with structural concepts. For many sociologists the body was considered the preserve of anthropology, and the impaired body lay within the exclusive expertise of the medical profession (Hughes and Patterson, 1997). Structural perspectives in sociology reinforced the Cartesian mind–body dualism, that is, the idea that the mind and the body are separate, and that one does not influence the working of the other. The 1990s, however, saw a move away from such ideas, with a realization that our body impacts on, and is influenced by, social structure (Nettleton and Watson, 1998). This coincided with technological developments in medicine and sports science, for example, which made viewing and manipulating the body possible to a greater extent than ever before. Antenatal screening, organ transplantation, athletes using exercise and diet to reach peak physical performance are all examples of how bodies are the object of scrutiny.

Let us consider the way in which we view our bodies. Three hundred years ago women's bodies were seen as attractive if they had plenty of flesh, especially around the breasts and hips. A thin woman in those times might well have felt inadequate and dissatisfied with her body. Today the opposite is true, and many women strive for a thin body with little extra flesh. It is those who are deemed overweight and those who cannot achieve the perceived ideal who are more likely to be unhappy with their bodies. Increasing consumerism and rejection of imperfection has seen a recent rise in the scope and amount of plastic surgery carried out, attempts to manipulate the body to conform to ideas of perfection. So social structure influences the way we view our bodies. However, this cannot be divorced from biological processes such as ageing, which impact on how we construct ideas of the body.

Turning to the social model of disability, Hughes and Patterson (1997) argue that the social model has focused entirely on disability (social discrimination) while leaving impairment (the body) within the realm of medical science. It rejects the part played by physical impairment in disability, thereby acknowledging the dualism. Although not denying the crucial importance of structural oppression, some writers argue for impairment to be included within a sociology of disability. Living in constant pain, for example, may impact on a person's ability to engage in 'normal' activity as much as discrimination. Similarly, Crow (1997, p. 71) calls for a recognition of the implications of impairment: 'What this renewed social model of disability does is broaden and strengthen the current social model, taking it beyond grand theory and into real life.' In other words, both the interpretive sociology of the body and structural oppression have a part to play in explaining the lives of those living with disability.

7   Implications for nursing

Nursing and much of nursing research have tended to focus on the experience of having a chronic condition and on the individual aspects of disability. Emphasis has been on how disabled people manage the effects of their impairment. Whilst this research is valuable, it has tended, in the main, to ignore the socio-political elements of disability. This has meant that the focus of nursing care has attempted to change *individual* disabled people rather than to change the *environment* in which disabled people live. This, it could be argued, has served to reinforce the notion of difference between disabled and non-disabled people. However, this is perhaps inevitable given that nursing is aimed at individual care. Nursing care does not, normally, extend to campaigning for social change. Also, individual disabled people want to be treated as such; they want individual care and they want that care to be based on evidence so as to ensure that the best care possible is provided. This means that nurses do need to know and understand what it means to an individual who acquires an impairment, or how an individual with an impairment lives his or her life. They also need to be a source of knowledge and provide disabled people with information about the day-to-day management of their impairment.

However, this does not mean that nurses should eschew the socio-political approach to disability. There are elements of the social model that they could, and indeed should, incorporate into their practice. As well as ensuring the physical accessibility of their premises, nurses should start by examining their own practices and procedures, rather than assuming that it is only and always the disabled person who is the problem. For example, when dealing with people with a learning difficulty who exhibit what is termed 'challenging behaviour', the question should be asked 'Whose challenging behaviour, the nurse's or the patient's?' Unless such an approach is taken nurses run the risk of constructing and reinforcing difference.

Activity 7.4   **Working with disabled people**

(a)   What do you think are the most important issues for nurses working with disabled people?

(b)   Should you concentrate on providing them with information about how to manage their impairment or should you examine how you can help them overcome the barriers that they meet?

(c)   Is the latter activity too political for nurses? Should nursing only concentrate on medical issues?

---

agents   individual's who have the capacity to act outside of (structural) constraints

Nurses should treat disabled people as **agents** who are capable of expressing views and having preferences, and they should try to meet these preferences wherever possible. This can raise some difficult issues. For example, do people with learning difficulties who do not want to take medication have a right not to do so, regardless of the consequences? Or do the nurse and those who care for that person have a duty to ensure that the person takes medication, regardless of that individual's wishes? These and similar issues need to be addressed when dealing with disabled people, and if this is to be done successfully it is essential that the problem is located in the right place. Impairment is not the problem, the problem is the way that people with impairment are treated.

Summary and Resources

Summary

- Disabled people experience discrimination throughout their lives. For example, they are denied equal access to the built environment, to educational opportunities, to transport and to housing.

- The traditional sociological approach to disability focuses on the experience and impact of impairment on an individual. It argues that having an impairment can cause *biographical disruption*.

- The social model of disability argues that disability arises as the consequence of the way that society is organized. There is no link between impairment and disablement. One is biological in origin, the other is social.

- The social model of disability states that to improve the life chances of disabled people we should focus on changing society rather than changing the individual.

- Critiques of the social model argue that the experience of impairment can also be disabling, and that this has been downplayed.

- Nursing, in the main, focuses on changing the individual rather than on changing society.

Questions for Discussion

1. Disabled people are more likely to experience unemployment and low pay, and more likely to experience prejudice and discrimination. What effect do you think that these experiences may have on health?

2. How can nurses provide individual care and yet still adopt the social model of disability within their practice?

3. On your next placement, make a list of all the barriers you find to providing the best care for people with impairments.

Further Reading

C. Barnes and G. Mercer: *Disability*. Cambridge: Polity, 2003. This book provides a concise and accessible introduction to the key concepts of disability. It concentrates on examining disability as a form of social oppression, drawing links with writings on the exclusion of women, minority ethnic groups and lesbians and gay men.

M. Priestley: *Disability: A Life Course Approach.* Cambridge: Polity, 2003.
This books explores important issues and debates in disability studies and examines how disability is experienced across the life course. It contains sections on birthrights, childhood, youth, adulthood, old age and dying. There are case studies throughout the book illustrating key issues together with suggestions for discussion.

C. Barnes, G. Mercer and T. Shakespeare: *Exploring Disability: A Sociological Introduction.* Cambridge: Polity, 1999.
This book provides a more detailed, and more sociological, analysis of the key concepts in disability studies. It is recommended for those who wish to read more about the development of sociology of disability and is a slightly more advanced text than those described above.

References

Albrecht, G. 1993: *The Disability Business.* London: Sage.

Barnes, C. 1992: *Disabling Imagery and the Media.* British Council of Organisations of Disabled People and Ryburn Publishing. www.leeds.ac.uk/disability-studies/archiveuk/Barnes/disabling%20imagery.pdf.

Barnes, C. and Mercer, G. (eds) 1997: *Doing Disability Research.* Leeds: Disability Press.

Barnes, C., Mercer, G. and Shakespeare, T. 1999: *Exploring Disability: A Sociological Introduction.* Cambridge: Polity.

Bury, M. 1979: 'Disability in society: towards an integrative perspective.' *International Journal of Rehabilitation Research,* 2, 33–40.

Bury, M. 1982: 'Chronic illness as biographical disruption.' *Sociology of Health and Illness,* 4, 167–82.

Bury, M. 1991: 'The sociology of chronic illness: a review of research and prospects.' *Sociology of Health and Illness,* 13, 451–68.

Bury, M. 1996: Defining and researching disability: challenges and responses. In C. Barnes and G. Mercer (eds), *Exploring the Divide: Illness and Disability,* Leeds: Disability Press, pp. 17–37.

Bury, M. 1997: *Health and Illness in a Changing Society.* London: Routledge.

Crow, L. 1997: Including all of our lives: renewing the social model of disability. In C. Barnes and G. Mercer (eds), *Exploring the Divide: Illness and Disability,* Leeds: Disability Press, pp. 55–73.

Davis, J., Watson, N. and Cunningham-Burley, S. 2000: Learning the lives of disabled children: developing a reflexive approach. In P. Christensen and A. James (eds), *Research with Children: Perspectives and Practices,* London: Falmer, pp. 201–24.

Dingwall, R. 1976: *Aspects of Illness.* London: Martin Robertson.

Gerhardt, U. 1989: *Ideas About Illness: An Intellectual and Political History of Medical Sociology.* Basingstoke: Macmillan.

Hughes, B. and Patterson, K. 1997: 'The social model of disability and the disappearing body: towards a sociology of impairment.' *Disability and Society*, 12(3), 325–40.

Hurst, R. 2000: 'To revise or not to revise.' *Disability and Society*, 15(7), 1083–8.

Keith, L. 2001: *Take up thy Bed and Walk: Death, Disability and Cure in Classic Fiction for Girls.* London: Women's Press.

Morris, J. 1991: *Pride Against Prejudice.* London: Women's Press.

Morris, J. 1993: *Independent Lives? Community Care and Disabled People.* London: Macmillan.

Nettleton, S. and Watson, J. 1998: The body in everyday life: an introduction. In S. Nettleton and J. Watson (eds), *The Body in Everyday Life*, London: Routledge, pp. 1–23.

Oliver, M. 1990: *The Politics of Disablement.* Basingstoke: Macmillan.

Oliver, M. 1992: 'Changing the social relations of research production.' *Disability, Handicap and Society*, 7(2),101–15.

Oliver, M. 1996: *Understanding Disability: From Theory to Practice.* Basingstoke: Macmillan.

Oliver, M. and Barnes, C. 1998. *Disabled People and Social Policy from Exclusion to Inclusion.* London: Longman.

Parsons, T. 1951: *The Social System.* New York: Free Press.

Pfeiffer, D. 2000: 'The devils are in the details: the ICIDH-2 and the disability movement.' *Disability and Society*, 15(7), 1079–82.

Radley, A. 1994: *Making Sense of Illness.* London: Sage.

Riddell, S. and Banks, P. 2001: *Disability in Scotland: A Baseline Study.* Glasgow: Disability Rights Commission Scotland Office.

Thomas, C. 1999: *Female Forms: Experiencing and Understanding Disability.* Buckingham: Open University Press.

Union of Physically Impaired Against Segregation 1976: *Fundamental Principles of Disability.* London: UPIAS.

US Census Bureau 2002: *Facts for Features.* CB02–FF.11, 12 July, Washington, D.C.

Watson, N. 2003: Daily denials: the routinisation of oppression and resistance. In S. Riddell and N. Watson (eds), *Disability, Culture and Identity*, London: Pearson Education, pp. 34–52.

Williams, S. 1996: 'The vicissitudes of embodiment across the chronic illness trajectory.' *Body and Society*, 2(2), 23–47.

Wood, P. 1980: *International Classifications of Impairments, Disabilities and Handicaps.* Geneva: World Health Organization.

World Health Organization 1980: *The International Classification of Impairments, Disabilities and Handicaps (ICIDH).* Geneva: WHO.

World Health Organization 1997: *The International Classification of Impairments, Activities and Participation (ICIDH-2).* Geneva: WHO.

World Health Organization 2002: *Towards a Common Language for Functioning, Disability and Health.* Geneva: WHO.

8 Social Class and Health

Terry O'Donnell

Key issues in this chapter

- A historical overview of the relationship between class and health.
- Class and the measurement of socio-economic difference.
- The extent and causes of health inequalities.
- The policies adopted to tackle health inequalities.
- Contemporary nursing, class and health.

By the end of this chapter you should be able to . . .

- Map the history of the relationship between class and health.
- Explain the concepts of class and understand the measurement of socio-economic difference.
- Discuss the evidence relating to class inequalities in health.
- Explore some of the policies used to tackle health inequalities.
- Understand the significance of class and health for nursing practice.

1 Introduction

Low incomes, poor environments and social deprivation are all associated with earlier death, and poorer health at all ages during life. The association between ill-health and material deprivation was first made in the early nineteenth century. During the last two decades of the twentieth century, the gaps

Box 8.1   **Health inequality in Britain**

- Life expectancy at birth for a boy is about five years less in the two lowest social classes than in the two highest, at 70 and 75 years respectively;

- each of the main disease groups shows a wide health gap among men, with those in the highest two social classes experiencing lower mortality than men in the lowest two;

- men aged between 20 and 64 from the bottom social class are three times more likely to die from coronary heart disease and stroke than those in the top social class;

- mortality from all major causes has been found to be consistently higher than average among unemployed men; unemployed women have higher mortality from coronary heart disease and suicide;

- children from manual households are more likely to suffer from chronic sickness than children from non-manual households;

- men in manual classes are about 40 per cent more likely to report a long-standing illness that limits their activities than those in non-manual classes;

- children from manual households are more likely to suffer from tooth decay than children from non-manual households.

Source: Department of Health, 1999.

between both the incomes, and the health, of the richest and poorest in our society actually widened (Acheson, 1998). Box 8.1 outlines some of the key health inequalities in Britain today.

In over two centuries of gathering hard evidence showing that disease and death are related to deprivation and disadvantage, we have often encountered political dispute about the validity of the research findings, how they should be interpreted and whether, and how, governments should act to improve the people's health. It is only since the very end of the twentieth century that we have had concerted efforts by a British government both to tackle health inequalities, and to do so using strategies clearly informed by the full range of research findings, rather than just selecting those findings that it found acceptable.

This chapter begins with a brief historical overview of the relationship between class and health. It will explore the sociological concept of 'class' and discuss the ways in which socio-economic difference has been measured. Drawing on current research evidence it will examine the extent and the causes of health inequalities and review some of the policies adopted to tackle health inequalities. Lastly, this chapter will explore how class and health inequalities are relevant to contemporary nursing practice.

2   Modernization, class and health

modern describes a kind of society that began in eighteenth-century Europe, in which scientific knowledge, technology, progress and individualism are highly valued

class the major form of social stratification in modern societies

As the nineteenth century opened, Britain was already on an increasingly fast track towards becoming a new kind of social formation – a **modern** society in which wealth was increasingly created through industrial manufacture. The population of England and Wales doubled from 9 million to 18 million between 1801 and 1851, by which time more than half of these people lived in towns and cities (Mathias, 1983). It is during this early period of modernization and industrial growth that the term and concept of **class** came into increasingly common usage.

Class

Working class came to describe the masses who depended on working for either a capitalist, or a member of the aristocracy. Very long hours were worked for wages that were often inadequate to meet even the most basic necessities of rent and food. The aristocracy were the main landowners, although some also invested in the new industry, and were considered to be the upper class. The capitalists owned the new forms, or means, of industrial production including factories, workshops, raw materials and transport; they were considered to be middle-class. This class also included owners of shops, farmers and the members of the growing professions such as doctors, lawyers, accountants and clergymen.

The earliest theoretical account of this new class society was provided by Marx – a structural theorist – in 1848, and the relationship between what he called the bourgeoisie and the proletariat is discussed in chapter 1.

Health

The main causes of death in the nineteenth century were infectious diseases such as respiratory tuberculosis, typhoid and cholera. For much of this century, it was believed that these diseases were caused by bad air coming from the filth generated by the living and working conditions. This polluted air was called miasma and its presence was detected by bad smells.

A growing number of studies showed that the killer diseases infected the working class in greater numbers, and killed them more often, than the middle and upper classes. The studies varied in their explanations of why this was so, and what should be done. Chadwick's report (1842), the *Inquiry into the Sanitary Condition of the Labouring Population of Great Britain*, was the result of a national statistical survey that showed:

- mortality rates were highest for the poorest;
- urban dwellers were more adversely affected than those living in rural areas;
- the poorer classes lived in the most unsanitary areas.

Chadwick, who believed in miasma theory, argued for schemes to safely dispose of the filth he believed to be an inevitable consequence of modernization. Most social reformers in this time focused only on the environmental impact of the Industrial Revolution and sought to improve the physical condition of homes and workplaces.

Engels, a close collaborator of Marx, took a different perspective. His study of working-class life and death, mainly in the Manchester area, was published as *The Condition of the Working Class in England* in 1845. He used several sources, including official reports from the Registrar-General for England and Wales, to document working-class mortality. He observed appalling living and working conditions and argued that they were the result of actions by the propertied classes. Engels argued that the propertied classes failed to deal with the pollution they caused in their workplaces, imposed hazardous working conditions for which they paid very low wages, and provided poor housing that lacked appropriate basic services, and for which they charged high rents. Furthermore, Engels argued that these actions, driven by profit, were directly responsible for the patterns of disease and early death in the working class and that they amounted to what he termed 'social murder'.

It was not until the last two decades of the nineteenth century that the full extent and causes of poverty were fully explored. Charles Booth (Fried and Elman, 1971) and Seebohm Rowntree (1902) showed that poverty was mainly caused by incomes below subsistence levels, either from low wages or from inadequate provision for when people could not work. They also showed that poverty undermined individual efforts to struggle for respectability, health and well-being. Nonetheless, governments tended more heavily towards the view that poverty was caused by the personal shortcomings of poor people and how they chose to live.

3 Understanding class

By the early twentieth century, it was evident that, far from polarizing into just two classes as Marx predicted, we had moved instead to a

social stratification   the
division of society into
levels that form a
hierarchy with the most
powerful at the top

complex of groups ranked in relation to ideas about their social and
economic differences; this is also known as **social stratification**. Both
the working class and the middle class contained sub-groups
reflecting significant differences in relation to such matters as size
and security of income, housing circumstances, schooling
experiences and their perceived social prestige. Weber (1958) (see
also chapter 1) provided a theoretical basis for understanding this
growing complexity by distinguishing between class situation and
status situation. Like Marx, he viewed a person's class situation as
determined by her or his position in the markets for capital and
labour. Those owning property, such as shares and land, are placed
on the capital side of the main economic divide, whilst the possession
of more, or less, valued skills, or educational credentials, puts the
majority on the labour side of the main economic divide. According
to Weber, we also have a status situation that groups us with similar
others according to the social value placed on our styles of life, which
includes our tastes, our social networks, and our consumption
practices, both for goods, such as cars, and for services, such as
education. Weber took the view that our life chances are shaped not
only by our class situation, but also by our status situation, which has
an important impact on our well-being.

Various schemes of social and occupational classification,
described below, have been developed to try to allocate us to a place in
these socio-economic hierarchies.

Social and occupational classifications

Rose and Pevalin (2001) identify two major traditions of socio-
economic classification in Britain. The dominant one, in terms of its
use in the analysis of official data, especially in relation to life, health
and death, comes from successive generations of government
statisticians. This tradition produced the Registrar-General's Social
Classification (RGSC) in 1911. This classification was modified in
1921 and in 1980, and renamed in 1990 (see box 8.2). The other
tradition was formed by British sociology as it analysed the various
expressions of class identity, and changes in the British class
structure, from 1945 onwards.

Contemporary sociological analysis of class

The early compilers of the RGSC believed that society consisted of a
definite social hierarchy that ranked people according to their
inherited and innate abilities. These beliefs about the social structure
have increasingly limited its validity as a measure of socio-economic
difference for sociologists today. Sociology is interested in the
relations between the classes, and has developed sociological
classifications to study social mobility, in particular. In doing so, it

---

Box 8.2   **Registrar-General's social class based on occupation**

Class   *Description of occupations*
I   Professional: accountants, doctors, lawyers
II   Managerial and technical/intermediate: managers, senior technicians, school teachers, police officers, nurses
IIIN Skilled non-manual: clerk, secretary, waiter, shop assistant
IIIM Skilled manual: HGV and PSV drivers, fitters, electricians
IV   Partly skilled: warehouse workers, machine tool operators
V   Unskilled: labourers (e.g. building, roads, tunnels construction), cleaners

Important notes
- People are assigned to a class on the basis of what they state as their occupation.

- Each job is assigned to a specific class, but if, within an occupation, persons are supervisors or managers, they are placed in a higher class than the others holding that job.

- People in the Armed Forces are treated separately and put in an additional group: Occupied – other.

- People known to be employed, but who have provided inadequate details, are also placed in Occupied – other.

- People who say they have never worked or who give no information are put in an additional group: 'Unoccupied'.

---

has identified many limitations of the RGSC. Concern about these limitations, combined with the impact of ongoing class analysis within sociology led to a thorough review of the RGSC in 1994, and its replacement by a new scheme, the National Statistics Socio-economic Classification (NS-SEC), from 2001 (see box 8.3).

The NS-SEC classification was developed from the Goldthorpe schema (Goldthorpe 1980; 1997) produced by sociologists in the 1980s and revised in the 1990s. This scheme separates employers who buy and direct the work of others, and the self-employed who work for themselves, from employees who account for up to 90 per cent of the economically active population. Employees clearly have only the fact that they work for someone else in common. They otherwise differ with regard to:

- stability of their job and income;
- size of that income;
- prospects for advancement and promotion;
- pension provisions and other indirect elements of remuneration;

Box 8.3	National Statistics Socio-economic Classification [NS-SEC]

1 Higher managerial and professional occupations

  1.1 Large employers and higher managerial occupations: health service managers, company directors
  1.2 Higher professional occupations: doctors, teachers, social workers, university lecturers

2 Lower managerial and professional occupations: nurses and midwives, journalists, police officers, laboratory technicians

3 Intermediate occupations: dental nurses, secretaries

4 Small employers and own account workers: publicans, farmers, restaurateurs

5 Lower supervisory and technical occupations: train drivers, plumbers, electricians

6 Semi-routine occupations: hairdressers, shop assistants, security guards

7 Routine occupations: waiters, cleaners, labourers, couriers

8 Never worked and long-term unemployed

- specialized knowledge and expertise and how these are valued;
- relative importance of educational qualifications compared with competences acquired in organizations;
- authority over others;
- personal autonomy and control over the job.

By seeking to take account of these crucial lines of difference, the NS-SEC reflects contemporary socio-economic differences in the labour market and work situations. It may be useful to identify the class position of nurses and to consider some of the differences identified above.

The research discussed below also shows that these differential experiences of employment markets and job characteristics influence our experiences of health and disease, both directly and indirectly.

The Black Report

The value of the RGSC scheme for identifying and tracking health differentials is most clearly shown in the *Inequalities in Health Report*, commissioned by a Labour government and published in 1980. It is popularly known as the Black Report and gives a detailed analysis of

Activity 8.1   **Obesity and social class**

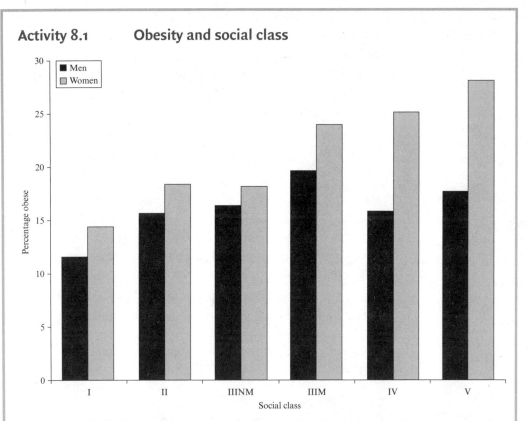

Prevalence of obesity in men and women from each of the six social classes measured by the Health Survey for England 1998

Source: NAO (National Audit Office), 2001.

(a)   What social classification is being used in this chart and how does obesity vary by social class?

(b)   Explain how food poverty contributes to obesity.

(c)   Are there other factors that might help to explain the connections between obesity and social class?

(d)   What role can nurses play in reducing obesity and alleviating food poverty?

official statistics showing that a clear gradient of inequality runs all the way from the richest to the poorest (Townsend et al., 1988). Class V had worse health and died sooner, and in greater numbers, from the major causes of death – heart disease, cancers and strokes – than Class IV, and so on in a straight line up to Class I, which had the lowest death rates, the longest life expectancy, and the best health. Death from skin cancer was the only clear exception to this pattern. The health gap between Classes I and II combined and Classes IV and V combined widened between 1948 and the mid-1970s. The gap was

Box 8.4	**The Black Report 1980, explaining the findings**

Artefact explanation

The difference between classes was unintentionally enlarged by the techniques used to measure class and the methods of managing the statistics.

Evaluation There are some technical problems, but the findings are likely to be real. The Longitudinal Study and the Whitehall Studies subsequently endorsed the reality of widespread health inequalities.

Social selection explanation

People's class is determined by their health, not the other way round. It is all part of a natural pattern whereby the least able occupy the least demanding and rewarding jobs.

Evaluation Only an insignificant amount of downward mobility is caused by illness. A range of subsequent studies point to a complex interaction between individual biology, psycho-social stresses and material disadvantage that accumulates across the life course.

Behavioural/cultural explanation

Poor health is caused by individual behaviours within personally chosen lifestyles. Middle-class culture tends to embrace health-enhancing behaviours whilst working-class culture seems to value health-detracting behaviours, such as smoking and unhealthy dietary choices.

Evaluation Individual health-detracting behaviours are involved and feature more heavily amongst working-class people. However, they were produced in an impoverished socio-economic environment that makes daily life a constant struggle to make ends meet. The behaviours should be understood as coping mechanisms, and as efforts to obtain some pleasure and enjoyment within generally adverse circumstances. However, some health-detracting behaviours are not only more common in the lower RGSC and NS-SEC classes, but also do more damage to them. For example, Whitehall II showed smokers in the highest Civil Service job grades had less heart disease and longer life expectancy than smokers in the lowest Messenger grades.

Materialist/structuralist explanation

Poor health and earlier death are dimensions of marked socio-economic inequalities in society as a whole. In particular, they stem from low and insecure incomes, unemployment and unstable employment, poor working conditions, and poor housing in materially and culturally under-resourced neighbourhoods.

Evaluation The Black Report identified this as the dominant explanation. The Acheson Report, drawing on data from the 1990s, validated this analysis. There is no serious, empirical basis for questioning its central thesis that tackling health inequalities means tackling social inequalities. This perspective has informed wide-ranging government policy since 1999.

Activity 8.2   **Mental disorders in childhood and social class**

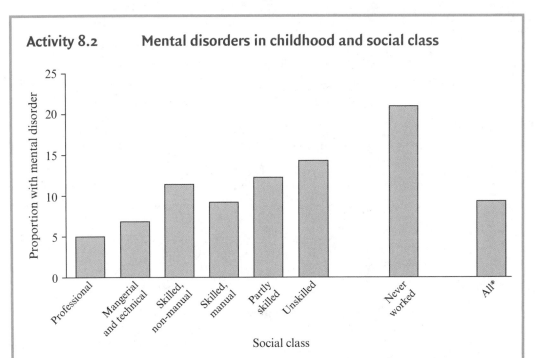

*   No answers, members of the Armed Forces, full-time students are excluded from the six social class categories but included in the 'All' category.

Mental disorder, people aged 5 to 15, by social class of family, Great Britain, 1998

Source: Drever et al., 2000; Office for National Statistics, 'Mental health of children and adolescents', press notice.

(a)   How much more likely are children in unskilled families to have a mental disorder than children in professional families?

(b)   How much more likely than the national average are children in families where the head of the household has never worked to have a mental disorder?

(c)   What factors do we need to take into account when trying to explain these patterns, and how do these factors influence nursing practice?

particularly wide for infant death (under 1 year) and child death (under 15 years).

The Black Report concluded that Britain's health inequalities were determined by inequalities in the distribution of wealth, power and status. The report evaluated four possible approaches to explaining its findings (see box 8.4) but was neither welcomed, nor implemented, even partially, by the Conservative government to which it reported in 1980.

4　Tackling health inequalities in the twenty-first century

The 1990s ended with a combination of research developments and governmental commitment to act on research evidence that together offer real prospects of achieving some reductions in health inequalities by the end of the first decade of the new century. These key developments are outlined in box 8.5.

The Acheson Report observes that average mortality has fallen in the last 50 years, but that unacceptable health inequalities still exist, and, in some instances, have widened. Indeed, some populations in the UK still have the same levels of early death as the national average during the 1950s. Acheson supports the view that health inequalities are a dimension of wider social inequalities. These shape neighbourhood and community environments as well as patterns of work, and they influence individual lives from conception onwards.

Contemporary explanations of health inequalities

Research begun in the 1990s is developing our knowledge of the pathways that link the bodies of individuals to their life experiences, including their material resources, and how these are all shaped by the social structure (see also chapter 1). It is through these complex, connected mechanisms that the less affluent, especially the poor, become sicker, at an earlier age, than the more affluent. Bartley (2004) gives a detailed account of the psycho-social explanation, the life-course explanation (introduced in chapter 6) and the neo-materialist explanation, and discusses how these can inform each other and thus provide the potential for deepening our understanding.

Psycho-social explanation

Contemporary ways and conditions of life produce social stresses that affect social classes unevenly, and members of these groups have uneven access to material and personal resources to manage these stresses. Such stresses do not only affect mental well-being. They also affect the body through the cardiovascular, endocrine and immune

Box 8.5	Key developments on health inequalities: 1990s–present

- Wilkinson analysed mortality and morbidity data from several countries and found that the widest gaps in health inequalities were to be found in those countries that had the widest gaps in incomes (Wilkinson, 1996).

- The Office for National Statistics published a Health Inequalities Decennial Supplement in 1997 containing evidence-based accounts of health and mortality in children, unemployment and mortality, illness and health behaviours in adults and data from the Longitudinal Study (Drever and Whitehead,1997).

- A new Labour government was elected in May 1997 and set up an Independent Inquiry into Inequalities in Health led by Acheson, which reported in 1998.

- A new public health strategy, *Saving Lives: Our Healthier Nation*, was published in July 1999, which accepted the recommendations of the Acheson Report and identified some immediate strategies to reduce health inequalities, for example Health Action Zones (HAZs) and Healthy Living Centres.

- In 2002, the Cross-Cutting Review identified a long-term strategy to reduce health inequalities involving all areas of government and calculated its costs (HM Treasury and Department of Health, 2002).

- The Government published *Tackling Health Inequalities – A Programme for Action* in 2003. It is a 3-year plan to lay the foundations for achieving various challenging targets for reducing health disadvantage in key areas such as infant mortality and deaths from heart disease, cancers and suicide by 2010 (Department of Health, 2003).

systems. Siegrist et al. (1990) argue that *socio-emotional distress* occurs when a high workload is matched with job insecurity, poor promotion prospects and low control. They suggest such effort–reward imbalance at work predicts heart disease and its precursors, such as raised blood pressure and high fibrinogen levels. Psychoneuroendocrine and psychoneuroimmune mechanisms may thus contribute to diseases such as cancers and, especially, heart disease. Additionally, negative experience of hard-to-manage stress, for example, ever increasing debt, often induces harmful coping mechanisms like smoking, high levels of alcohol consumption, and unhealthy eating patterns. Ability to change these health-damaging behaviours is restricted by access to important resources of money, time and supportive outlets such as gyms, health clubs and community networks. Kaplan et al. (1996) argue that high levels of psycho-social stress not only reflect exposure to antisocial behaviour,

social cohesion a sense of belonging to wider society

violent crime and reduced **social cohesion**, but also help to produce and maintain patterns of reduced social participation. However, these stresses occur in poor neighbourhoods. They are *ecological* experiences, which means they characterize places rather than individuals.

Lynch et al. (2000) use an airline travel metaphor to illustrate the shortcomings of the psycho-social explanation. They point out that first-class passengers on long-haul flights have more space, better food and seats that recline into beds, and so tend to arrive relatively refreshed. Economy-class passengers lack these advantages and are likely to arrive feeling a bit rough. The problem is more likely to be that they could not sleep in cramped conditions than that knowledge of the better provisions in first class kept them awake.

Nurses and other health care professionals can contribute to projects in deprived areas that aim to empower communities as well as to address some of the direct effects of poverty. Such projects involve the members of the community as decision makers and include setting up credit unions and food co-operatives that provide access to cheaper, healthy foods, training people to run health and fitness courses in their neighbourhoods, and providing free community transport to social events as well as to clinics and hospitals. In addition, nurses and their colleagues can avoid contributing to disempowerment by ensuring that service users from all communities across the life span are fully informed, active participants rather than passive recipients.

Life-course explanation

The health effects of adverse socio-economic circumstances accumulate from conception, through childhood and adolescence, to adulthood and life in later years. Early work by Barker et al. (1989) led to the concept of *foetal programming*, which argues that poor maternal nutrition, and the generally poor health associated with living in poverty, affect the developing baby during pregnancy. Material and social disadvantage for adults are thus reflected in the lower birth weight and poor health of their children, for example, in higher levels of asthma. Bartley et al.

longitudinal describes a research study that follows the same group of people over time

(1994) found that **longitudinal** study data showed low birth weight itself predicted socio-economic disadvantage through childhood and adolescence. Additionally, poor socio-economic conditions in childhood have been shown to have an independent effect on both adult health and adult socio-economic status. Indeed, the highest health risks have been found in those who both grow up in, and remain in, disadvantaged material circumstances (Van de Mheen et al., 1998).

Health problems in adult life do not result in downward mobility but poor health in childhood and youth, combined with poor socio-economic circumstances, can produce a downward spiral. Health care is delivered at specific points in time. However, the life-course perspective asks those working in health care to recognize that illness and health-damaging behaviours occur in social contexts to people who are living their lives in good or poor circumstances, and with varying degrees of control over their lifestyles. Nurses are especially well placed to take account of the whole person with an ongoing life story and to challenge **victim blaming** within their practice. Victim blaming oversimplifies the pathways through which major diseases such as coronary heart disease, diabetes and cancers occur in particular individuals and may lead to low self-esteem which can further detract from health.

victim blaming considering people to be individually responsible for their own ill-health

Neo-materialist explanation

Adverse socio-economic and psycho-social environments and the risky exposures and experiences associated with them are the material productions of social formations. These social formations have historically produced an unequal distribution of personal income and wealth, which, in turn, shapes unequal access to the infrastructure of markets for food, transport, housing, health care, education and lifestyle consumption. In Britain, for example, the least affluent 50% of the population receive only 25% of total income, and the poorest 10% have only 3% of total income (Drever et al., 2000). More than 3 million children live in households whose income is less than 60% of the average (**median**) income. By contrast, the richest 10% of the population receive 25% of total income. It is these structured inequalities that produce **social exclusion** and low levels of **social capital**. Researchers working within this explanatory approach warn against putting too much emphasis on social cohesion, social participation and self-esteem, so that the consequences of inequality become the focus of attention rather than the need for structural change (Lynch et al., 2000). They point out that losing sight of the unequal social structure whilst working on what socially excluded and materially deprived communities can do for themselves may be a subtle form of victim blaming. From a neo-materialist perspective, it is income inequality together with inequitable distribution of public resources such as health services, schooling and social welfare provisions that produces health inequalities. These wider inequalities are themselves produced by economic and political processes operating at a macro-level and as such require major social interventions to create effective change. Professional organizations, such as the Royal College of Nursing and the British Medical Association, recognize the importance of the neo-materialist perspective, study evidence in its support and debate the impact of economic structures on health. All individual members of such organizations may follow and participate in these activities.

median the midpoint. So the median income is the point at which half of all incomes lie above, and half below

social exclusion the impact of poverty and low income on involvement in mainstream social life

social capital community spirit, social cohesion, social networks, social trust, shared values and civic participation

Activity 8.3   **Learning disability and economic disadvantage**

A study based in three day centres in Northern Ireland by McConkey and Mezza (2001) looked at the views of both care workers and people with learning disabilities about possibilities for, types of, and benefits from, paid employment. Some of their key findings are outlined below.

Experience of work or training for work

- 42 per cent of the 275 day centre attendees had previously had an unpaid job or done work experience.
- 33 per cent had previously had a vocational training placement provided by a voluntary organization.
- 17 per cent had previously had some other placement set up by a day centre.
- 25 per cent were currently doing a specific job in a day centre.
- 22 per cent were currently on a further education college course.
- Only 1.5 per cent (four people) had ever had paid employment.

Aspirations of people with learning difficulties

- Significantly more people who had done two or more placements wanted a paid job compared with those who had no, or limited, work experience.
- Twice as many people who were on an FE course, or had been in the last year, wanted a paid job compared with those who had not been to college.
- Those who wanted a paid job were significantly younger than those who didn't.
- Overall, 85 of the day centre attendees said they wanted a paid job.

Key workers' perceptions about suitability of clients for paid employment

- Staff rated 38 per cent of those who wanted a job as being capable of doing one, 29 per cent as unlikely to cope, and said they were unsure about the prospects of the rest.
- Staff preferred the chances of those who they rated as above average in self-care skills, those who had been on three or more work experiences, and those who had above average skills in reading, writing, and time- and money-management skills.
- Staff thought the main obstacles to clients holding down jobs were poor concentration, poor communication skills and understanding, and lack of motivation.
- Staff also identified instances where they thought parents might be a negative force in their adult child's work prospects.

(a)   In what ways might current patterns of attendance at day centres
       be unhelpful for clients' prospects of holding down paid work?

(b)   Consider the roles that work-derived income and social contacts
       from work might play in relation to both the well-being and the
       socio-economic position of people with learning disabilities. You
       might want to think about this for both those living with their
       parents and those living in supported independent settings. You
       may also find it helpful to think about applying the concepts of
       social exclusion and social capital to your analysis.

Health care and the inverse care law

The inverse care law is a phrase first used by Julian Tudor Hart to
describe how those who have most need of NHS care health services
actually obtain them later, and in smaller amounts, whilst those who
have less need use more, and often better, health services (Hart,
1971). Hart did not carry out a systematic review of evidence but
rather observed his working environment as a GP and coined the
phrase to make a political point. However, reviews of subsequent
research have shown the description of an inverse pattern within
health care to be largely accurate (Watt, 2002). For example, a
detailed review by Dixon et al. (2003) has shown that hip
replacements are 20 per cent less frequent among lower socio-
economic groups, despite around 30 per cent higher need, and that a
one-point move down a seven-point deprivation scale resulted in GPs
spending 3.4 per cent less time with the individual concerned.

The review shows that these inequities result from two sorts of
disadvantage: those that make access to services difficult, such as lack
of transport and available time away from work, and those that make
consultations less productive, such as patients being less assertive
about demanding information, participation in treatment decisions,
and appropriate referrals for further treatment. Nurses have an
important role to play in helping to restore patients' 'voice' by
listening, and by encouraging more talk and self-expression. They
may also act as mediators and advocates for patients in encounters
with other health care professionals.

Activity 8.4   **Living on the Seacole**

The Seacole Estate was built in the late 1960s on the outer edges of a medium-sized town in the Midlands. The estate has a population of 7,000 living in low-rise houses, maisonettes and a few blocks of flats of three to six storeys. The jobless rate in Seacole is above the national average and the jobs done by those residents in work tend to be low-paid, putting household incomes below the national average. There is a fairly dilapidated shopping centre with one small independent supermarket and two other food stores. The nearest large supermarket is about four miles from the estate.

Most of the Seacole children go to one of the two primary schools on the estate and then to a very large secondary school that also draws from some neighbouring estates. Parents seem to be fairly happy with their children's primary schooling. Whilst it is still usually quite difficult to get parent participation in the school's governing body, attendance at parents' evenings has increased in the last couple of years and some parents have occasionally helped out during the school day. The secondary school, however, does not enjoy a good reputation with either parents or its students. Neither does it perform well in relation to national figures on educational attainment or attendance. There are currently six teacher vacancies that the school is finding difficult to fill.

Residents complain about a growing pattern of mostly 11–15-year-olds 'hanging out' in some specific locations. The young people are held to be at best noisy and at worst aggressive and threatening in their behaviour towards those living nearby. The young people themselves complain about a complete absence of social venues or activities for them locally, and lack of affordable transport into town.

Studies have shown that Seacole residents have a high reportage level when asked if they have been victims of crime in the last three years. A small number of under-16-year-olds – mainly boys – have persistent offender records, usually for crimes committed on or near the estate.

(a)   Describe what you would expect the broad patterns of ill-health to be in Seacole and say why you think so.

(b)   Identify some government projects and initiatives to do with supporting families and engaging communities that might be helpful in tackling the social inequalities that exist in Seacole.

(c)   Explain how the concepts of social exclusion and social capital might be useful in understanding the social difficulties outlined above.

(d)   How can nursing contribute to tackling these social inequalities?

Summary and Resources

Summary

- Class, socio-economic differences and health inequalities have been a persistent feature of modern societies.

- Health inequalities are produced through complex pathways, but good explanations take account both of how life experiences are socially produced, and of how they have an impact inside our bodies.

- Nurses, individually and as a profession, can contribute to tackling health inequalities at many levels; this involves tackling wider social inequalities.

- Effective policies to reduce health inequalities need to be informed by research.

Questions for Discussion

1   'Beer, fags and chips – that's the size of the problem.' What kind of explanation of health inequalities does this view reflect? See the explanations identified in the Black Report (box 8.4). Which of these explanations do you find most convincing? Which of these explanations do you think are most widely accepted amongst nurses? What implications might this have for practice?

2   'In our society the attainment of adult status is marked by employment, moving into your own home, entering relationships and marriage. Yet our services for adults have barely begun to address these issues for the bulk of the people who use them' (McConkey, 2001, p. 371). McConkey is referring to service users who have learning disabilities. Do you agree or disagree with his view? What bearing do the areas he mentions have on well-being and health for people with learning disabilities? How can nurses contribute to enhancing not only the health of people with learning disabilities, but also their experience of life-changes?

3   The life-course perspective shows how health disadvantage accumulates through life from before conception through to later years. Can nursing intervention across the life course help to make a difference? How can the education and training of nurses enable them to develop an awareness of inequalities and an 'inequalities imagination'? Can anything be done by nurses who subscribe to neo-materialist explanations of health inequalities?

Further Reading

M. Bartley: *Health Inequality: An Introduction to Theories, Concepts and Methods.* Cambridge: Polity, 2004.

This is a detailed exploration of research methods and findings on health inequality at the beginning of the twenty-first century. It is a difficult, but thorough, account and will be useful to those who wish to probe further.

P. Bywaters and E. McLeod (eds): *Working for Equality in Health.* London: Routledge, 1996.

This is an older, edited publication. It is included here because the contributors are all either specialized researchers in health inequalities or practitioners with direct professional experience of the health impacts of wider social inequalities (and sometimes both). The various chapters are still relevant in this first decade of the twenty-first century.

I. Christie, M. Harrison, C. Hitchman and T. Lang: *Inconvenience Food: The Struggle to Eat Well on a Low Income.* London: Demos, www.demos.co.uk/catalogue/inconvenience food, 2002.

Inconvenience Food is the short report from a research study into the difficulties faced by low-income families, in both urban and rural settings, in their efforts to obtain an adequate diet.

H. Sutherland, T. Sefton and D. Piachaud: *Poverty in Britain: The Impact of Government Policy since 1997.* York: Joseph Rowntree Foundation, 2003.

This review examines many sources of evidence in its assessment of government policies aimed at reducing inequalities.

References

Acheson, D. 1998: *Independent Inquiry into Inequalities in Health Report.* London: Stationery Office. At www.archive.official-documents.co.uk/document/doh/ih/ih.htm.

Barker, D. J. P., Martyn, C. N., Osmond, C., Hales, C. N. and Fall, C. H. D. 1989: 'Growth in utero, blood pressure in childhood and adult life, and mortality from cardiovascular disease.' *British Medical Journal*, 298, 564–7.

Bartley, M. 2004: *Health Inequality: An Introduction to Theories, Concepts and Methods.* Cambridge: Polity.

Bartley, M., Power, C., Blane, D., Smith, G. D. and Shipley, M. 1994: 'Birth weight and later socio-economic disadvantage: evidence from the 1958 British cohort study.' *British Medical Journal*, 309, 1475–8.

Benzeval, M., Judge, K. and Whitehead, M. (eds) 1995: *Tackling Inequalities in Health: An Agenda for Action.* London: King's Fund.

Black Report 1980: *Inequalities in Health: Report of a Research Working Group*, chair Sir Douglas Black. London: Department of Health and Social Security.

Chadwick, E. 1842: *Inquiry into the Sanitary Conditions of the Labouring Population of Great Britain.* London: W. Clowes and Sons.

Department of Health 1999: *Saving Lives: Our Healthier Nation.* London: Stationery Office.

Department of Health 2003: *Tackling Health Inequalities – A Programme for Action.* London: DoH. At www.dh.gov.uk.

Dixon, A., Le Grand, J., Henderson, J., Murray, R. and Poteliakhoff, E. 2003: 'Is the NHS equitable? A review of the evidence.' *LSE Health and Social Care Discussion Paper*, 11. London: London School of Economics.

Drever, F., Fisher, K., Brown, J. and Clark, J. 2000: *Social Inequalities.* London: Stationery Office. At www.statistics.gov.uk/statbase/Product.asp?vlnk=5771

Drever, F. and Whitehead, M. 1997: *Health Inequalities Decennial Supplement* 15. London: Stationery Office. At www.statistics.gov.uk/downloads/theme_health/DS15_HlthInequals_v2.pdf.

Engels, F. 1999: *The Condition of the Working Class in England*, ed. D. McLellan. Oxford: Oxford University Press, 1999. First published 1845.

Fried, A. and Elman, R. M. (eds) 1971: *Charles Booth's London.* Harmondsworth: Penguin.

Goldthorpe, J. H. 1980: *Social Mobility and Class Structure in Modern Britain.* Oxford: Clarendon.

Goldthorpe, J. H. 1997: The 'Goldthorpe' class schema: some observations on conceptual and operational issues in relation to the ESRC review of governmental and social classifications. In D. Rose and K. O'Reilly (eds), *Constructing Classes: Towards a New Social Classification for the UK*, Swindon: ESRC and ONS, pp. 40–8.

Hart, J. T. 1971: 'The inverse care law.' *The Lancet*, 1, 405–12.

HM Treasury and Department of Health 2002: *Tackling Health Inequalities – Summary of the Cross-Cutting Review*, No. 29854, London: DOH. At www.dh.gov.uk/Home/fs/en.

Kaplan, G. A., Pamuk, E., Lynch, J. W., Cohen, R. D. and Balfour, J. L. 1996: 'Income inequality and mortality in the United States: analysis of mortality and potential pathways.' *British Medical Journal*, 312, 999–1003.

Lynch, J. W., Smith, G. D., Kaplan, G. A. and House, J. S. 2000: 'Income inequality and mortality: importance to health of individual income, psychosocial environment, or material conditions.' *British Medical Journal*, 320, 1200–4.

Mathias, P. 1983: *The First Industrial Nation: An Economic History of Britain 1700–1914.* London: Routledge.

McConkey, R. and Mezza, F. 2001: 'Employment aspirations of people with learning disabilities attending day centres.' *Journal of Learning Disabilities*, 5(4), 309–18.

McConkey, R. 2001: 'Book reviews.' *Journal of Learning Disabilities*, 5(4), 369–74.

National Audit Office 2001: *Tackling Obesity in England*. London: Stationery Office. At www.nao.gov.uk/publications/nao_reports/00-01/0001220.pdf.

Rose, D. and Pevalin, D. J. 2001: *The National Statistics Socio-economic Classification: Unifying Official and Sociological Approaches to the Conceptualisation and Measurement of Social Class*, ISER Working Papers 2001–4. Colchester: University of Essex.

Rowntree, B. S. 1902: *Poverty: A Study of Town Life*. London: Macmillan.

Siegrist, J., Peter, R., Junge, A., Cremer, P. and Seidel, D. 1990: 'Low status control, high effort at work and ischemic heart disease: prospective evidence from blue-collar men.' *Social Science and Medicine*, 31(10), 1127–34.

Townsend, P., Davidson, N. and Whitehead, M. 1988: *Inequalities in Health: The Black Report and the Health Divide*. Harmondsworth: Penguin.

van de Mheen, H., Stronks, K. and Mackenbach, J. P. 1998: 'A lifecourse perspective on socio-economic inequalities in health: the influence of childhood socio-economic conditions and selection processes.' *Sociology of Health and Illness*, 20(5), 754–77.

Watt, G. 2002: 'The inverse care law today.' *The Lancet*, 360, 252–4.

Weber, M. 1958: *The Protestant Ethic and the Spirit of Capitalism*. New York: Charles Scribner's Sons.

Wilkinson, R. 1996: *Unhealthy Societies: The Afflictions of Inequality*. London: Routledge.

9 Race and Ethnicity

Lorraine Culley and Simon Dyson

Key issues within this chapter

- Concepts of race and ethnicity.
- Ethnic differences in health status.
- Ethnicity and healthcare services.
- Cultural competence and reflexive practice.

By the end of this chapter you should be able to . . .

- Distinguish between concepts of 'race' and ethnicity.
- Describe ethnic differences in health status and understand possible explanations for these.
- Understand the significance of culturally appropriate health care services.
- Critically assess the relevance of cultural competence and reflexive practice.

1 Introduction

According to the 2001 census (Office for National Statistics, 2003), approximately 7.9 per cent of the population of the United Kingdom (4.6 million people) describe themselves as belonging to a minority ethnic group. Indians are the largest minority group, followed by people of Pakistani origin, Black Caribbeans, Black Africans and Bangladeshis. An increasing number of people describe themselves as having mixed ethnic origins (15 per cent of the minority ethnic population). This chapter begins with a brief discussion of the concepts of race and ethnicity within sociology and an exploration of ethnic differences in health status in the UK. A number of different explanations for the ethnic patterning of health are evaluated.

The chapter goes on to raise a number of issues relating to the use of health care services by minority ethnic communities and argues that health care practitioners need to ensure that they are working in ways which respond positively to cultural diversity. It concludes by suggesting that nurses should strive to provide culturally appropriate care at an individual level and that this needs to be supported by institutional policies and practices which demonstrate a clear commitment to meeting the needs of religious and cultural minorities as service users and as employees.

2   Concepts of race and ethnicity

race   a biological distinction between different groups of people, determined by genetic make-up

The terms **race** and ethnicity are widely used but their meaning is the subject of considerable controversy and a good deal of confusion. Scientists have rejected the idea of the existence of distinct biological races within the human species, since there is considerable genetic or physical variation within so-called 'races' and a great deal of genetic overlap between them (Mulholland and Dyson, 2001). Scientists have also challenged fundamentally the idea that there is a direct link between biology and behaviour. Nevertheless, ideas about racial differences continue to be very influential, since many people behave 'as if' races existed and use such ideas to justify racist behaviour. Even though races do not exist, **racism** is a reality. This can be defined as a set of ideas, actions and structures which operate to promote the exclusion of people by virtue of their being deemed members of different racial groups (Goldberg, 1993). Some sociologists retain the term race, but put it in inverted commas ('race') to denote that, as a social rather than a biological phenomenon, it can still have a major impact on life chances.

racism   an ideology or practice which is predicated on a belief in the existence of a hierarchy of 'races', based on inherited biological characteristics, and which promotes the social exclusion of people by virtue of their being deemed members of different racial groups

ethnicity   a socially constructed difference used to refer to people who see themselves as having a common ancestry, often linked to a geographical territory, and perhaps sharing a language, religion and other social customs

The concept of **ethnicity** is preferred by many sociologists; this refers to socially constructed difference. Although there is no universally accepted definition of ethnicity, the concept is generally used in sociology to refer to people with a common ancestry, usually linked to a particular geographical territory, and perhaps sharing a language, religion and other social customs (Fenton, 1999). The relative importance of these will differ between individuals. We should not assume that because a person accepts a particular ethnic label that it is possible to produce a list of characteristics which would apply to all who might identify themselves in this way. It is also important that ethnicity is not confused with nationality, which is a specific legal citizenship status (e.g. British).

Ethnicity can be said to refer to issues of both structure and identity. For example, the health of minority ethnic groups is heavily influenced by structural factors such as social disadvantage and poverty. At the same time, ethnicity as identity refers to the ways in which people identify with cultural traditions which provide both meaning and boundaries between groups (Karlsen and Nazroo, 2000). It may be worth reviewing the distinctions between theories of social structure and social action presented in chapter 1. Such traditions might contribute to health variations in a number of different ways, through, for example, influencing health-related behaviours such as smoking and drinking alcohol. There is, however, a tendency to 'pathologize' minority ethnic groups in terms of seeing them as representing deviant cultures or adopting lifestyles which give rise to health problems. Before we look at some of the ethnic differences in health status, let us explore ethnicity in the context of identity.

Activity 9.1   **Exploring identity**

(a)   How would you describe your identity? Think of four or five ways in which you could describe yourself.

(b)   How would you define your *ethnic* identity? What aspects of your identity are important in this definition?

(c)   If a patient was described to you as 'Asian', would this be relevant to the care you provide?

Think about the following:

(d)   Which identities are more important to you?

(e)   How would you describe your sense of belonging?

(f)   How might others categorize you?

We all have ethnicity, but are not defined solely by it. Individuals have multiple identities – as man or woman, young or older person, nurse, midwife, student, husband, mother, daughter, Pakistani or Irish. Different aspects of your identity might be important in different contexts. Even within our sense of ethnic identity, different aspects of this may be more or less significant in any given context. This is sometimes referred to as 'situational ethnicity'. By this is meant that as the individual moves through daily life, what is important in ethnic identity can change according to variations in the situations and the audiences encountered. Our behaviour is heavily influenced by cultural norms, but we should think of these as flexible guidelines rather than rules that rigidly determine our behaviour (Ahmad, 1996). It is important to bear in mind that ethnic identities are subject to change and redefinition; cultures are constantly changing and evolving as they interact with each other, and so they cannot be easily captured in a cultural checklist. Attempts to do this may lead to harmful stereotyping.

Although there is a tendency to define members of minority ethnic communities primarily by their ethnic identity, it is important to note that minority ethnic groups are not homogeneous. There are divisions of social class, age and gender, for example, which may be very important for health and health care. There is also considerable diversity *between* groups commonly defined as minority ethnic groups (Modood et al., 1997). The category 'Asian', for example, though commonly used, masks an enormous diversity of ethnic identities and tells us very little about family origins, language, religion or diet. A 'British Asian' person may have family origins in India, Pakistan or Bangladesh. Their first language may be English, Gujarati, Urdu, Punjabi, Sylheti, Bengali or one of several others. They may be Hindu, Muslim, Sikh, Christian, Jain or of no faith. They may be vegetarian or meat eaters. Diversity within and between ethnic groups extends to all aspects of life, including family and household structure, education, housing, employment, and indeed health status, as we now go on to consider.

3 Ethnic differences in health status

The health statuses of minority ethnic groups in the UK appear to be worse than the health status of the white majority population. However, health experiences are not *caused* by ethnicity. Ethnicity, as a socially constructed category, draws our attention to particular types of discrepancies, but it does not in itself tell us the *mechanisms* by which peoples are rendered less healthy.

Methodological problems

There are two broad ways of measuring inequalities in ethnic health: mortality (who dies prematurely) and morbidity (who gets ill), but both measures have problems. First, mortality rates tend to concentrate on older generations and thereby primarily on immigrants, rather than on the younger generations, the majority of whom are British-born. Second, use of mortality rates tends to understate inequalities. This is because the occupation listed on the death certificate of migrants may be the highest occupational level achieved (perhaps teacher in country of origin) rather than their occupation in Britain (perhaps unskilled factory worker) owing to downwards occupational mobility at the time of migration. Third, the country of birth does not identify differences in life chances *between* groups within that country.

Attempts to measure morbidity may be based on survey questions that ask for self-reported health. However, these surveys rely upon the respondent understanding symptoms, seeking health services, remembering symptoms and/or health service utilization and being willing to report any of this to an interviewer. If different ethnic groups report health differently in any systematic way then this causes problems for analysis. We must bear these limitations in mind when interpreting data on inequalities in ethnic health.

Patterns of mortality in minority ethnic groups

Inequalities in health are frequently presented through a concept called the Standardized Mortality Ratio (SMR). The SMR compares the mortality rates of two populations, taking account of differences in their age structure. The SMRs in table 9.1 express age-adjusted death rates for each migrant group in ratio to the death rates for the whole resident population of England and Wales, which is set, by definition, at 100. SMRs greater than 100 indicate a higher age-adjusted death rate than this population. SMRs less than 100 indicate a lower age-adjusted mortality than this population. There are, however, many pitfalls in interpreting the relationship between ethnicity and health.

Table 9.1 Standardized Mortality Ratio (SMR) adjusted for marital status, for selected causes, by country or region of birth and by sex, 20–64 years, 1991–1993

	SMR adjusted for age and marital status		
	Ischaemic heart disease	Cerebrovascular disease	Lung cancer
Caribbean			
Women	92	161[a]	32[a]
Men	54[a]	145[a]	53[a]
Indian subcontinent			
Women	173[a]	135[a]	34[a]
Men	161[a]	183[a]	51[a]
All Ireland			
Women	126[a]	116[a]	140[a]
Men	112[a]	120[a]	148[a]
Scotland			
Women	125[a]	128[a]	160[a]
Men	114[a]	106	141[a]
England and Wales[b]			
Women	100	100	100
Men	100	100	100

[a] SMR statistically significantly different from 100.
[b] All people resident in England and Wales.
Source: Adapted from Maxwell and Harding, 1998, p. 21, cited in Dyson and Smaje, 2001, p. 44.

It is important not to read figures off from the table as evidence of an 'ethnic' effect as the figures are not controlled for socio-economic status. 'Ethnicity' never causes health status in and of itself, but the identification of an apparent 'ethnic effect' after controlling for other relevant factors can help us to sharpen our ideas about possible causal mechanisms. Note also that table 9.1 refers only to country of birth (those born outside of England and Wales) which is not the

---

Activity 9.2   **Interpreting Standardized Mortality Ratios**

Examine table 9.1 and answer the following questions:

(a)   What does table 9.1 tell us about premature death amongst minority ethnic groups?
(b)   Are the patterns of inequalities the same for men and women?
(c)   Are the patterns of inequalities the same for each disease?
(d)   Do Caribbean-born women have better heart health than the standard for women?
(e)   Do Caribbean-born women have better heart health than Caribbean-born men?
(f)   Do men and women from India suffer worse heart health than other groups?
(g)   Do white people all enjoy lower death rates?

---

same as ethnic group. Around half of the minority ethnic population of Britain is British-born. Note also that this table refers to premature death, not illness.

Patterns of morbidity in minority ethnic groups

Although relying on reported health, table 9.2 does have the advantage of being based on ethnic classification directly rather than country of birth.

The overall inequality in self-reported health for 'ethnic minorities' as a whole masks considerable variation between groups. Those of Caribbean and especially those of Pakistani/Bangladeshi descent have higher levels of self-reported ill health, those of Indian and Chinese origin have levels at or below the white group. On the one hand, the raised level for those of overall 'South Asian' descent

Table 9.2 Respondents reporting various conditions, by self-defined ethnic group (percentages)

	Self-reported fair or poor health	Reported heart disease	Reported hypertension (women)	Reported hypertension (Men)	Reported diabetes	Reported respiratory symptoms
White (including Irish)	27	4.2	12	11	1.7	27
Ethnic minorities	32	4.0	12	10	5.7	18
Caribbean	34	3.7	21	13	5.3	23
All South Asian	32	4.2	8	9	6.2	16
Indian Asian/African Asian	27	3.3	6	10	4.7	15
Pakistani/Bangladeshi	39	6.0	13	8	8.9	18
Chinese	26	3.0	6	4	3.0	12

Source: Nazroo, 1997, pp. 192–5.

underplays the very high levels of reported ill-health for Pakistanis/Bangladeshis. On the other hand, it also hides the similar levels of reported morbidity between whites and Indians.

South Asians are often said to have worse heart health than whites, but this appears to be made up of very high rates amongst those of Pakistani/Bangladeshi descent (especially the younger age groups), whilst levels of heart health in Indians appear to be equal to those in whites. Caribbeans report similar levels of heart health as whites and Chinese better heart health than whites.

Overall, whether the measurement is mortality or morbidity the health of minority ethnic groups is generally worse, though there are important counter-trends both in terms of ethnic categories (Indians), and disease categories (cancers and respiratory diseases). We now turn to a review of some of the explanations that have been offered for these differences in the health of ethnic groups.

4   Explaining ethnic patterns in health status

There are several competing and complementary theories that have been offered as a possible explanation of the patterns of health among minority ethnic groups. Following Activity 9.3, we briefly consider some of these factors and discuss the mechanisms whereby social status may impact on health status.

Activity 9.3   **Explaining health inequalities**

Examine tables 9.1 and 9.2 and consider what possible explanations there might be for the patterns of ethnic inequalities in health which are represented.

Genetic factors

Although scientists reject the concept of distinct races, this does not mean completely rejecting genetic factors as possible explanations of health variations between ethnic groups. At the same time, we need to beware of focusing too much on conditions in which genetic factors play a large contributory part, such as sickle cell, at the expense of conditions that affect all ethnic groups, such as heart disease, hypertension or diabetes. To the extent that conditions such as heart disease have any genetic component, such components may be *associated with but not caused by* the racialized identities with which social groups are labelled.

Migration

There appear to be higher levels of ill-health among migrants than among the population as a whole (Nazroo, 1997). However, the evidence does not suggest such levels of ill-health are caused by the processes of migration, nor by 'carry-over' of previous poor health (since the overall health of migrants is at least as good as British-born ethnic minorities of the same age). It does suggest that relatively healthy individuals migrate to work in poorly paid occupations in deprived environments, compounded by racism, so that there is a relative decline in their health over time. The evidence from Nazroo (1997) is also consistent with the socio-economic explanation that emphasizes the direct migration to conditions of poverty, poor environment and racial harassment. This argument is further strengthened by the work of Williams (1993) who suggests that increased length of time in Britain increases the level of poor health amongst migrants.

Racism

Racism may be said to affect health adversely in three ways. First, through *racism in health service provision and delivery*. This may be individual racism or **institutional racism**. Second, there is the *indirect effect of racism* (past or present) in areas of social life in which life chances are known to be linked to health. This would include immigration laws, the implementation of the social security system, and racism in housing, employment and education (see chapter 15 for discussion of racism and housing). And third, there are the *possible direct effects of racism* on health, such as the effect of racism in creating internalized anger and in raising blood pressure. Racism is an indirect cause of overall ethnic differences in health and can be a significant immediate cause, for example in the case of a racially motivated physical assault.

institutional racism occurs when institutional policies, procedures and practices intentionally or unintentionally give rise to discriminatory outcomes and reproduce disadvantage

Access to services

Ethnic patterns in the use of health services are important in their own right as an index of the quality of service provision, but may also affect health status. There are various possible explanations for different patterns in utilizing health services. In terms of factors influencing clients seeking services these include the health beliefs and knowledge of the population; their knowledge of and attitudes towards health services and what is termed social structure (see chapter 1 for further discussion of this). In terms of the provision of services there is the overall distribution of health care resources, racism in service delivery and quality of care.

Nazroo (1997) has suggested that, broadly speaking, minority ethnic groups consult GPs as often as whites, but have less equal access to hospital and community nursing care. A more detailed discussion can be found in Smaje (1995a), Smaje and Le Grand (1997) and Nazroo (1997).

Materialist explanations

There are strong positive associations between socio-economic status and health status in the general population (see chapter 8). Minority ethnic groups are, in general, associated with lower socio-economic status, and therefore would be expected to have poorer overall health on those grounds. However, controlling for socio-economic status does not itself greatly diminish the relationship between ethnicity and health (Smaje, 1995b). It seems that what are required in order to assess the interaction of ethnicity and material factors in patterning health are more specific and direct measures of material deprivation.

Nazroo (1997) provides survey evidence of ethnic variations *within* given levels of income, rates of unemployment and types of housing tenure. He develops a standard-of-living index based on accommodation (amount of overcrowding), access to amenities (such as indoor toilet) and access to consumer durables (such as a refrigerator). He finds that for reported ill-health this standard-of-living index reduces differences between ethnic groups very significantly in a manner which traditional controls for socio-economic status (class or housing tenure) do not. Furthermore, even the standard of living index is a relatively crude measure of deprivation, the implication being that more sophisticated and/or more direct measures of material inequalities may account for the majority of apparent differences in reported ill-health between different ethnic groups.

In summary it seems that material deprivation, when measured relatively directly rather than by weak analytical concepts such as class, accounts for much of the variation in the reported health status of different ethnic groups. But accepting the general strong association does not necessarily tell us about the precise mechanisms which are at work.

Culture

Attempts to understand health inequalities as a product of cultural differences have been very problematic. They tend to draw upon a very rigid view of **culture**, which is seen to determine behaviour in a very direct way. This can lead to health education campaigns which perceive minority ethnic communities as dangerous to their own health.

culture a shared set of values, perceptions and assumptions based on shared history, language or other learned experiences

The emphasis on cultural difference ignores the extent of similarities between different ethnic groups. Cultures are not static, but are continually changing and evolving. Culture is a product of gender, class and other power relations as much as of ethnicity, to which it is too often reduced. Finally, culture may be a source of nurturing and strength.

Mediating material factors and culture: social standing

Material factors are strongly associated with health status, but we understand little of the *mechanisms* by which this association may be effected. Wilkinson (1996) argues that material factors are mediated in a number of ways in affecting health, including the health of minority ethnic groups. These mediators include: *social cohesion* (material inequality weakens social cohesion generally and leads to a poorer quality of life and greater levels of psychosocial stress for all of us); *social support* (which may have a health-protecting effect); and *social status in a hierarchy* (those at the bottom of a hierarchy being more likely to suffer chronic psychological stress).

5   Ethnicity and health care services

There is some evidence of the differential use of primary and secondary health care services among different ethnic groups, although some of this is contradictory with examples of both under- and overutilization (Smaje and Le Grand, 1997). Carrying out research on this issue is difficult owing to the inadequacy of ethnic data collection in the NHS and the complexity of the relationship between health needs, demand for health care and supply of health services.

Activity 9.4

Ethnic differences in health service utilization – palliative care

Hill and Penso (1995) studied access to palliative care services by minority ethnic groups in three parts of the country with large minority ethnic populations. They discovered a low uptake of services in all three areas. Consider the possible explanations for this. Try to categorize reasons into the possible ethnic differences in need for services, demand for services and supply factors.

(a)   Are there features of the minority ethnic population which mean that they are likely to have a lower need for cancer services?

(b)   What might affect the demand for palliative care services from minority ethnic populations?

(c)   Might there be differences in access to services for minority ethnic communities (supply factors)?

(For a detailed discussion of these issues see Smaje and Field, 1997.)

What the example of palliative care services demonstrates is the complex relationship between need, demand and supply. As Smaje and Field (1997) have argued, while there is less 'need' for palliative care services within most minority ethnic groups, primarily because of the younger age structure of the minority ethnic population, the apparently lower levels of utilization probably stem from a range of additional factors, including differences in patterns of informal care in some minority communities and ethnocentrism or perhaps racism in the provision of services.

A lack of culturally appropriate services may seriously disadvantage some service users. This is a problem identified not just in palliative care, but across a range of service provision in children's health (Cooper et al., 1998), disability and social services (Ahmad, 2000), mental health (Bhugra and Bahl, 1999), health promotion (Douglas, 1995), maternity services (Bowler, 1993), care of the elderly (Pharoah, 1995) and in social services provision (Ahmad and Atkin, 1996). As Henley and Schott (1999) have argued, the health care needs of minority ethnic groups are broadly the same as those of white people. If people do not use services, it is more likely to be because there is inadequate information about what services are available and how to use them or because they are provided in a way which is not culturally appropriate. It could also be the case that people have had negative experiences of using services in the past and that there are language barriers and poor general communication.

Ethnicity and mental health

The issue of ethnicity and mental health is one surrounded by controversy, so that it is very difficult to attempt an adequate summary in the space available here. We have already indicated the many problems of inadequate data which exist in relation to ethnicity and physical illness. In the case of mental illness this is further compounded as the very definition of what constitutes mental illness is itself contested. There is evidence of differential rates of admission to psychiatric hospitals for some minority ethnic groups and some conditions, but interpreting the significance of this is difficult and contentious. For example, there are suggestions that an apparent ethnic difference may in fact reflect the fact that cross-cultural misunderstanding may lead to inadequate diagnosis. There is also evidence of differential treatment once a diagnosis is made, but again adequately explaining these differences poses serious problems. An analysis of this issue is beyond the scope of this chapter, and the reader is referred to the discussion of ethnicity and mental illness by Iley and Nazroo (2001).

This section has argued that there are many potential barriers to service access across all sectors of care which relate to wider structural and resource issues beyond the immediate control of individual practitioners. There remains, however, a need for all health professionals to ensure that they are working in a non-discriminatory way and responding appropriately to cultural diversity. It is not possible here to review in detail the many ways in which culture and experience may influence beliefs about health and illness or health behaviour (see Henley and Schott, 1999). Rather, the next section briefly indicates how nurses in all branches can prepare themselves to respond in a culturally competent way to a multi-ethnic society.

6   Cultural competence and reflective practice

Several research studies have suggested that health care providers across a range of services may sometimes portray negative attitudes to minority ethnic clients and patients and that the quality of care received may be compromised (Gerrish et al., 1996). Users report both satisfaction with services and a range of negative experiences. Many of the latter relate to problems of communication and the failure to respond adequately to cultural and religious needs (Culley, 2001). Evidence shows that good communication is essential to improving health outcomes, yet poor communication is a common source of complaints about treatment across a range of services. Effective inter-cultural communication requires a set of skills and competencies which need to be learned and practised alongside clinical skills. For example, it is necessary to develop the capacity to respond to diversity in an open and reflexive manner, recognizing and respecting difference and paying attention to possible cultural factors (ethnicity, age, sex, education, etc.) which may influence communication (Gerrish et al., 1996).

Communication is not reducible to language alone (Robinson, 1998). Nevertheless, language barriers are significant for some users. Poor communication is likely to lead to worsening health outcomes and, in the case of mental health problems especially, the lack of a common language can lead to misdiagnosis and ineffective and harmful treatment (Bradby, 2001). Although most British-born patients speak good English, those who have migrated are less likely to be fluent, though this will depend on age, length of time and age of arrival in Britain as well as general level of education and opportunities in Britain. Nurses need to familiarize themselves with the special skills needed to communicate across a language barrier. Working with interpreters, for example, requires training if the communication is to be well managed. Unfortunately, there are often situations in which interpreters are not available. While this is clearly fraught with problems, there are ways of reducing potential harm to patients, although you should always have a professional interpreter for important conversations. For example you should maintain a sympathetic and unhurried manner and a reassuring tone of voice (avoid total silences); simplify your English and speak slowly and clearly (but do not shout); demonstrate things rather than simply relying on the written word and always check that the person understands what you are saying. Ensure that you keep good notes so that questions do not have to be repeated by different professionals (see Henley and Schott, 1999).

There are many checklists which act as guides to different religious and ethnic groups. Although useful in some contexts, they are open to misuse, leading to a failure to determine individual needs, and to stereotyping (Culley, 2000). People cannot be neatly divided into cultural groups and their behaviour predicted. The checklist approach ignores the enormous range of differences that exist within an ethnic group.

The key to providing culturally appropriate care at the individual level is to follow the advice of Henley and Schott (1999, p. 76): 'The only person who can tell you what will or will not be right for them is the patient. If we really want to find out, we have to ask.' This is not always easy and there is a skill to asking effective and sensitive questions and in responding positively and respectfully to people who might express values and wishes very different from our own. However, a commitment to patient-centred care means reflecting on our own assumptions and values, considering possible variations in people's needs and wishes, and identifying the implications of these for our day-to-day practice (Henley and Schott, 1999).

Providing good individual care in any branch of nursing is about good communication; this requires enabling patients to explain their needs and wishes. At the same time, consulting and listening are equally important at the organizational and policy level. Although the above discussion has focused on elements of individual care, institutional processes are equally important in determining the adequacy of service provision to minority ethnic communities (Gerrish et al., 1996). Individual practitioners must be supported by effective policies, adequate resources and well-informed managers and educators if the needs of religious and cultural minorities are to be met. Improving the quality of care means listening to users, for individual nurses and for health care planners and managers. Without the active and meaningful involvement of minority ethnic service users, it is highly likely that provision will continue to be reflective of the needs of white, middle-class patients and families.

Summary and Resources

Summary

- The concepts of race and ethnicity are contested in sociological theory, but highly relevant for an understanding of contemporary health care.

- There are ethnic differences in patterns of morbidity and mortality in Britain which may be explained by a combination of social and economic factors.

- There is a growing body of evidence which suggests that health services are not always adequately meeting the needs of minority ethnic groups.

- Nurses and other health professionals need to work towards overcoming potential barriers to effective care and develop the skills for working with diverse communities.

Questions for Discussion

1   In relation to your area of practice, consider the implications for health care if, because of a language barrier, patients and relatives cannot discuss symptoms and prognoses, ask questions or raise anxieties.

2   Consider the possible influence of religion on people's lives and in relation to your own area of practice; discuss how religious beliefs might affect attitudes towards illness and treatment.

3   Describe the ways in which health professionals in your area of practice can access the views of service users from minority ethnic communities.

4   Working with colleagues, devise a vision of what equal access and equal provision in your area of practice would look like and consider what changes may be required, both individually and institutionally, to achieve this.

Further Reading

L. A. Culley and S. Dyson (eds): *Ethnicity and Nursing Practice.* London: Palgrave, 2001.
This expands on the discussion in this chapter. It examines sociological theories of ethnicity, race and racisms, inequalities in physical and mental health, and issues of ethnic monitoring and interpreting, and considers specific areas of nursing and midwifery practice.

A. Henley and J. Schott: *Culture, Religion and Patient Care in a Multi-ethnic Society.* London: Age Concern, 1999.
This is an extremely useful resource for providing, planning or managing care in all health care settings. It describes ways of identifying cultural and religious needs and offers sensitive and practical ways of meeting them whilst cautioning against the dangers of stereotyping.

L. Robinson: *'Race', Communication and the Caring Professions.* Buckingham: Open University Press, 1998.
This examines inter-ethnic communication and discusses the ways in which prejudice and stereotypes function as barriers to effective communication between social and health care workers and clients from ethnic minorities.

References

Ahmad, W. I. U. 1996: The trouble with culture. In D. Kelleher and S. Hillier (eds), *Researching Cultural Differences in Health*, London: Routledge, pp. 190–219.

Ahmad, W. 2000: *Ethnicity, Disability and Chronic Illness.* Buckingham: Open University Press.

Ahmad, W. and Atkin, K. (eds) 1996: *'Race' and Community Care.* Buckingham: Open University Press.

Bhugra, D. and Bahl, V. (eds) 1999: *Ethnicity: An Agenda for Mental Health.* London: Gaskell.

Bowler, I. 1993: '"They're not the same as us": midwives' stereotypes of South Asian descent maternity patients.' *Sociology of Health and Illness*, 15(2), 457–70.

Bradby, H. 2001: Communication, interpretation and translation. In L. Culley and S. Dyson (eds), *Ethnicity and Nursing Practice*, London: Palgrave, pp. 129–48.

Cooper, H., Smaje, C. and Arber, S. 1998: 'Use of health services by children and young people according to ethnicity and social class: secondary analysis of a national survey.' *British Medical Journal*, 317, 1047–51.

Culley, L. 2000: Working with diversity: beyond the factfile. In C. Davies, L. Finlay and A. Bullman (eds), *Changing Practice in Health and Social Care*, London: Sage/Open University Press, pp. 131–42.

Culley, L. 2001: Nursing, culture and competence. In L. Culley and S. Dyson (eds), *Ethnicity and Nursing Practice*, London: Palgrave, pp. 109–27.

Douglas, J. 1995: Developing anti-racist health promotion strategies. In R. Bunton, S. Nettleton and R. Burrows (eds), *The Sociology of Health Promotion*, London: Routledge, pp. 70–7.

Dyson, S. and Smaje, C. 2001: The health status of minority ethnic groups. In L. Culley and S. Dyson (eds), *Ethnicity and Nursing Practice*, London: Palgrave, pp. 39–65.

Fenton, S. 1999: *Ethnicity: Racism, Class and Culture*. London: Macmillan.

Gerrish, K., Husband, C. and Mackenzie, J. 1996: *Nursing for a Multi-ethnic Society*. Buckingham: Open University Press.

Goldberg, D. 1993: *Racist Culture*. Oxford: Blackwell.

Harding, S. and Maxwell, R. 1997: Differences in mortality of migrants. In F. Drever and M. Whitehead (eds), *Health Inequalities*, London: Office for National Statistics, pp. 108–21.

Henley, A. and Schott, J. 1999: *Culture, Religion and Patient Care in a Multi-ethnic Society*. London: Age Concern.

Hill, D. and Penso, D. 1995: *Opening Doors: Improving Access to Hospice and Specialist Care Services by Members of Black and Ethnic Minority Communities*. London: National Council of Hospice and Specialist Palliative Care Services.

Iley, K. and Nazroo, J. 2001: Ethnic inequalities in mental health. In L. Culley and S. Dyson (eds), *Ethnicity and Nursing Practice*. London: Palgrave, pp. 67–89.

Jenkins, R. 1997: *Rethinking Ethnicity*. London: Sage.

Karlsen, S. and Nazroo, J. 2000: Identity and structure: rethinking ethnic inequalities in health. In H. Graham (ed.), *Understanding Health Inequalities*, Buckingham: Open University Press, pp. 38–57.

Maxwell, R. and Harding, S. 1998: 'Mortality of migrants from outside England and Wales by marital status.' *Population Trends*, 91, 15–22.

Mullholland, J. and Dyson, S. 2001: Sociological theories of 'race' and ethnicity. In L. Culley and S. Dyson (eds), *Ethnicity and Nursing Practice*, London: Palgrave, pp. 17–37.

Modood, T., Berthoud, R., Lakey, J., Nazroo, J., Smith, P., Virdee, S. and Beishon, S. 1997: *Ethnic Minorities in Britain: Diversity and Disadvantage*, London: Policy Studies Institute.

Nazroo, J. Y. 1997: Health and health services. In T. Modood, R. Berthoud, J. Lakey, J. Nazroo, P. Smith, S. Virdee and S. Beishon, *Ethnic Minorities in Britain: Diversity and Disadvantage*, London: Policy Studies Institute, pp. 224–58.

Office for National Statistics 2003: 'Ethnicity: Population Size.' At www.statistics.gov.uk/cci/nugget.asp?id=273.

Pharoah, C. 1995: *Primary Health Care for Elderly People from Black and Minority Ethnic Communities*. Studies in Ageing. London: HMSO/Age Concern Institute of Gerontology, King's College.

Raleigh, V. S., Kiri, V. and Balarajan, R. 1997: 'Variations in mortality from diabetes mellitus, hypertension and renal disease in England and Wales by country of birth.' *Health Trends*, 28(4), 122–7.

Robinson, L. 1998: *'Race', Communication and the Caring Professions*. Buckingham: Open University Press.

Smaje, C. 1995a: *Health, 'Race' and Ethnicity: Making Sense of the Evidence*. London: King's Fund.

Smaje, C. 1995b: 'Ethnic residential concentration and health: evidence for a beneficial effect?' *Policy and Politics*, 23(3), 251–69.

Smaje, C. and Field, D. 1997: Absent minorities? Ethnicity and the use of palliative care services. In D. Field, J. Hockey and N. Small (eds), *Death, Gender and Ethnicity*, London: Routledge, pp. 166–86.

Smaje, C. and Le Grand, J. 1997: 'Ethnicity, equity and the use of health services in the British NHS.' *Social Science and Medicine*, 45, 485–96.

Wilkinson, R. G. 1996: *Unhealthy Societies: The Afflictions of Inequality.* London: Routledge.

Williams, R. 1993: 'Health and length of residence among South Asians in Glasgow: a study controlling for age.' *Journal of Public Health Medicine*, 15(1), 52–60.

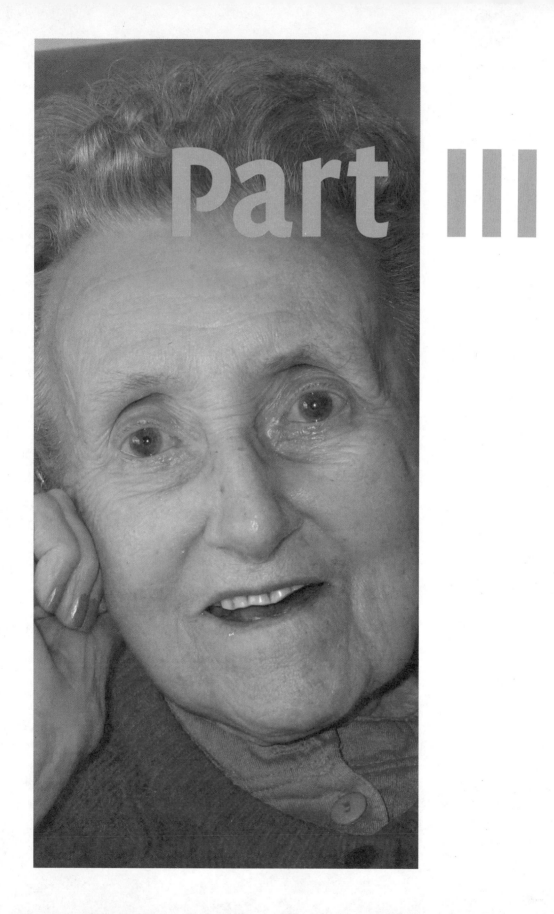

Part III

Where does Care Take Place?

There are often both implicit and explicit assumptions that nursing work is located primarily within the hospital. Historically, and to date, the organization and funding of health care has constructed and maintained this myth. It is further reinforced by the media with its focus on the more acute and 'sexy' side of health care work – the popular medical dramas *Casualty* and *Holby City* are illustrative examples of this.

Of course, nurses work in a variety of places, for example, in the community, in people's homes, in schools as well as in hospitals and other institutions. However, nurses are not the only ones who provide care for those who are ill. Much of it is provided by a range of health workers including families and, particularly, women. The three chapters in this section focus on the care provided within and by families, the community and institutions.

Chapter 10, 'The Family, Health and Caring', focuses on the contribution made by the family both to health and well-being *and* to ill-health. It begins by unpacking 'common-sense' views of the nuclear family, demonstrating the diversity that exists within family life. It then introduces some key sociological perspectives on the family. This chapter considers the role of the family in maintaining health, focusing on the care and caring work carried out both within and by family members. The chapter concludes by exploring the ways in which families can cause ill-health, for example, via domestic violence, or the burden of caring for the chronically ill.

In chapter 11, 'Primary Care in the Community', various definitions of primary care are explored. The chapter then considers the history of general practice and its role within health care. A policy overview and a brief history of the development of primary care are also given. This chapter concludes by encouraging you to reflect on the role of nurses within primary health care teams.

In 'Hospitals and Other Institutions' (chapter 12) a sociological critique of 'institutions' is given, focusing on the process of institutionalization. Different types of institution are considered and a brief historical overview is given; the development of the general hospital, the asylum and the children's hospital are discussed. Finally, this chapter examines the shift to community care and explores the role of residential care homes, nursing homes and hospices. You are encouraged to recognize the importance of institutions in providing care, the different types of institutional care that exist and the problems that arise through institutionalization.

All of the chapters within this section encourage you to reflect on what we mean by 'caring', who cares, and where care takes place.

10 The Family, Health and Caring

Geraldine Brown and Corinne Wilson

Key issues in this chapter

- The concept of 'the family'.
- Sociological perspectives on the family.
- Health and the family.
- The family and caring.

By the end of this chapter you should be able to . . .

- Understand the nuclear family and family diversity.
- Discuss sociological perspectives on the family.
- Explore the link between family life, health, illness and caring.
- Recognize the need to challenge common-sense ideas around the family.

---

1 Introduction

This chapter considers the links between the family, health, illness and caring. It begins by exploring some of the debates around families and then moves on to highlight some of the relevant issues when considering the impact of the family on health, illness and caring. The aim of the chapter is to draw your attention to the fact that sick people are often part of a family, and families can play an important role in patient care. However, families also hold the potential to make people sick!

In recent times, there has been an ideological shift in the way that we think about the family. In particular, there has been a conscious move away from all-encompassing, state-provided health care, to an emphasis on self-care and care by families. It appears that the family has a greater role in health care than ever before, but what are the consequences of this shift? How are families coping with this increased pressure to care for the sick and maintain the health of the nation? It has been suggested that with increases in unemployment, poverty and one-parent families and the greater involvement of women in paid work, the ability of the family to take on an even greater role in health care is in question (Locker, 1986). The family has an increasingly major role in health care; however, before we can begin to consider this we must first ask, What is 'the family'?

Activity 10.1   **Defining the family**

It is useful, before you even begin to read further in this chapter, to start thinking about how you would define the family.

(a)   Write down what immediately comes into mind when you think about the family.

(b)   Who are the members of your family?

(c)   How important are the people you have identified as members of your family in your everyday life?

---

2   The concept of 'the family'

> Most of us are born into families and spend, whether we choose or not, most of our childhood and teenage years within 'our family'. (Bernades, 1997, p. 1)

Look at what you have written down for activity 10.1. What is important to recognize is that, as Coote et al. (1998, p. 104) argue, 'In real life, "family" means different things to different people each according to his or her personal experience'. So it is possible for two, or more, individuals to talk about 'family', whilst talking about very different experiences.

Common sense and 'the family'

There is a common-sense understanding of what we mean when we talk of 'the family'. Common-sense understandings of the family mask the complexities of family life (see chapters 1 and 2 for further discussion of 'common-sense' understandings). This masking perpetuates and maintains images of supposedly normal families and the naturalness of roles ascribed to individual family members. It prevents us from understanding the impact of differences such as gender, class, ethnicity, racism, sexuality, and so on, on family life. Thinking about the family sociologically enables us to unpick these overarching common-sense understandings. Sociological explanations of the family challenge common-sense assumptions and understandings and allow us to recognize that society, today, throughout history and across cultures, encompasses a diversity of family forms. It also enables us to question the 'natural' roles assumed by individual family members, for example, women's innate ability to care. With specific reference to the purpose of this chapter, understanding the diversity of family life is important; as Bond and Bond (1986, p. 140) argue, 'the family provides the most important social context within which health is maintained and illness occurs and is resolved'.

For health professionals who are moving beyond common-sense understandings, recognizing the complexities of family life is important when providing a more holistic approach to health care.

3 Sociological perspectives on the family

The 'universal' nuclear family

An important starting point is to recognize that families are social, not natural, phenomena; therefore, they change over time and are influenced by social, economic and political developments. However, in Western societies there has existed a powerful assumption of a universal family form. The concept of 'the family' has rested on the

nuclear family the nuclear family comprises merely parents (or parent) and their dependent child(ren)

◄ image of a **nuclear family** consisting of a husband, wife and their dependent children, living together and connected by mutual affection, care and support (Elliot, 1986). Elliot claims that this family type has been powerful and influential and exists as a standard of how sexual, emotional and parental responsibility should be structured. There now exists an enormous body of work that contains many different explanations pertinent to the existence, the functions and the role of 'the family' in society, some of which are considered below.

Functionalist perspectives on the family

One of the most prominent and influential sociological attempts to explain the existence of the family was put forward by Talcott Parsons (1955) (see also chapter 1). Parsons's theory about the family was prominent in the 1950s and 1960s and was based on research carried out with American middle-class families. From Parsons's perspective, it is argued that families exist because of the functions they perform and, consequently, families have evolved over time because of the role they play in helping us meet the social and economic demands of society. However, what is crucial in the functionalist analysis is the

kin groups the social relationships and lineage groups bound together through a system of well-defined customs, rights and obligations. Kin relationships may either derive from descent or be established through affinity

notion of the evolution of the nuclear family. These small **kin groups** have evolved to fit the needs of an industrial economy. Prior to the rise of industrialization, Parsons suggests, there existed large kin groups that performed a variety of functions vital to the group's survival. The smaller kin group – the nuclear family – emerged from the fact that the family was no longer required to perform many of the functions required before industrialization, for example, economic, education, health and welfare functions. The functions were increasingly shifting away from the family to become the responsibility of the newly developing state institutions, such as education and health care. It is these smaller kin groups that Parsons argues were better able than large kin groups to perform the specialized functions essential to the maintenance of society.

An extended kin group

The nuclear family consists of a breadwinner/husband and a homemaker/wife and dependent children. There is a clear distinction between the roles of the wife/mother and the husband/father. The husband/father role is to provide economically for his family. The wife/mother role is primarily concerned with looking after the well-being of the husband and children. In the functionalist account, these roles arose out of the biological differences between women and men and primarily out of women's reproductive capability. For example, Parsons (1955) argues that the two most important functions performed by the nuclear family are the socialization of children and the provision of psychological support for adults. As Cheal (2002) argues, functionalism is a theoretical approach that emphasizes the positive benefits of families; that is, the socialization of children enables them to grow into valuable, productive, law-abiding members of society.

Critiques of functionalist perspectives

Functionalist accounts, like those of Parsons, have not been without their critics. The assertion made by Parsons that industrialization brought about a decrease in family size has been challenged. Research done by Laslett (1972), for example, demonstrates that household size remained fairly constant and that, before industrialization, the nuclear family was predominant. He suggests that from the Middle Ages the most common family form was that of the nuclear family, and this appears to have been the norm even in the most rural of families. There is also the suggestion that geographical mobility was a common occurrence in pre-industrial society; for example, children were often sent away to go into domestic service or take up apprenticeships. This challenges Parsons's notion that the nuclear family evolved to fit the needs of an industrial society. With regard to the **extended family** or wider kin networks, Laslett points out that owing to high mortality rates, very few children were likely to have parents alive when they got married, again challenging the idea that the nuclear family evolved from larger kin groupings. Laslett argues that the pre-industrial nuclear family was able to adapt relatively easily to industrialization.

extended family a family group consisting of three or more generations of relatives living either within the same household, or in close proximity

In contemporary Western societies, the maintenance of health and well-being is sometimes not believed to be a vital function of the modern nuclear family. In Britain, the National Health Service (NHS) dominates the provision of health care, yet, despite this, we know that the health services do not act alone. For example, when we are ill, our contact with the NHS is often limited to making a brief visit to the doctor's surgery. Indeed, there are few of us requiring long-term specialist hospital care. The tending of those who are ill and recovering from illness and the care of the long-term sick and disabled is, on the whole, done by families and, in particular, women. There is an implicit recognition that without this informal care, medical institutions would not be able to cope. Furthermore, with policy developments within the health arena, for example community care and its underlying principles, it is possible to argue that this function has never been lost and the assumption remains that care will be provided by the family (see chapter 12 for further discussion of non-institutional care). It is also important to note that the duty on the family to care is not imposed just upon the nuclear family but on all families, and particularly on all wives, mothers and daughters.

Feminist perspectives on the family

Not all sociologists have described the family in a positive light. Feminist accounts have recognized the implications of the nuclear family for all women's lives (see also chapter 5). The separation of the home from the workplace that emerged in the nineteenth century has implications for all women and their role within families. The legacy of nineteenth-century domestic ideology and the image of the 'angel in the home' (Hall, 1982, p. 18) impact upon women's roles today. Victorian middle-class ideology (see chapter 1 for a definition of ideology) identified mothers and wives who went out to work as endangering the whole of society. Engels (1845), for example, wrote that the wife's employment would not dissolve the family entirely but turn it upside down. If the wife supports the family and the husband sits at home and looks after the children and performs domestic tasks the result will be the unsexing of the sexes. Engels goes on to argue that men would be left without their masculinity and women without their 'true' femininity (see chapter 5 for a definition of these terms). What is evident here is the linking of masculinity to paid work and femininity to domestic labour and childcare. It is important to note the similarities with functionalist allocation of gender-specific roles with the emphasis on the 'naturalness' of women's role as rooted in her biology.

When talking about families, Engels was not referring to all family forms but to a specific family form, the nuclear family. Engels's thoughts reflect those held by many middle-class commentators of the time. These sentiments were reinforced through legislation, for example the Factory Acts of the 1840s which limited children's and women's employment. This further reinforced the notion of women's role and encouraged their economic dependence upon the husband/father (Barrett and McIntosh, 1991).

At the end of the nineteenth century, with the recognition in political circles that the working-class male child was a national asset, the health and welfare of children became entrenched in state practices. Connections were made, not to structural inequalities, but to immoral mothers who neglected their children by going out to work. The responsibility for the health of children and, implicitly, the future health of the nation, was placed firmly in women's hands. It became increasingly clear that women's role within the family was to care not just for dependent children but also for her husband.

By the twentieth century normal family life had come to be defined by the breadwinning husband and the domesticated wife. Women's role was firmly located within the private sphere and women were responsible for caring for the family in health and, usually, in sickness. The role of men was located within the public sphere, as the

material relating to economic factors ◄ economic provider responsible for financial stability and the **material** well-being of the family. These gender-specific roles have implications when we consider issues relating to family life, health, illness and caring.

Feminist critics of the family have highlighted how male breadwinning and the accompanying family wage ideology has prohibited, and continues to prohibit, women from gaining equal access to paid work. The dependence of women and children on a

The nuclear family

male breadwinner creates a damaging power imbalance within the family. These inequalities are maintained by the state through social and economic policies that assume families contain a male breadwinner and a woman who is responsible for childcare and domestic work (Pahl, 1999). As Jackson (1997, p. 328) argues, 'family ties are ties of economic co-operation of support and dependency, but also inequality and exploitation'.

The representation of the family as heterosexual (whereby the only sexual relations to be sanctioned were those between husband and wife for the purpose of reproduction), class-specific (the family form of the new middle classes), and gender-specific (with its particular division of labour), has had far-reaching consequences. While this ideal may not have been the reality for many poor working-class families in the twentieth century, it was pervasive at that time, and while it is not the reality for a great many people today, its legacy lives on (Jagger and Wright, 1999).

Activity 10.2   **The legacy of the nuclear family**

(a)   How important do you think the legacy of the nuclear family is today?

(b)   Can you think of any examples of how the ideology of the nuclear family impacts on everyday life?

(c)   How might the legacy of the nuclear family affect patient care?

Diversity and family form

This ideal becomes problematic when one takes into consideration the diversity of family life that exists in the UK today. The 2001 census gives us an indication of this diversity. The census statistics show there are 21,660,475 households in England and Wales and 30 per cent of these are one-person households. Almost half of the one-person households are one-pensioner-only households and three-quarters of these (2,366,000) are occupied by a woman living alone (www.statistics.gov.uk/cci/nugget.asp?icl=350). So it is evident that a large number of people do not live in a nuclear family.

The issue here is that if welfare, and in particular health policy, rests on the implicit assumption that maintaining health and caring are important functions of the family, and 'the family' is viewed in the context of the nuclear family, then we need to consider the implications for all those people who do not live in this type of family and do not have access to the resources the family provides.

It is acknowledged that health care comes from a variety of sources, for example the state, private markets, volunteers, family and friends; however, the care provided by family and friends is recognized to be the most fundamental (Graham, 1999). As the Griffiths Report (1988) states, 'Families, friends and other local people provide the majority of care in response to needs that they are uniquely well placed to identify and respond to. . . . The proposals take as their starting point that this is how it should be' (p. 5). So it is clear that, while in the UK we do have state-provided health care in the form of the National Health Service, state-provided health care

A modern family?

cannot exist without the large amount of caring work carried out in and by the family. We could suggest that it is important to draw on informal sources of caring, and indeed families can be a vital source of support to some people. But, as will be demonstrated, these normative assumptions can have serious consequences for individuals caring and being cared for within the family. Relying on the family to provide an informal network of care can be problematic. It is important not to assume that all families have the propensity to provide informal care.

Activity 10.3   **Diversity, the family and health**

Read the following extract from an article published in the *Observer* newspaper.

Nuclear family goes into meltdown
'The nuclear family of mum, dad and 2.4 kids is splitting up. Researchers have coined a name for the emerging British household – the Beanpoles. They "live together" and have 1.8 children. As Britons live longer, divorce rates rise and couples have fewer children, the traditional family – married parents with two or more children – is giving way to cohabiting couples with a single child. A new study by the London-based research group Mintel shows family groups are getting "longer and thinner – like a beanpole".

While 20 years ago the average extended family comprised three "nuclear" generations, family groups are now made up of four generations of often cohabiting couples, each with an average of 1.8 children.

"The family is undergoing radical changes under the pressure of an aging population, longer lifespans, increased female working, the tendency to marry later in life, the falling birth rate and the rising divorce rates," the study says.' (John Arlidge, in the *Observer*, Sunday 5 May 2002)

(a)   Consider the implications for future health care provision by the family.

(b)   What significance might this have for nurses (in their professional *and* personal lives)?

4   Health: an everyday responsibility?

The family provides the most important social context within which health is maintained, and illness occurs and is resolved (Bond and Bond, 1986). If we start by considering the way the family maintains health, we can suggest that the family performs an extensive range of health tasks as part of its everyday routine. Domestic tasks such as shopping, cooking, cleaning and washing are tasks that we, as family members, often take for granted because we associate them with daily living. However, they are pivotal in maintaining the health of individual family members and are often the focus of state-backed health promotion campaigns.

If we think about food, diet is an important factor in maintaining health. A report by the World Health Organization in 1990 recommends that we should be eating five portions of fruit or vegetables each day. It is an official recognition of the importance of the relationship between diet and health, and these recommendations have been incorporated into government initiatives in the UK. It is widely accepted that what we eat affects our health, not just in the short term, but in relation to long-term health.

While malnutrition and its impact on health remain a concern, statistics show that obesity affects more people in the developed world; for example, in the UK 21 per cent of women and men are categorized as obese (Department of Health, 2002). In terms of the implication for health, obesity is considered a significant factor in the increase in coronary heart disease and various cancers. It is also linked to diabetes, hypertension, osteoarthritis, reduced mobility and a generally poorer quality of life. In addition, there is growing recognition that obesity impacts on emotional well-being because of the social stigma attached to being overweight (Department of Health, 2002). There is also growing concern about the increasing numbers of children diagnosed as obese. Consequently, whilst the government and a plethora of health organizations are actively promoting the need for us to eat healthily, the institution that carries the main responsibility for the provision, preparation and consumption of food is the family. In so saying, while it may be argued that the task of providing and preparing food is a family one, this is somewhat misleading. The task of preparing food has, on the whole, been the responsibility of women.

Research has demonstrated that obesity in all ages is more prevalent in socio-economic class V (Department of Health, 2002). This suggests a link between income and a healthy diet or, more importantly, the ability to provide a healthy diet. This ability will affect a family's health in different ways. For example, Doyal (1995) points out that women will often go without food to ensure that other family members are fed, thus maintaining the health of the family at the expense of their own health. However, what is important to note here is that even in the most financially secure of families, women and children who are economically dependent on a male breadwinner can be at risk of suffering poorer health since not all families redistribute income equally (Pahl, 1999).

While it is important to recognize the role of the family in promoting good health, and ensuring that family members adopt a health-promoting lifestyle, we cannot ignore the fact that families do make people sick.

5 The family and caring

Families play an important role in caring for the sick. As mentioned previously, most of us have minimal contact with formal health institutions and when we are ill the majority of our care takes place within the family. It is estimated that there are six million carers in England and Wales, saving the public purse an estimated £34 billion

(Princess Royal Trust, 2003). Caring for the sick can often be very demanding and time-consuming. While it may involve the normal daily tasks we associate with caring for the well, they often need to be performed more frequently. In addition, although family carers do not constitute a homogeneous group and there are clear generational and cultural differences, amongst others, there are some general characteristics that can be identified amongst carers, for example:

- high levels of stress;
- inadequate financial circumstances;
- poor health;
- feelings of isolation;
- inadequate housing;
- marital breakdown. (Department of Health, 2001)

Once again the role of caring for the sick frequently becomes the responsibility of female family members, as this role can be perceived as an extension of the normal caring that women perform within the family. Some of the factors identified above may adversely affect women to a greater extent than other family members. While most illnesses may be considered minor and requiring a relatively short period of care, caring for the chronically ill, the terminally ill, the disabled and the elderly can be a long-term commitment that can have a significant impact on family life. Families often take on this role because there is a lack of appropriate services for those with complex health care needs.

To illustrate the point we are making here it will be useful to consider the effect of childhood asthma on families. Statistics suggest that one in eight children has asthma and that this figure has increased six-fold in the last 25 years (www.asthma.org.uk). Research carried out with families with an asthmatic child (Nocon and Booth, 2001) identifies the multiple impact asthma has on family life, demonstrating how the health status of one family member can adversely affect both the material and emotional well-being of all family members. For example:

- parents often take less well-paid jobs closer to home to be nearer their children;
- emergency care can mean a loss of earnings due to time off work;
- one-off costs (e.g. new bedding) and regular costs (e.g. hospital visits) can be a financial drain;
- asthma attacks can cause disrupted sleep for all family members leading to tiredness, irritability and lack of concentration.

Caring is often perceived to be a natural means of demonstrating love and support, and something that is carried out unstintingly. However, while families can offer a significant amount of support in times of ill-health, the burden of caring for a family member or being cared for by the family can exacerbate existing illness or make other family members sick.

Writing about terminal illness, Davies et al. (1994) suggest that the whole family should be the focus of care and recommend that nurses should be aware of, and adjust their practice to take account of, the disruptive effects of illness on family functioning. Arguably, such a focus is not only applicable to families caring for someone with a terminal illness, but to all families with caring responsibilities.

Over the past 30 years there has been an increasing amount of literature highlighting what has been called the 'hidden side' of family life. This literature has put the family under scrutiny and uncovers the risks many women, and children, face every day from family life; there is also now an increasing body of work that focuses on violence perpetrated against men. What is increasingly evident is that sociology, together with other disciplines, has been instrumental in challenging the dominant ideology that portrays family life as nurturing and harmonious. Giddens (1989) claims that home is, in fact, the most dangerous place in modern society.

If we look first at domestic violence, it estimated that one in four women will experience domestic violence at some point in their lives. Domestic violence features in at least one in every four divorces in England and Wales, and every year over 63,000 women and children spend at least one night in a refuge (Cabinet Office, 1997). In a speech, the Minister for Women, Sally Morgan (2001), pointed out that one woman dies approximately every three days as a result of domestic violence and furthermore that 'a man who is capable of violence towards his wife or partner is also capable of violence towards his children'.

While there is a wealth of research on the effects of domestic violence on women's health, there has been little research on the impact of domestic violence upon the health of children in the family. However, research that does exist points out that children witnessing domestic violence can present with a range of health problems, ranging from physical assaults, to anxiety, depression and eating disorders (Hendessi, 1997).

As most physical abuse occurs in the privacy of the family home it remains invisible. It is suggested that most physical assaults on children are not reported as crimes, and parents who perpetrate these assault are not defined as abusive. Despite development in children's legislation, children are not protected by law unless the assault goes beyond 'reasonable' chastisement, which usually means causing serious physical injury (Davis and Bourhill, 1997). However, what is important to note is that when children are killed it is usually by their parents. Cheal (2002) suggests abusive parents kill children of all ages, but those at greatest risk are very young children who are more likely to die when they are exposed to severe physical abuse. Accurate figures on abuse as a cause of death in children are very difficult to

Activity 10.4   **Families can harm your health**

Read the following extract from an article published in the *Observer* newspaper:

Half of all 'elder abuse' inflicted by relatives
'Thousands of old people are being physically, sexually and psychologically abused in their own homes by relatives and those paid to look after them, according to a new survey.

Of more than 2,400 complaints made, almost half concerned abuse inflicted by relatives, with 28 per cent perpetrated by a paid worker and 11 per cent by a friend of the victim.

"Most cases of elder abuse in Britain take place in the victim's own home and are perpetrated by family or paid carers," said Gary Fitzgerald, chief executive of Action on Elder Abuse (AEA), an independent charity that conducted the study. "The frequency of abuse in the homes of old people is terrifying."

According to the survey, one in three old people suffers from some form of psychological abuse; one in five is physically abused and the same number conned out of their savings; more than 10 per cent are neglected and 2.4 per cent sexually abused.

One victim, 78 year old Margaret Panting, was found dead in the Sheffield home of her former son-in-law five weeks after he removed her from her sheltered housing accommodation to look after his three children.

"This is a case of elder abuse," said pathologist professor Gary Rutty, who found more than 100 injuries on Panting's body when he examined it after death last July, including cigarette burns under her arms and razor cuts on her stomach.

Peter Biggin and his sons, Martin, 18, and Nathan, 16, were arrested on suspicion of murder, a charge that was dropped last month when the court said it could not be proved who was responsible for the injuries. All three deny the charges.' (Amelia Hill, in the *Observer*, Sunday 21 July 2002).

(a)   To what extent do you think that the family can make you sick?
(b)   What do you think might be some of the methodological problems encountered when researching abuse of older people, or other vulnerable groups?
(c)   To what extent is the home the most dangerous place in modern society?
(d)   Can nurses make a contribution to making the family a safer place?

come by, but the implication for children's physical health and emotional well-being cannot be overstated.

It is important when thinking about abuse within the family that we recognize that this abuse is not always perpetrated by men against women or by parents against their children, but can also take the form of women abusing men or a child abusing a parent, and can occur within same-sex relationships, or between siblings (Bernardes, 1997).

Families play an enormous role in providing care for others, but families can also harm your health.

Summary and Resources

Summary

- The ideology underpinning the nuclear family is still pervasive, but the reality today is that many of us live in families that bear little resemblance to this form.

- The ideology of the nuclear family has played an important role in informing the organization and delivery of health care in Britain. Nurses should be sensitive to this and avoid stereotyping families according to this ideology.

- Families are pivotal to the maintenance of health, but at the same time are facing an increasing responsibility to care for the sick; this can place an increasing pressure on family members of which nurses should be aware.

- Some family members, particularly women, are perceived to be 'naturally' more inclined to caring and nurturing roles, with the majority of the health task role being deemed their responsibility.

- Whilst families can be of vital support for many individuals, there are also occasions when families can affect health negatively and it is important to recognize that not everyone's experience of family life is positive.

Questions for Discussion

1 Is it important for health professionals to challenge common-sense (or traditional) ideas about 'the family'? How may they do this?

2 Why and how do families play an important role in maintaining health?

3 Why is it important to consider the diversity of family life when thinking about care of the sick?

Further Reading

G. Allen (ed.): *The Sociology of the Family: A Reader.* Oxford: Blackwell, 1999.
An edited book which contains material pertinent to understanding family and families, and issues that relate to the family and health.

J. Bernardes: *Family Studies: An introduction.* London: Routledge, 1997.
A very useful book that considers issues in relation to family and families.

H. Graham: *Women, Health and Family*. Brighton: Wheatsheaf, 1984.
An interesting book that considers the relationship between women's role in the family and health.

References

Aldridge, J. 2002: 'Nuclear family goes into meltdown.' *Observer*, 5 May. At www.guardian.co.uk/Archive/Article/ 0,4273,4407597,00.html.

Barrett, M. and McIntosh, M. 1991: *The Anti-Social Family*. London: Verso.

Bernardes, J. 1997: *Family Studies: An Introduction*. London: Routledge.

Bond, J. and Bond, S. 1986: *Sociology and Health Care*. New York: Churchill Livingstone.

Brannen, J., Dodd, K., Oakley, A. and Storey, P. 1994: *Young People, Health and Family Life*. Buckingham: Open University Press.

Cabinet Office 1997: *Living without Fear: An Integrated Approach to Tackling Violence against Women*. London: HMSO.

Cheal, D. 2002: *Sociology of Family Life*. Basingstoke: Palgrave.

Coote, A., Harman, H. and Hewitt, P. 1998: Family policy: guidelines and goals. In J. Franklin (ed.), *Social Policy and Social Justice*, Cambridge: Polity, pp. 105–14.

Davies, B., Reimer, J. and Martens, N. 1994: 'Family functioning and its implications for palliative care.' *Journal of Palliative Care*, 10(1), 29–36.

Davis, H. and Bourhill, M. 1997: 'Crisis': the demonization of children and young people. In P. Scraton (ed.), *'Childhood' in 'Crisis'?* London: UCL Press, pp. 28–57.

Department of Health 2001: *Counting Families In*. London: HMSO.

Department of Health 2002: *Tackling Obesity in England*. London: HMSO.

Doyal, L. 1995: *What Makes Women Sick: Gender and the Political Economy of Health*. Basingstoke: Macmillan.

Elliot, F. 1986: *The Family: Change or Continuity?* London: Macmillan Education.

Engels, F. 1845: *The Condition of the Working Class in England in 1844* (ed. D. McLellan. Oxford: Oxford University Press, 1999).

Giddens, A. 1989: *Sociology*. Cambridge: Polity.

Graham, H. 1999: The informal sector of welfare: a crisis in caring? In G. Allen (ed.), *The Sociology of the Family*, Oxford: Blackwell, pp. 283–300.

Griffiths, R. 1988: *Community Care: Agenda for Action: A Report to the Secretary of State for Social Services*. London: HMSO.

Hall, C. 1982: The home turned upside down? The working-class family in cotton textiles 1780–1850. In E. Whitelegg, M. Arnott, V. Beechey, L. Birke, S. Himmelweit, D. Leonard, S. Ruehl and M. A.

Speakman (eds), *The Changing Experience of Women*, Oxford: Martin
   Robertson, pp. 17–30.
Hendessi, M. 1997: *Voices of Children Witnessing Domestic Violence: A Form
   of Child Abuse*. Coventry Domestic Violence Focus Group.
Hill, A. 2002: 'Half of all "elder abuse" inflicted by relatives.' *Observer*,
   21 July. At http://observer.guardian.co.uk/uk_news/story/
   0,6903,759118,00.html.
Jackson, S. 1997: Women, marriage and family relationships. In V.
   Robinson and D. Richardson (eds), *Introducing Women's Studies*,
   Basingstoke: Macmillan, pp. 323–49.
Jagger, G. and Wright, C. 1999: *Changing Family Values*. London:
   Routledge.
Jary, D. and Jary, J. 1991: *Collins Dictionary of Sociology*. Glasgow:
   HarperCollins.
Laslett, P. 1972: Mean household size in England since the sixteenth
   century. In P. Laslett and R. Wall (eds), *Household and Family in Past
   Time*, Cambridge: Cambridge University Press, pp. 125–58.
Locker, D. 1986: The family, social support and illness. In D. Patrick
   and G. Scambler (eds), *Sociology as Applied to Medicine*, 2nd edn,
   London: Balliere Tindall, pp. 135–47.
Morgan, S. 2001: Speech to the Women's Aid Federation of England,
   26 September, at http://archive.cabinetoffice.gov.uk/ministers/
   2001/Speeches/Sally%20Morgan/WAFE%2026.9.htm
Nocon, A. and Booth, T. 2001: The social impact of childhood
   asthma. In B. Davey, A. Gray and C. Seale (eds), *Health and Disease:
   A Reader*, 3rd edn, Buckingham: Open University Press, pp. 51–87.
Pahl, J. 1999: The family and the production of welfare. In J. Baldock,
   N. Manning, S. Miller, and S. A. Vickerstaff (eds), *Social Policy*,
   Oxford: Oxford University Press, pp. 154–87.
Parsons, T. 1955: *Family Socialization and Interaction Process*. Glencoe, IL:
   Free Press.
The Princess Royal Trust for Carers 2003: *Annual Review 2002/3*.
   London: Princess Royal Trust for Carers. At www.carers.org/
   downloads/annualreview.pdf.
World Health Organization 1990: *Diet, Nutrition and the Prevention of
   Chronic Disease*. Geneva: WHO.
www.asthma.org.uk/news/
www.statistics.gov.uk/census2001/

11 Primary Care in the Community

Mike Filby

Key issues in this chapter

- Defining primary care.
- The role of general practice.
- Policy developments within primary care.
- Nursing, primary and community care.

By the end of this chapter you should be able to . . .

- Explore different definitions of primary care.
- Understand the history of general practice and the role it plays within the modern health service.
- Discuss policy developments within primary care.
- Recognize the position of nursing in primary and community care.

---

1 Introduction: what's going on in primary care

Life in any part of the National Health Service can rarely be described as dull but these are particularly interesting times for primary care. A rapid process of organizational change at the turn of the millennium has seen the establishment of authoritative primary care organizations (PCOs) for the first time since the creation of the NHS in 1948. **Primary Care Trusts** (PCTs) have substantial resources to commission and provide a wide range of health care services to citizens in the community. They commission hospital services from acute trusts for their populations and in 2004 75 per cent of the NHS budget was being channelled through PCTs. They also have substantial

Primary Care Trusts primary care organizations within the NHS. First created in 2000 and established across the whole of England by April 2002

National Service Frameworks introduced in 1998, NSFs typically comprise a set of service standards, implementation guidance and performance measures which are intended to apply nationally

◄── obligations in relation to local population health improvement and the implementation of **National Service Frameworks** and other central government service yardsticks.

It will be some time before it can be judged whether such a shift to a 'primary care-led NHS' is real or illusory. Nevertheless, the new organizational framework and other policy initiatives have significantly altered the landscape of primary care and, as with all such changes, present opportunities and threats to nurses and other health care professionals. Nurses have not been slow in taking up the challenge of opportunities and in some areas of high health need they have taken over practices employing GPs and other staff (Houghton, 2002). A further example of the change in primary care may be gauged from box 11.1.

Box 11.1   **Shirley NHS walk-in centre**

Just a few feet away from Shirley High Street in Southampton, a small revolution is taking place in primary care. Shirley is one of 40 or so walk-in centres (WICs) dotted around the country, some, like this one, in stand-alone premises, others co-located in NHS, social or commercial settings but presenting more like the front end of a building society than a traditional primary care surgery. The key features are that they are open-access – no appointment needed, located for the convenience of the public – and that they are run and staffed by nurses. They have also proved popular with the public. Shirley WIC saw 25,000 patients in its first year and is currently running at 120 a day. The majority (80 per cent) are diagnosed and treated on the premises for a range of minor illness and injury; the remainder are referred to their GP, accident and emergency or another service.

Patients are guaranteed an initial assessment within 15 minutes, undertaken by the shift leader, an experienced G-grade nurse often with a background in primary care or accident and emergency. Three other G- or F-grade nurses with two health care assistants make up the shift team and follow up the initial assessments if necessary in a consulting room.

The challenge of autonomous practice is very real for the nurses at Shirley: there are no medics on hand for a backstop view and their notes and assessments are open to scrutiny by GPs and others on referral. Despite initial scepticism from the medical community, the PCT is sufficiently impressed by the contribution of the WIC to establish a second in the east of the city.

Source: Based on a research visit and interview undertaken by the author on 9 June 2003.

Innovation in primary care: the effects on nursing

Nationwide service innovations such as NHS Direct and NHS Walk-in Centres are essentially nurse-led services designed to facilitate increased access to primary care and to deflect unnecessary pressure from other services in secondary care. The government has extended the provision and scope of these services from original pilot areas and the services have proved relatively popular with the public.

Nurses, then, are among those at the forefront of innovation and development in primary care, demonstrating the commitment, competence and expertise required to fashion and lead patient- and population-responsive services. Moreover, the changing demographic profile of doctoring in primary care suggests that this trend is set to accelerate; a range of services in primary care will increasingly depend on the availability of skilled nurses to run them.

However, at the other end of the continuum many nurses, practice nurses in particular, find their professional aspirations and development possibilities restricted, their employment conditions poor and work experience infused with traditional gender expectations and power relations (for a further discussion of gender relations see chapter 4). A central reality of primary care is that small, male-dominated businesses remain at the heart of service delivery.

These are two faces of primary care. They reflect the problem of variability in provision and quality which is high on the Government's modernization agenda for primary care, as represented in the National Plan which noted the 'huge gap between the best and the rest in the NHS' (Department of Health, 2000, p. 27) while 'The development of primary care services is the key to the modernisation of the NHS' (p. 79). It also promised that 'Nurses will have new opportunities' in primary care (p. 19).

In the discussion which follows attention will be drawn to the meaning of primary care, the critical role of general practice in the structuring of primary care, the more recent development of primary care policy and the link with community care. The chapter concludes with some critical speculation on the position and politics of nursing in primary care.

2   What is primary about primary care?

'Primary' care is not a natural given of reality, rather the outcome of the interaction of different ways of speaking about health and health care. For example, starting with the Conservative government's White Paper *Primary Care: Delivering the Future* (Department of Health, 1996), official policy discourse on primary care both became more prominent and tended to expand the notion of primary care. Indeed, the term 'primary care', as opposed to 'primary health care' or even 'primary medical care', symbolized a move towards a more inclusive discourse on primary care, albeit one that stopped short of including social care.

Peckham and Exworthy (2003) provide a very good account of how definitions of primary care have reflected ideas about levels of care, activities, functions and geographical provision and how these interact with ideologies of health and health care. They draw attention to the fact that the notion of primary care originated in the Dawson Report published in 1920 (Dawson, 1920), referring to a 'level' of care in an ascending hierarchy of specialism. This is reflected in the 'point of first contact' conception of primary care which becomes the received definition. This conceptualization by levels can be explored in Activity 11.1.

Service provision within primary care

An enormous range of services is now being provided by PCOs and these look set to expand with the acceptance of a new GP contract in 2003. The organizing rationale, for example in managing chronic illness in the community or services for older people, centres on providing care and support for patients at home. Many such people have entered secondary care directly as an acute emergency and are being referred back for some package of ongoing care. Clearly, this is related to the process of de-institutionalization of health care (Vetter, 1995) and to the capacity of nurses, therapists and doctors to provide complex care outside of hospital (see also chapter 12). The historical emphasis on 'first contact' as the defining feature of primary care also owes something to the specific British context of the NHS where access to specialist services requires referral from a GP. However, in other countries individuals have more freedom, albeit related to economic resources, to seek care directly from a specialist. Residents of inner cities in Britain, which are not over-provided with health care services, frequently use their local hospital accident and emergency (A & E) department as their point of first and preferred contact. Does this make the A & E department a primary care service?

This example demonstrates the differing definitions of primary care by patients and health care practitioners. As Williams (2000) has

Activity 11.1   Primary care: activity and assumptions

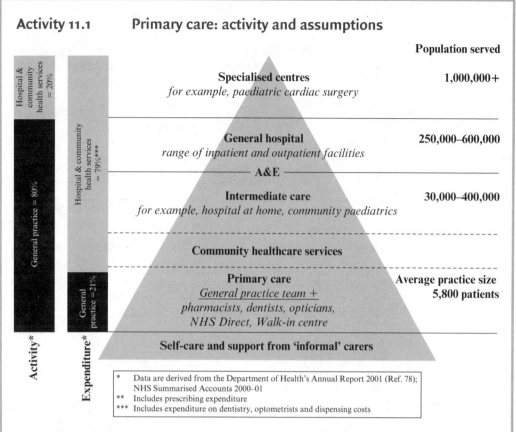

The position of general practice in relation to all health services
Source: Audit Commission.

Consider the figure above.

(a) What does this tell us about the relationship between activity and cost in different sectors of health care?

(b) What assumptions does the chart make about the role of general practice in primary care? How does this fit in with current policy?

shown, while health care professionals in the field have few difficulties in subscribing to the value and values of primary care, their occupational histories and cultures mean that they often accent these in different ways. District nurses are more likely to see primary care as bringing health care near to where people live, whereas GPs and practice nurses are prone to emphasize the provision of a range of services under one (practice) roof, and this is related very much to what they actually do as primary care practitioners.

An increasing emphasis in health policy concerns the role of PCOs in the improvement of population health and the imperative to work

Activity 11.2   **Primary care meanings**

During your practice placements make a mental note of spontaneous references to primary care among professionals and patients.

(a)   Try to identify similarities and differences in the working meanings that different role holders reflect.

(b)   Exchange informal notes with your peers from your own and other branches of nursing; are there any systematic differences and does it matter if there are?

in partnership with agencies across a spectrum of public, including non-health, provision, in achieving this (see also chapter 13).

From the above discussion it could be argued that the search for a neat and fixed definition of primary care is probably unhelpful. What falls within the ambit of primary care will continue to evolve as the boundaries between service areas become more fluid.

3 General practice

Primary care has increasingly moved into the policy spotlight in recent years but the role of the peculiar institution of general practice, as suggested above, is critical to an understanding of primary care in Britain. It is not simply that general practice is 'part of a complex web of primary care services' (Audit Commission, 2002, p. 12), but that general practice has a determining impact on the shape and texture of this sector of health care, and indeed on the structure of primary care nursing. As the Audit Commission report itself notes, for many people primary care and general practice are one and the same thing. This represents something of a triumph for a branch of doctoring which for most of its history remained in the shadow of more prestigious varieties of hospital-centred medicine. Whilst general practice has evolved, it still survives in its historically recognizable form, yet it does seem likely that the scope and pace of change in general practice will increase in the current policy climate.

Despite the tragic consequences of the activities of one murderous GP in south Manchester, general practice continues to receive a relatively good press and patient satisfaction levels with general practice tend to be high. The position of general practice also continues to be affirmed in official policy statements. The NHS Plan praised GPs as a source of strength for the NHS (Department of Health, 2000). In policy commentary, general practice has been referred to as the 'lynchpin of primary care' (Sibbald, 2000, p. 14), and an authoritative analysis of general practice concluded 'that UK general practice is indeed a major jewel in the NHS crown' (Moon and

North, 2000, p. 175). The Audit Commission (2002) report also drew attention to the comprehensiveness of cover afforded by general practice and its celebrated **gatekeeping** role with respect to access to more specialized services, which is often seen as a major factor in the relative cost-effectiveness of the NHS as a whole.

gatekeeping   the key role which general practitioners have traditionally played in managing access of patients to secondary and other health care services

Yet general practice has been a source of government frustration, particularly around variations in quality of services. As Maynard (2002, p. 19) commented wryly, 'Like pub food, general practice varies enormously from the excellent to the deadly'. Lurking in the concerns about quality are issues of accountability and control and these have become more pronounced as primary care has assumed more strategic importance for the NHS as a whole. The relationship between the government and general practice has therefore been an ambiguous one, conditioned by what might be called the historic settlement of 1948 which saw the creation of the NHS and institutionalized the modern form of general practice.

The development of general practice

While the history is complex (see Parry and Parry, 1976; Moon and North, 2000), general practice can be said to have emerged in the early nineteenth century from the jumbled ranks of apothecaries and surgeons providing services to the expanding urban middle classes. Despite being incorporated in the medical establishment through the Medical Registration Act of 1858, general practice continued to occupy a lowly position in the medical hierarchy for the ensuing century. The national insurance reforms of 1911 provided the beginnings of a more secure economic position for general practice through the system of capitation payments based on patient lists, while continuing to allow GPs considerable autonomy in carrying out their business.

Nervous about the role of the state and the pre-eminence of hospital medicine (Moon and North, 2000), GPs initially resisted the plans for the creation of the NHS. This was finally overcome by the concession to allow GPs to retain their status as independent contractors. This essentially means that GPs (albeit through a collective agreement) would contract with the state to provide a range of care for patients but not be directly employed by it; capitation payments remained central to what became an increasingly complicated system of remuneration as successive governments attempted to buy service development in primary care.

It is difficult to overestimate the importance of the independent contractor status for the emergent mentality of general practice and the consequent impact on the development of primary care nursing. For example, GPs through the General Medical Services Committee mounted a determined and successful campaign against the proposals of the famous Cumberledge Report (Department of Health and Social Security, 1986) (see Sibbald, 2000). This report proposed the establishment of nurse-managed neighbourhood nursing teams comprising practice and district nurses, health visitors and other community nurses based on localities of up to 25,000 people and effectively transcending the 'surgery walls'. It flew, perhaps naively, (too) directly in the face of economic and power relations in general practice and was sidestepped by the government. The 1990 GP contract and the development of **GP fundholding** (GPFH) expanded the profile of primary care and nursing services but these were being shaped by the interests of general practice (Wilson, 2000).

GP fundholding introduced in 1990, it meant that GP practices were able to hold budgets to purchase care for their patients; abolished in 1999

It is therefore important to be aware that the organization of doctoring in the community as 'general practice' is a specific historical and political outcome. Recent policy developments signal an attempt to introduce more diversity in organization and provision to meet the particular circumstances of local communities and to adjust for the trends in the doctoring population.

4 Policy overview: towards the primary care-led NHS

Primary Care Trusts were consolidated in April 2002 as the standard-issue PCO throughout England following the publication of *Shifting the Balance of Power: Securing Delivery* (Department of Health, 2001), which also abolished district health authorities and regional offices of the National Health Service Executive. These were replaced with strategic health authorities. Parallel (but different) developments were in train in Scotland and Wales.

The creation of these organizations in primary care represents the realization of change prefigured by the Labour government's White Paper *The New NHS, Modern, Dependable* (Department of Health, 1997). In policy terms, however, the increasingly sharp focus on primary care emerges a decade or so prior to the Labour programme which, while formally abolishing the marketization of health care, developed some of the emerging ideas for the structuring of primary care. The policy developments reflect the central dilemma for successive governments bequeathed by the politics of the 1948 NHS Act, whereby the providers remained essentially small private businesses, contracting their services to the NHS. Issues of development, direction, compliance, accountability, quality are difficult to manage in this sort of relationship and can only be crudely addressed in the contracting process, although the 2003 GP contract is focused much more on quality.

The introduction of the internal market following the 1990 NHS and Community Care Act established the distinction between purchasers and providers of care and, most significantly, introduced the system of GP fundholding. Successive waves of GPs took up this option so that by the time fundholding was abolished in 1998, 75 per cent of patients were covered by these arrangements. Establishing GPs with purchasing power was intended to lever in more responsiveness and efficiency in the providers (hospital and community trusts) but also to modify the GP gatekeeping role, adding the responsibility for allocating resources to the power of referral to secondary care. This may be seen as the beginning of the incorporation of GPs into the process of service development.

However, as Peckham and Exworthy (2003, p. 76) note, 'reform was being conducted by primary care but not for primary care'. The notion of a 'primary care-led NHS' was coined in 1994 on the back of further development of the fundholding system; a government 'listening exercise' resulted in a White Paper, *Choice and Opportunity: Primary Care – The Future*, followed by legislation in the last days of the Conservative government, the NHS (Primary Care) Act (1997). The thrust of policy was towards making the frameworks within which primary care services could be developed more flexibly, particularly in areas with client groups (a topical example would be refugees) that had not been well served by the traditional arrangements for general practice. Thus the Act allowed the setting-up of what are known as

Personal Medical Services (PMS) pilots
introduced following the 1997 NHS (Primary Care) Act; operates through a local contract to provide specific services to meet locally identified needs

Personal Medical Services (PMS) pilots; significantly, it was the incoming Labour government of 1997 that implemented this policy.

While the evaluation of PMS is mixed, one area of relative success has been the development of new nursing roles especially in the nurse-led pilots which have 'inverted the traditional hierarchy between doctors and nurses' (Lewis et al., 2001, p. 120), as nurses have taken on clinical leadership and management while also attempting to democratize the operation of primary care teams.

Activity 11.3　**A primary care-led NHS**

Go to your local GP surgery or Health Centre and look for evidence that the NHS is becoming a primary care-led service.

- Ask the receptionist for a practice leaflet, or look at the posters on the walls. What services are being offered other than appointments to see a GP?
- Are there other health professionals based there whom you can see?
- Are there specialist clinics taking place?

From PCGs to PCTs

The creation of free-standing primary care organizations is one of the notable developments of health policy in recent years under the Labour government. In carrying out its pledge to abolish the internal market and GP fundholding, however, the government retained the distinction between purchasing – replaced by the wider concept of commissioning – and provision of services. This was embodied organizationally in the creation of primary care groups (PCGs), themselves situated on a ladder of increasing autonomy and responsibility. Thus four levels of primary care organization were differentiated culminating in primary care trusts. The creation of PCGs also reflected the belief that the shaping of local services was best done by those intimately connected with the health needs of local populations, that is, doctors and nurses. Most of the 482 PCGs created in April 1999 were at 'level two', that is, they were given devolved powers for managing a budget but they were still formally a sub-part of the district health authority. They were geographically based organizations encompassing all the GP practices in a given area which, ideally, reflected a 'natural community' population of 100,000, though this varied enormously in practice.

The governance arrangements were also novel in that the PCG board was to include two nurse representatives as well as GPs, a lay and a social services representative. The expectation was that there would be a gradual evolution to PCTs. However, government frustration with the performance of the NHS as a whole led to the acceleration of the timetable to the effect that all PCGs were to become (merged) PCTs by April 2002.

The functions of PCTs are essentially the same as those of their predecessors. These were about:

- improving (and addressing inequalities in) the health of their community;
- developing primary and community health services, through investing to improve the quality of care and the integration of services;
- commissioning secondary services. (NHS Executive, 1999)

The governance arrangements were somewhat more complex, however. PCTs have a board which has a lay chair and a majority of non-executive lay members reflecting the local community served, and includes representatives of the Professional Executive Committee (PEC). Members of this committee are essentially nominated by different professional constituencies (which in turn may involve some elective process). Nurses, along with other non-medical professionals, are thus represented on the PEC, as are social services.

The changes heralded by *Shifting the Balance* engendered a certain amount of organizational chaos as PCTs rushed to formation and the health authorities were restructured. The ethos of localism has become more difficult to sustain as PCTs encompass generally larger populations and a number of differing localities and communities. The burden of expectation placed on PCTs by government has been enormous and the imposition of central targets has tended to unbalance the commitment to responsiveness to locally determined health needs. Whether the government will show enough patience to allow these organizations to settle to their task is an open question.

Primary care and community care

Interestingly, as primary care came to prominence in the 1990s, it increasingly overshadowed its policy twin, community care, which had arguably been the organizing concept in social policy in the 1980s and early 1990s. As Lewis (1999) observes, both concepts have recent and similar histories but paradoxically they have been dealt with separately in policy terms, whereas on the ground their implications for users, patients and professionals are closely linked.

The watershed in community care policy occurred with the implementation (in 1993) of the 1990 NHS and Community Care Act. However, community care discourse can be seen to emerge in the late 1950s. The concern then was with the role and costs of the large, long-stay hospitals housing primarily the mentally ill and those with learning difficulties. In the inquiries and reports which followed, little attention was paid to the content of community care which often simply meant care outside of large institutions, and could therefore include smaller residential units 'in the community'. The term also increasingly came to be seen as doubly ambiguous: what was meant by 'community' and what was meant by 'care'? The disabling effects of large closed institutions are discussed in chapter 12. However, it is generally accepted that the underlying driver for change towards community care was the economic cost of maintaining long-stay institutions.

This impetus increased in the 1980s in a Britain fuelled by the Thatcher government's monetarist approach to (reducing the financial burden of) the welfare state. In addition, the 'new right' ideologies in respect of individual self-reliance readily translated into a notion of care by the community and family care, rather than on behalf of the community through local public provision. However, at this time the 'discovery' of informal care and the exploitation of women implied by family care also became increasingly exposed in the policy literature (see also chapter 10). The 1990s saw the development of the market in the provision of social care in the community and some trialling of new forms of provision. The main target groups continued to be the mentally ill, the learning-disabled and 'the elderly'. Older people indeed moved increasingly centre stage as the dubious notion of 'bed blocking' in the acute sector achieved increasing policy prominence.

The revolution in community care embodied in the reforms of the 1990 Act was also triggered by economic considerations, primarily the hundredfold increase in the public costs of private residential – including nursing homes – care during the previous decade (Gorman and Postle, 2003). However, the model of community care which emerges is, they argue, a very specific one. The implementation of community care in the form of care management – the management of individualized care packages – represents a distortion of the wider vision of community care. Community care as care management continues to reflect aspects of the Thatcherite project in terms of the emphasis on the managerial control of the costs of care, its individualized emphasis and the creation of a market in social care. Care managers (typically social workers) assess the needs of users, frame a package of care in response to this and then seek to contract with independent providers for the care. Gorman and Postle point to a number of contradictions resulting from this emphasis, not least the effective erosion of real choice for users and the short-circuiting of the assessment process necessitated by the resource realities. It would be inaccurate to say that many people in receipt of care had not increasingly benefited from this form of care organization but the relevance of the term 'community' to this regime of care is not self-evident.

The community care reforms tended to weaken the position of nurses working in the community as the lead responsibility for the negotiation of care packages with users and carers fell to social services. In addition, the reforms entailed an increasingly sharp distinction between health care and social care; the significance was that while the former remained free at the point of delivery, social care involved charging and means-testing. There were thus system pressures towards tighter definition of what counted as health care in the community and on the roles of those providing it. At the same time the internal market meant that GP fundholding practices took a much more calculating view of the services they were willing to purchase from 'community nursing'. District nurse roles, for example, were redefined around narrower and more targeted tasks, and these would increasingly exclude aspects of social care (Kelly and Symonds, 2003). Indeed, Kelly and Symonds argue that the history of community nursing since the early nineteenth century is one of somewhat passive adaptation to emergent discourses such as those of the new community – and primary – care. As Malin et al. (1999)

Activity 11.4   **Community care in action**

During your practice placement seek an opportunity to attend a multi-disciplinary discharge care planning meeting.

(a)   Reflect on the roles of the professionals, the patient/user and close relatives in determining the plan outcome.

(b)   Consider the sense in which the outcome might be described as care by the community.

suggest, community nurses, albeit lacking the power resources of other groups, have been largely reactive and apolitical with respect to issues of the organization of care.

5   Nursing, general practice and primary care

Finally, let us return to where we began and the opportunities and potential for nurses and nursing in the new context of primary care. As we have seen, the positioning of primary care at the heart of the health care system has entailed the creation of managerially driven primary care organizations, increased demands on primary care fuelled by national priorities and local circumstances, a proliferation of services, and many innovations in the way services may be organized, such as through the PMS pilots. All this is taking place in the context of a national shortage of GPs, the occupational group which has traditionally dominated and determined the shape of primary care, and nursing in primary care.

Although nursing roles in primary care have been by no means static, to date they have tended to reflect the interests and changing responsibilities and workloads of GPs. As Ashburner and Birch (1999) demonstrate, new nursing roles such as that of 'nurse practitioner' were conditioned by the circumstances of particular GP practice interests and as a result varied considerably in title and content. Such roles tended to embody an ambiguous notion of nurse autonomy; that is, nurses were subject to the overall control of the doctor while working without direct supervision. On the whole, GPs have successfully resisted genuine autonomy in nursing practice even in areas where medical issues are not relevant (Ashburner and Birch, 1999) and, by default, they have thus determined the paths of nursing development.

Issues of power and autonomy have similarly characterized one of the central myths of primary care, the **primary care health team** (PCHT). This is not to say that there are not many examples of effective collaboration between health professionals working in primary care and in general practice; many professionals deploy excellent team-working skills in particular contexts. Clearly also, where there is a complex division of labour involving many different skills and roles, as in health and social care, the need for effective collaboration in delivering care to patients and clients is paramount. However, many studies have shown that, in practice, effective teamwork in PCHTs was limited, despite its high moral and rhetorical value among participants (Wiles and Robinson, 1994). Not least is the ambiguous position of GPs in relation to the 'team' and on the whole GPs have shown themselves to be reluctant team players (Wall and Owen, 1999), as might be predicted from the culture of the independent contractor. As Wilson (2000) suggests, it would indeed be surprising if the complex historical, occupational and policy

Primary Care Health Team   centred on the general medical 'practice' and incorporating medical and nursing personnel

context of primary care did other than result in tensions around independence and power in teams.

'Modernization' within primary care

The new organizational framework and the 'modernization' agenda are also part of this context and it seems likely that a series of developments around the reconfiguration of services will mean that teamwork remains important but is unlikely to be focused on the traditional, GP-practice-centred PCHT model. Teams are more likely to be fluidly constructed around particular projects, such as patient groups or pathways which will cut vertically across sectors; some of these may involve medical practitioners, many will be nurse-led. The PMS pilots have provided the opportunity for non-medical, community-based professionals to provide specific health services. GPs who may provide a specialist clinic for a group of practices will develop a team for that purpose only, for example. As Wilson (2000) argues, networks of professionals may represent forms of collaboration and communication more appropriate for the new context while continuing to draw on teamwork skills.

Whether the opportunities for nursing presented by the new context are realized depends on many interacting factors. Not least is the 'political' organization of nurses. In order to influence the direction of change, nurses in primary care will be required to develop a more united front and shared analysis than in the past. This is difficult not least because of the way nursing in general practice has been shaped by medical practitioners; individual nurses have an interest in their specific positions as nurse practitioners or practice nurses and an identity with the 'practice'. An additional complication is the way community nursing has historically related to practice and became increasingly determined by it during the 1990s. There is a key role now for nursing leadership at all levels in primary care trusts to develop and articulate nursing strategy. Under the constitution of PCTs, nurses have representation on the Professional Executive Committee and opportunity to shape policy, but as ever this requires effective networking and communication.

The drift of organizational reform in primary care through the establishment of PCTs is to insist on greater management of the primary care agenda and corporate responsibility for it among the stakeholders. The development of services is intended to reflect the health needs of patients and communities and collectively determined priorities at national and local level and not simply those of the producers. While it is clear that, in the early days, PCT managements have been concerned to keep the GPs on board, there is, nevertheless, an unmistakeable drive towards innovation and diversity in forms of provision in the context of 'modernization', and the exercise of managerial leverage. The implementation of the new 2003 GP contract will tend to reinforce these trends, though GP culture will lag considerably behind any changes in behaviour which it may bring about.

While a clearing in medical domination may emerge for the development of nursing agendas, these will have to chime effectively with the corporate agenda of the PCT. Eluding managerial dominance while emerging from that of general practice will be a notable challenge.

Summary and Resources

Summary

- Primary care has moved towards the centre of the health care policy stage in the last decade.

- The institution of general medical practice has been a crucial determinant of the shape of primary care and nursing in primary care and will continue to be a key stakeholder.

- New primary care organizations have been established to introduce more strategic management and development of primary care services.

- The newly developing scenario in primary care will present opportunities for nursing development and nurse-led services, but medical domination of the politics of nursing in the community will continue in the absence of more pro-active nursing organization and leadership at the local level.

Questions for Discussion

1   The distinction between primary and secondary care is a taken-for-granted one among commentators and practitioners alike in health care and firmly rooted in health policy. Is it still relevant in a patient-centred service?

2   A 'primary care-led NHS' has been a key policy slogan of health service reform since 1997; what evidence would you point to from your practice experience to show that this is, or is not, happening?

3   The implementation of care in the community in the 1990s saw a hardening of the distinction between health and social care; does this distinction help or hinder the delivery of care? Hint: think about discharge planning for patients.

Further Reading

A. Kelly and A. Symonds: *The Social Construction of Community Nursing*. Basingstoke: Palgrave Macmillan, 2003.
Kelly and Symonds present a challenging insight into primary care through their principal focus on the development of community nursing and the discourses and policies which have shaped it over time.

N. Malin, J. Manthorpe, D. Race and S. Wilmot: *Community Care for Nurses and the Caring Professions*. Buckingham: Open University Press, 1999.

This book offers an excellent overview of the development of community care policy and practice over the past three decades and discusses a number of key practice issues, with particular emphasis on the implications for health care professionals.

G. Moon and N. North: *Policy and Place; General Medical Practice in the UK.* Basingstoke: Macmillan, 2000.
This text analyses policy and politics in the NHS in terms of the impact on, and influence of, general medical practice in the community. The discussion offers an insight into the power relations between elements of the medical profession and nurses in particular, and the reflection of these in the development of primary care in Britain.

S. Peckham and M. Exworthy: *Primary Care in the UK.* Basingstoke: Palgrave Macmillan, 2003.
This text provides a comprehensive and authoritative discussion of the development of primary care policy in the United Kingdom. It also discusses the organization of primary care and a number of key contemporary issues in primary care such as interprofessional working.

References

Ashburner, L. and Birch, K. 1999: Professional control issues between medicine and nursing in primary care. In A. L. Mark and S. Dopson (eds), *Organisational Behaviour in Health Care: The Research Agenda*, Basingstoke: Macmillan, pp. 63–76.

Audit Commission 2002: *A Focus on General Practice in England*. London: Audit Commission.

Dawson, B. 1920: *Report on the Future Provision of Medical and Allied Services*, Cmd 693. London: HMSO.

Department of Health 1996: *Primary Care: Delivering the Future*. London: HMSO.

Department of Health 1997: *The New NHS, Modern, Dependable*. London: HMSO.

Department of Health 2000: *The National Plan*. London: TSO.

Department of Health 2001: *Shifting the Balance of Power: Securing Delivery*. London: DoH.

Department of Health and Social Security 1986: *Neighbourhood Nursing: A Focus for Care. The Cumberlege Report. Report of the Community Nursing Review*. London: HMSO.

Gorman, H. and Postle, K. 2003: *Transforming Community Care: A Distorted Vision?* Birmingham: Venture Press.

Houghton, M. 2002: 'We bought our own GP.' *Nursing Times*, 98(13), 28–9.

Kelly, A. and Symonds, A. 2003: *The Social Construction of Community Nursing*. Basingstoke: Palgrave Macmillan.

Lewis, J. 1999: 'The concepts of community care and primary care in the UK: the 1960s to the 1990s.' *Health and Social Care in the Community*, 7, 333–41.

Lewis, R., Gillam, S. and Jenkins, C. 2001: *Personal Medical Services Pilots*. London: King's Fund.

Malin, N., Manthorpe, J., Race, D. and Wilmot, S. 1999: *Community Care for Nurses and the Caring Professions*. Buckingham: Open University Press.

Maynard, A. 2002: 'Crisis in General Practice.' *Guardian*, 22 August, Letters.

Moon, G. and North, N. 2000: *Policy and Place: General Medical Practice in the UK*. London: Macmillan.

NHS Executive 1999: *Primary Care Trusts: Establishment, the Preparatory Period and their Functions*. London: DoH.

Parry, N. and Parry, J. 1976: *The Rise of the Medical Profession*. London: Croom Helm.

Peckham, S. and Exworthy, M. 2003: *Primary Care in the UK*. Basingstoke: Palgrave Macmillan.

Sibbald, S. 2000: Primary care: background and policy issues. In A. Williams, *Nursing Medicine and Primary Care*, Buckingham: Open University Press, pp. 14–26.

Vetter, N. 1995: *Hospital: From Centre of Excellence to Community Support*. Aldershot: Gower.

Wall, A. and Owen, B. 1999: *Health Policy*. Eastbourne: Gildredge Press.

Wiles, R. and Robinson, J. 1994: 'Teamwork in primary care: the views and experiences of nurses, midwives and health visitors.' *Journal Of Advanced Nursing*, 20, 324–30.

Williams, A. 2000: *Nursing Medicine and Primary Care*. Buckingham: Open University Press.

Wilson, A. E. 2000: The changing nature of primary health care teams and interprofessional relationships. In P. Tovey (ed.), *Contemporary Primary Care*, Buckingham: Open University Press, pp. 43–60.

12 Hospitals and Institutions in the Community

Philip Shelton

Key issues in this chapter

- The emergence of the hospital.
- The hospital: the best place for care?
- Institutionalization.
- Institutions within the community.

By the end of this chapter you should be able to . . .

- Define the nature of an institution.
- Understand the historical development of hospitals, asylums and other institutions.
- Explore issues of discharge.
- Understand the nature of institutions within the community
- Be aware of contemporary issues around institutions for nursing practice
- Recognize the challenges of medicalized death in hospital.

1   Introduction

What is an institution? In what way does the institution have an effect on the delivery of care and the ways that patients receive care? Are hospitals the best place to be in order to get better? This chapter will consider the growth of institutions as ways of caring for the sick. It will also chart their recent history, demonstrating the relationship of hospitals to the

institutionalization   the ◄ medicalization and **institutionalization** of health care,
long-term incarceration
of individuals, whether   including the specialization of hospitals. The consideration of
compulsory, coercive or   hospitals as institutions will explore the structured
voluntary, for the purpose
of treatment, care and   relationships within hospitals, with particular emphasis on the
social control   place of the patient within these structures. There will also be
critical discussions of the effectiveness of the modern
hospital/institution in caring for the sick and in caring for the
dying. The NHS and Community Care Act (Department of
Health, 1990) reshaped the organization and subsequent
delivery of health and social care in the public, private,
informal and voluntary sectors. The impetus was for
convalescent and long-term care to take place within
community settings, either residential or the person's own
dwelling, freeing up secondary services for acute patients. The
decrease in reliance on hospital beds has only partially been
compensated for with the growth in the number of places in
residential services. The implications of this for nurses will also
be explored in this chapter.

2   What is an institution?

In sociological terms, the nature of institutions can be viewed in a
number of ways depending on context and function. Scott and
Christensen (1995, p. 33) suggest that 'institutions consist of
cognitive, normative, and regulative structures and activities that
provide stability and meaning to social behaviour'. In other words
institutions are more than just the buildings that create a hospital, an
asylum or a university. They also comprise the practices, procedures
and values that give them an identity. It may be worth reviewing
chapter 1 here, particularly the discussion of theories of social
structure and the importance of structures, rules and social roles.

While Scott and Christensen focus on the psychological, social
and political elements of organizational life, Erving Goffman
distinguishes between an institution and a 'total institution', the
latter he defines as: 'a place of residence and work where a large
number of like-situated individuals, cut off from the wider society for
an appreciable period of time, together lead an enclosed, formally
administered round of life' (Goffman,1961, p. 11). According to King
and Raynes (1968), institutionalization has the following four
features:

1   depersonalization;
2   social distance (between staff and inmates);
3   block activities (when all activities are rigidly organized at group level
    with little opportunity for individual preference);
4   a lack of variety in daily routine.

Other important factors are the appearance, size and structure of the accommodation, the furnishings and the atmosphere. Victorian edifices may rapidly induce gloom and despondency in those who come to live there, while a well-designed, bright, attractive modern building can have quite the opposite effect. However, in a resource-limited service like the NHS the desire to provide the personal domestic-like features of a small establishment has to be balanced against economic factors.

So whereas for most of us different activities, such as going to work, socializing or playing sport, are carried out in different settings, possibly with different people, within a total institution all aspects of life are carried out under one roof, or in one complex. Other characteristics of institutions include activities being planned to suit a rational goal, a privilege system where small rewards and punishments can be built around obedience to staff, and situational adaptations where rebellion can serve to raise morale, or inmates are converted to taking the staff's view of themselves and attempt to act the role of the perfect inmate.

For Goffman tuberculosis sanatoria, army barracks and mental asylums, amongst other organizations, constitute total institutions. These settings are not conducive to long-stay patients becoming independent and reaching their full potential, for reasons explored in section 5.

Nurses do not usually view themselves as working in institutions, as they are familiar with the routines of the hospital setting, may find the rules conducive to the smooth running of the ward, and do not always appreciate how alien it all seems to the patient. However, in institutions for older people, those with mental health problems or learning difficulties, traditionally procedures and practices have been very inflexible with no scope for patients to express individuality, or to deviate from routines set by the staff.

This can be viewed as a very controlling environment, and whilst sociologists do not necessarily agree about what constitutes an institution, they would see the need to examine the extent to which institutions can be seen as places of either care or control.

This section has examined sociological definitions of institution, and the inflexibility of total institutions. It has highlighted the idea that institutionalization is not compatible with the notion of individualized care.

3 Types of institution

The emergence of the general hospital

According to Dainton (1961), from as early as 1155 hospitals were developed by religious orders as institutions for the sick. Hospitals in their earliest form both provided care for the sick and acted as homes for orphans and others who were unable to care for themselves.

The dissolution of the monasteries (including their infirmaries) from 1535 to 1540 by Henry VIII and the resulting loss of their medical expertise acted as an impetus to the growth of the medical profession, which then developed outside its religious origins. The first indication of the organization of health services was the founding of the Royal College of Physicians in 1518, which then began licensing London doctors.

In 1601 the Poor Law was introduced whereby parishes became responsible for the care of old and chronically ill poor people and fatherless children. This led to the development of workhouses, some of which had a separate infirmary for the sick. The well-to-do, with servants to do their nursing, and able to afford a doctor to visit them, were treated in their own homes.

In the eighteenth century, social changes brought about by industrialization and urbanization of the population led to increasing numbers of both rich and poor. For the rich, philanthropic endeavours were a way of demonstrating their wealth, and subscribing to the building of voluntary hospitals, and other public buildings, such as schools, libraries and public baths, provided a visible and lasting monument. In the rapidly growing cities to which the poor were moving in large numbers because of the lure of work in the new industries, the care of the sick and vulnerable was not compatible with the need for wage earning, and these groups found themselves increasingly institutionalized. Poor living conditions and poverty led to a downturn in the health of the nation, especially with regard to infectious diseases, as previously isolated individuals and communities were brought into contact with one another (Vetter, 1995). The new voluntary hospitals were, however, very discriminating over who they would admit, and so most people were dependent on family or Poor Law institutions when sick.

Consequently both voluntary and Poor Law hospitals expanded and increased in number during the nineteenth century. Doctors who were members of the Royal Colleges dominated the voluntary hospitals, which developed into centres for research and teaching. Lobbying by the Poor Law Board, some members of the medical profession and philanthropists finally achieved an administrative separation of sick people and people with mental health problems from the workhouse, and into infirmaries or asylums.

So a two-tier system existed, with voluntary hospitals caring for surgical patients and accident victims, and Poor Law infirmaries housing the chronically and terminally ill, people suffering from infections, and anyone else not catered for by voluntary hospitals.

The emergence of the asylum

In 1808 the County Asylums Act gave permissive powers to the justices of each county to build asylums, and replace the few psychiatric annexes to voluntary general hospitals. The Poor Law Amendment Act (1834) required relief to be provided within institutions only, which meant that to receive any help from the state the destitute were obliged to enter the workhouse, which led to the construction of a huge network of workhouses.

The Lunatics Act of 1845 made the provision of asylums the responsibility of each county, and the number rose from nine in 1827 to 91 by 1910. Not only this but they also grew in size from an average of 166 patients in 1827 to 1072 in 1910 (Busfield, 1986). It is said that following the 1845 Act the sex ratio in the asylums altered, from being predominantly male to predominantly female, a situation that remains to this day. This was because the main category of patient was the pauper lunatic, and more women than men found themselves destitute, and labelled lunatics in order to remove them from being a drain on the parish rates.

The early mental hospital is a different institution from the general hospital in both its architecture and its locality. The asylum was located in the countryside, often remote from the nearest town, and tended to be self-sufficient. Inmates, as they were called, helped to nurse the old and frail, and worked on the farms and in the kitchens of the asylum. This originally provided a contrast to disorganized privately run asylums in the cities, which were often a source of tuberculosis and disease (Hardey, 1998).

By the end of the nineteenth century a nationwide system of asylums and hospitals had been created in the USA and in many European countries and their colonies, as well as in Britain. Whilst the hospitals and the asylums shared characteristics, it was the latter which were to prove the most problematic. They housed both 'lunatics' (people with mental health problems) and 'idiots' (people with learning disabilities) and little attempt was made to differentiate the needs of these two very different groups before the Mental Deficiency Act (1913). Contained within the same institutions were people suffering from neurological disorders, including epilepsy and dementia, and a variety of other individuals whose behaviour had prompted sharp moral and social rejection. Extramarital sex (by women), and homosexuality and masturbation (by both sexes) (Darby, 2003), had been characterized as types of 'moral insanity', which could provide a pretext for admission to the institution. The incarceration of this latter group is an obvious example of the use of institutions for the purpose of custody and social control, rather than benevolent care and protection.

Foucault, writing on the origins and political functions of institutions including hospitals (1973) and mental institutions (1967), suggests that institutions were born from a political imperative to segregate those sections of the population perceived as 'unproductive' within the developing capitalist economies of the eighteenth, nineteenth and twentieth centuries; this included the sick and those with mental health problems or learning difficulties.

The emergence of the children's hospital

In the eighteenth century the presence of children in hospital was rare; there was strong opposition from prominent doctors on the grounds that a child should not be separated from its mother, and mothers would not be able to have the time from work to be admitted with their children (Dainton, 1961). Interestingly, the idea that children and mothers should not be separated was abandoned during the twentieth century, and only revived following research on the needs of children in hospital in the 1960s. It was also recognized amongst the medical profession that children were more likely to develop infectious diseases (Higgins, 1952), which made hospitals reluctant to admit them. Instead, dispensaries were formed by doctors that enabled children to be treated in their own home. However, physicians did not always provide adequate supervision, which delayed the child's recovery. In addition the opportunity to study the effect of diseases on children was missed.

By the nineteenth century the limitations of the general hospital were apparent, and medical advances meant there was a need for more specialist hospitals. In contrast to general hospitals which had the backing of charitable laypeople aided by doctors, specialist hospitals were founded and controlled by doctors. The first British children's hospitals were opened in 1851 by Dr Charles West, who was convinced of the need for a hospital to provide care for children, despite the traumas of separation. In addition whilst specialist hospitals, including children's hospitals, were founded on the principle of helping the sick and advancing medical practice, other motives were a lack of opportunity for promotion within the voluntary hospital system and the chance for self-advancement in a new area.

The medical profession had developed into a unified profession by 1858. The elite were the voluntary hospital consultants, who had the opportunity to experiment on patients and develop skills in surgery, and other interventions. The old workhouse infirmaries were staffed by salaried doctors and were associated with care as opposed to cure. Specialist hospitals had developed to fill the gaps in provision left by the other hospitals' selectivity in admissions. By the inception of the NHS in 1948, however, many voluntary hospitals had lost much of their funding from donations, and were variable in the standards of care they offered. It was hospitals attached to medical schools that became the new elite institutions. The asylums were redesignated psychiatric hospitals, reinforcing the idea of a medical model of treatment, rather than custody and restraint.

Activity 12.1   **Care or control?**

(a) Think about the ways in which hospitals, as institutions, are about social control as much as they are about care (you might want to think about the control of patient routine, behaviour, and so on).

(b) To what extent, then, is the role of a nurse about control of the patient?

(c) Consider the ways in which institutions regulate and reinforce their own institutional norms. How might this impact on your ability to care for the patient?

4 Hospitalization

When the general public is questioned about health care, it is hospitals and acute interventions that are most commonly raised. For most people the NHS is its hospitals, and what happens inside them will colour their perceptions of it.

Hospitals are the very visible face of the NHS; they are where cutting-edge technology and heroic surgery take place. They are also the focus of political debates on the NHS, and the health sector by which politicians' success in running the NHS will be judged. Indeed, in the 2001 election campaign Tony Blair declared 'schools and hospitals first'. Not, you will note, 'education and the NHS first'. Hospitals are also important for providing clinical experience for students of the health professions.

hospitalization period of time as a patient confined to a hospital

Although the primary purpose of **hospitalization** is to care for the person's health and well-being, it also involves loss of both personal and physical privacy and the imposition of a number of restrictions. For example, not only are patients subject to the routines of the ward, they often find themselves in close proximity to each other, while intimate contact between health care provider and patient is unavoidable. There have been attempts to make certain wards more

palliative care care to meet the needs and expectations of patients who have a progressive life-threatening illness (and those of their families)

patient-friendly, particularly in paediatrics and **palliative care**. For example, the NHS Plan (Department of Health, 2000) suggests that children and young people should be provided with a range of equipment appropriate to their age, including a bedside TV with headphones, telephone and radio, provided free of charge wherever possible. In addition there should be facilities available for more active play, if the child wishes, and their condition allows.

However, hospitalization inevitably restricts normal activity. Some restrictions, such as those imposed by bed rest or traction, may be therapeutically desirable, while others, such as visiting times, may be related more to organizational than therapeutic concerns. We may have had our own personal experience of hospitals at some point in our lives, or know someone who has, and it is worth remembering that when a person becomes hospitalized they have to contend not only with their illness but also with an environment which is alien to them, and where they are expected to entrust their care to strangers.

Whilst surgery and treatment can be stressful, an additional aspect of hospitalization is Illich's (1979) concept of iatrogenesis (see chapter 3), which suggests that a patient's health may deteriorate as a direct consequence of becoming hospitalized; for example, poor hospital diet, or more likely an inadequate diet, can lead to malnutrition, or any misdiagnosis can lead to a delay in treatment.

The process of hospitalization can reflect aspects of institutionalization in that the patient is subject to the routine of the ward. However, for most people, the length of time spent in hospital is relatively short so it is difficult to argue that the patient's identity is being wholly subsumed within institutional life, unlike the area of mental health, as the next section illustrates.

5 Institutionalization and the asylums

The process of institutionalization described in section 12.2 has been typically played out in asylums. Whilst external factors, such as the nature of the buildings themselves, can influence institutionalization, Erving Goffman (1961) – influenced by theories of social action (see chapter 1) – broke new ground in the sociological understanding of institutions by focusing on the experiences of 'inmates' (patients). He made detailed observations of contact among inmates themselves and between inmates and the staff of the institution, and suggested that these interactions symbolized power relationships, status differences and unstated expectations. He argued that what he termed the institutional 'underlife' (p. 180) assumed an importance greater than the formal procedures and policies of the institution. He also coined the phrase 'total institution'. Whilst clearly no institution is totally disconnected from life outside, the use of this phrase does convey something of the flavour of the dominating and all-pervasive nature of the institution in the world of the inmate.

In many institutions the activities of daily life such as sleep and work take place under one roof governed by one authority. Each phase of a person's daily routine is rigidly fixed and carried out in the company of others, who are all treated alike. Enforced activities are part of an overall plan designed to fulfil the official aims of that institution. Inmates, who have restricted access to the world outside, are on admission stripped of 'habitual' supports, such as personal possessions (Goffman, 1961). It takes little thought to realize how well hospitals or homes providing continuing care can fit this pattern.

Most of these problems are not major and are often the result of staff becoming socialized within the prevailing culture of the

---

Activity 12.2 **The process of institutionalization**

'Clothing is anonymous. One's possessions are limited to toothbrush, comb, upper or lower cot, half the space upon a narrow table, a razor . . . [other] things are assiduously gathered, jealously hidden or triumphantly displayed.' (Cantine and Rainer, cited in Goffman, 1961, p. 269)

(a) Would it surprise you to learn that this extract is cited from prison literature? How far do you believe that it may describe the patient experience?

(b) Does it apply equally to all patients and all hospitals or hospital wards?

---

institution, colluding in the provision of routinized, traditional and often uncaring and unevaluated practices. However, evidence to support this notion of total institutions emerged particularly during the late 1960s in Britain, when a series of enquiries into allegations of ill-treatment in long-stay hospitals, for example Ely Hospital, Cardiff in 1969, were given prominence within the press. Scandals which have included physical and sexual abuse have been well documented (Martin, 1984), and the impact of their reporting has been to undermine public confidence in institutional provisions for those with chronic health problems and other long-term dependency needs.

Whilst Goffman documented the negative aspects of institutions including loss of liberty, loss of autonomy, and depersonalization, he did not want to entirely abolish the asylums. However, within the UK mounting criticism from influential professionals, spiralling public costs, changing demographics, and growing public outcry led the government to seek alternatives to large-scale institutional care.

6 Deinstitutionalization and the shift to community care

The idea of shifting the provision of care from institutions to the community had been considered by various governments over a number of years. The NHS and Community Care Act (Department of Health, 1990) was passed at a time when 11 years of neo-liberal political philosophies had led to a recasting of the definition of the purpose of public policy, placing an emphasis on individual responsibility and choice. As we have seen from the previous section, there were long-standing criticisms of the institution. Initially, community care was aimed at the elderly, the mentally ill and people with learning disabilities. However, the term has since been extended in official usage in two ways: to cover all sections of the population needing care, and to recognize the diversity of non-institutional care that might be available.

Delayed discharge

bed blocking   a pejorative term for 'delayed discharge' which depersonalizes the patient

delayed discharge   a term for 'bed blocking' but recognizing that difficulties with discharge lie with the system and not the individual

This diversity was also meant to provide the solution to the complex problem of what is commonly referred to as **bed blocking**. However, because this term is associated with placing the onus on the individual the practice will be referred to as **delayed discharge**. One reason why delayed discharge occurs is a steady decline in the number of acute hospital beds and its consequences or blockages in the system. This reflects a number of factors, in particular:

- the switch for older people, people with mental illnesses and those with learning disabilities from long-stay beds to care in the community;
- medical advances allowing for shorter lengths of stay (King's Fund, 2001);
- the congestion of beds, exacerbated by social services' inability to provide care within a residential setting.

Activity 12.3

Nursing student's experience on the ward: example of 'bed blocking'

"'And once the patient is in hospital, because there's a process we couldn't get the social workers on the ward, because the social workers needed to assess people before they could be discharged and we were waiting weeks and months, sometimes just for a social worker to come out and do an assessment. So obviously we couldn't set up a social package for the person to go home. People were tying up beds you know, on the medical ward because the social workers weren't there to complete the package or relatives were, it's free while they were in hospital.'" (Shelton, 2003)

(a)   What does the term 'bed blocking' imply compared to delayed discharge?

(b)   What do you think might be some of the other reasons for the delay?

(c)   What are the implications for the patient?

Community care is often perceived differently by local authorities and health authorities. For example, 'To the former it meant a reduction in the amount of residential accommodation, while to the latter, it could refer to alternatives to hospitals such as residential accommodation, nursing homes or sheltered housing' (Allsop, 1995, p. 103). This situation can be very stressful for the nurse, particularly if the patient's

operation has been a success but there is n...
package' in place. One of the consequences t...
remain in the hospital is iatrogenic in that ther...
such as methicillin-resistant staphyloccus aureus
Postponement can also lead the patient to experien...
and loss of confidence in relation to regaining their in...
home (Glasby, 2003). For long-stay patients, delayed dis...
have an adverse affect on their ability to become deinstituti...
making subsequent rehabilitation to independent living all t... ...re
problematic. Clearly the need for discharge planning is paramount, and
the role of nurses in this process is crucial.

There are a range of institutions to which a patient can be
transferred; the focus here is on four types of institutional care:
residential care, nursing care, group homes and hospices. The next
few subsections discuss some of the differences between institutions
and explore institutional experiences.

Residential care homes

Residential care homes are registered with the local authority and
intended for older people who, even with domiciliary support, cannot
manage to live in their own homes but who do not need intensive
nursing care. All provide accommodation, meals, personal care,
supervision of medication and care during normal short illnesses but
not constant nursing care. The NHS is responsible for providing
community health services (for example, district nursing, chiropody
and incontinence supplies) to people in residential homes on the
same basis as to people in their own homes.

Nursing homes

Nursing homes are registered with a strategic health authority and
required to have a registered nurse on duty 24 hours a day. Nursing
homes care for those who are more dependent than those whose care
needs can be met in a residential care home. For example, a nursing
home would be more suitable for a person needing some form of
continuing treatment, such as long-term care of a fistula.

While most people in nursing homes will be permanent residents,
their use as temporary accommodation in order to ease the problem
of delayed discharge has been proposed. What has been termed
intermediate care would free up acute beds, when a person's
discharge is being delayed while they wait for social service
assessment or because they are not quite ready for independent
living. A scheme in Liverpool uses beds in Health Authority-
accredited homes for terminal and intermediate care. These beds are
acquired on an *ad hoc* basis, and not more than five are used in one
nursing home at any time (Last, 2000).

However, a survey of 60 Primary Care Groups and Trusts in 2000 found that the biggest perceived obstacle to the development of intermediate care was obstruction from acute hospitals and consultants, who would not welcome the transfer of resources from the acute to the primary care sector (Light and Dixon, 2000).

Group homes

The deinstitutionalization of care has also affected individuals with learning disabilities and now an increasing number live within the community. Community settings for people with learning disabilities can take many forms, ranging from independent living to living in supported accommodation. Group homes can also vary in size, although small-scale staff housing is now the most common form of accommodation for people with learning disabilities in the UK (Perry et al., 2000).

The deinstitutionalization of people with learning disabilities is thought to increase community participation, community integration and quality of life (Myles et al., 2000) as well as encourage personal development and increased activity levels (Perry et al., 2000). However, research evidence suggests that whilst people with learning disabilities may be physically located within communities, they are still socially excluded from mainstream society, remaining 'socially outside, looking in' (Myers et al., 1998, p. 393). The location of group homes (for people with learning disabilities and mental health problems) has also often been met with resistance by local communities, resulting in the now well-established 'NIMBY' (not-in-my-back-yard) syndrome (Repper and Brooker, 1996; Cowan, 2003). Indeed, many studies have identified the problem of bullying and victimization of people with learning disabilities by members of their local communities (Mencap, 1999), including that which is perpetrated by children (Whittell and Ramcharan, 2000).

Hospices

A hospice is a registered charity catering for people with life-threatening and life-limiting conditions who require both respite and palliative care. There are specialist hospices which solely cater for children.

Hospices have been in existence for many centuries, but the hospice movement in the UK is associated with the opening of St Christopher's Hospice in South London by Dame Cicely Saunders in 1967. It was a response to the poor quality of care for dying people, both in institutions and at home, in a health system where acute interventions and cure dominate, and death may be seen as a failure. Glaser and Strauss (1965) described restricted and poor communication with dying people and the individual routes towards death in hospital which they termed 'dying trajectories'. They suggested that the uncertainty of some 'dying trajectories', set in the highly medicalized and routinized context of the hospital, posed problems for staff managing wards. In his classic contribution Sudnow (1967) suggested that once a patient had been defined as 'dying' medicine seemed to have little to offer, and medical and social contact were withdrawn from the dying person in a 'social death' which preceded biological death. Depersonalization of the dying can still be identified as a feature of hospitals and nursing homes in contemporary UK society, and reflects a shift in the way in which death and dying are conceptualized that took place around the middle of the nineteenth century. Death became more of an individual event, with fewer collective customs and rituals, and more secrecy surrounding it. Death and dying became taboo subjects, and this lack of open discussion heralded an era of fear and denial that has influenced the way in which dying people and their families are treated within health care. This view of death is not, however, universal, and on your placements you may well come across cultural approaches to death and dying that differ from those you are familiar with.

The hospice movement grew outside of the NHS in order to develop its own model of care, different from the institutionalized care of those dying in hospital. By 1997 there were over 200 hospices yet, despite this increase, particularly in domiciliary and out-patient care, death has become more institutionalized. The proportion of patients dying at home has fallen from a peak of 60 per cent in the 1960s to 24 per cent by 1997 (Bosanquet, 1997). In fact, as illness progresses the number of patients and their relatives wanting death at home decreases (Hinton, 1994). Again this reflects the notion of death as a medicalized event, that takes place away from public gaze.

Critics of the growth in the number of hospices claim that it has been unplanned and uncoordinated. They have been built wherever the funding can be raised, resulting in there being greater provision in wealthier areas, rather than where need is greatest. There is also the criticism that the focus of hospice care is cancer at the expense of other terminal illness, although this is not the case in specialist children's hospices. The association with Christianity has also led to calls for greater recognition of British multicultural society.

Questions have also been raised about the 'medicalization' of hospices with the increasing influence of doctors in the institutions and the status given the medical perspective (James and Field, 1992). Seale (1989) had already doubted whether hospice care was significantly better than hospital care for the dying, but in a later piece of work on palliative care he concedes, 'satisfaction with that [hospice] care reported by respondents after the death is very high, and generally higher than that of respondents for patients in conventional care' (Seale, 1991, p. 151).

Activity 12.4   **The process of deinstitutionalization**

'Once in the lounge patients had to be removed again at regular
intervals to be reordered or taken to the toilet. Then they went to
lunch, to the toilet, back to bed for two hours, up again for late
tea, to the toilet, into dinner, to the toilet, to the lounge, to the
toilet and finally to bed. During the night, auxiliaries undertook
two-hourly rounds in which each patient was checked and their
body ordered as necessary.' (Lee-Treweek, 1997, p. 54)

(a)   The above is an account of life for residents in a nursing home. Is
it inevitable that patients/clients in institutions become
institutionalized?

(b)   Can you think of ways in which institutionalization may not be
negative for patients?

(c)   As a nurse, how might you address institutionalization within
your work setting?

(d)   How could you help a patient who experiences problems with
deinstitutionalization?

---

normalization a
therapeutic philosophy
which emphasizes
individual patient choice
and the importance of
'homelike' environments

The challenge to these institutions comes from therapeutic
philosophies such as **normalization**, and these have had considerable
impact on traditional models of institutional care. Underpinning this
is the belief that the consumers of health care should have the same
life choices as any other citizen and that the ways in which users of
health care services may be different from others should be valued,
rather than seen as evidence of deviance from assumed norms.
Normalization has had its greatest impact in the field of learning
disability, but its influence has also extended to the fields of mental
health, physical disability and the care of frail elderly people.

In summary, there are institutional alternatives to conventional
hospitals, particularly for those with long-term and life-limiting
conditions. The process of deinstitutionalization is a complex
phenomenon involving not only the building but also the
environment, the atmosphere, staff attitudes and standards of care.

Summary and Resources

Summary

- Institutions have been central to Britain's health and social care service provisions and will continue to be so.

- Institutionalization occurs in both health and social care settings, depriving the patient of their autonomy.

- Whilst community care attempted to counter the problems of life within large institutions, there remains the problem of ensuring that institutionalization is not simply re-created, albeit within smaller settings.

- Alternative institutional care is now offered within hospices and homes, which attempt to provide more individualized care, but these community settings generate their own problems.

- The institutionalization of dying in Western societies has led to a reconceptualization of death as a private affair, with few collective rituals.

Questions for Discussion

1 What are the characteristics of an institution?

2 Would you say that hospitals are healthy places to stay? Give reasons for your answer.

3 Think about the process of discharge for a patient you have nursed. What went well? What went badly? How could these problems have been overcome?

Further Reading

R. Jack (ed.): *Residential versus Community Care: The Role of Institutions in Welfare Provision.* London: Macmillan, 1998.
This provides a useful account of the ways in which institutional care in a community setting can parallel and reinforce patients' hospital experiences.

D. Pilgrim and A. Rogers (eds): *A Sociology of Mental Health and Illness.* 2nd edn. Buckingham: Open University Press, 1999.
This provides a comprehensive overview of sociological approaches to mental health and illness. It explores the ways in which mental illness is viewed by the law and institutions and is an excellent introduction to the world of sociology applied to mental health.

W. Scott: *Institutions and Organizations*. 2nd edn. London: Sage,
2001.
If you are interested in current approaches to organization theory this
provides a comprehensive and historical overview with a review of
empirical research.

References

Abel-Smith, B. 1964: *The Hospitals, 1800–1948: A Study in Social
    Administration in England and Wales*. London: Heinemann.
Allsop, J. 1995: *Health Policy and the National Health Service*. Harlow:
    Longman.
Bosanquet, N. 1997: 'New challenges for palliative care.' *British
    Medical Journal*, 314, 1294.
Busfield, J. 1986: *Managing Madness: Changing Ideas and Practice*.
    London: Hutchinson.
Cantine, H. and Rainer, D. (eds) 2000: *Prison Etiquette: The Convict's
    Compendium of Usual Information*, new edn. Carbondale: Southern
    Illinois University Press.
Cowan, S. 2003: 'NIMBY syndrome and public consultation policy:
    the implications of a discourse analysis of local responses to the
    establishment of a community mental health facility.' *Health and
    Social Care in the Community*, 11(5), 379–86.
Dainton, C. 1961: *The Story of England's Hospitals*. London: Museum
    Press.
Darby, R. 2003: 'The masturbation taboo and the rise of routine male
    circumcision: a review of the historiography.' *Journal of Social
    History*, 36(3), 737–57.
Department of Health 1990: *Community Care in the Next Decade and
    Beyond: Policy Guidance*. London: HMSO.
Department of Health 2000: *The NHS Plan*. London: HMSO.
Foucault, M. 1967: *Madness and Civilization: A History of Insanity in the
    Age of Reason*. London: Tavistock.
Foucault, M. 1973: *The Birth of the Clinic*. London: Tavistock.
Glasby, J. 2003: *Hospital Discharge: Integrating Health and Social Care*.
    Abingdon: Radcliffe Medical Press.
Glaser, B. G. and Strauss, A. L. 1965: *Awareness of Dying*. New York:
    Aldine de Gruyter.
Goffman, E. 1961: *Asylums: Essays on the Social Situation of Mental Patients
    and Other Inmates*. Harmondsworth: Penguin.
Hardey, M. 1998: *The Social Context of Health*. Buckingham: Open
    University Press.
Higgins, T. 1952: *Great Ormond Street 1852–1952*. London: Odhams
    Press.
Hinton, J. 1994: 'Can home care maintain a quality of life for patients
    with terminal cancer and their relatives?' *Palliative Medicine*, 8,
    183–96.

Illich, I. 1979: *Limits to Medicine: Medical Nemesis: The Expropriation of Health.* Harmondsworth: Penguin.

James, N. and Field, D. 1992: 'The routinization of hospice: charisma and bureaucratization.' *Social Science and Medicine,* 34(12), 1363–75.

King, R. and Raynes, N. 1968: 'An operational measure of inmate management in residential institutions.' *Journal of Social Sciences and Medicine,* 2, 41–53.

King's Fund 2001: *General Election Briefing.* London: King's Fund.

Last, S. 2000: 'Bed spread.' *Health Service Journal,* 10 August, 22–3.

Lee-Treweek, G. 1997: 'Women, resistance and care: an ethnographic study of nursing work.' *Work, Employment and Society,* 11(1), 47–65.

Light, D. and Dixon, M. 2000: 'A new way through.' *Health Service Journal,* 10 August, 24–5.

Martin, J. 1984: *Hospitals in Trouble.* Oxford: Blackwell.

Mencap, 1999: *Living in Fear.* London: Mencap.

Myers, F., Ager, A., Kerr, P. and Myles, S. 1998: 'Outside looking in? Studies of the community integration of people with learning disabilities.' *Disability and Society,* 13, 389–413.

Myles, S., Ager, A., Kerr, P., Myers, F. and Walker, J. 2000: 'Moving home: costs associated with different models of accommodation for adults with learning disabilities.' *Health and Social Care in the Community,* 8(6), 406–16.

Perry, J., Lowe, K., Felce, D. and Jones, S. 2000: 'Characteristics of staffed community housing services for people with learning disabilities: a stratified random sample of statutory, voluntary and private agency provision.' *Health and Social Care in the Community,* 8(5), 307–15.

Repper, J. and Brooker C. 1996: 'Public attitudes towards mental health facilities in the community.' *Health and Social Care in the Community,* 4(5), 290–9.

Scott, W. and Christensen, S. (eds) 1995: *The Institutional Construction of Organizations: International and Longitudinal Studies.* London: Sage.

Seale, C. 1989: 'What happens in hospices: a review of research evidence.' *Social Science and Medicine,* 28, 551–9.

Seale, C. 1991: 'A comparison of hospice and conventional care.' *Social Science and Medicine,* 32, 147–52.

Shelton, P. 2003: 'The application of sociological knowledge to nursing practice for pre-registration students.' Paper presented at the British Sociological Association Medical Sociology Conference, York.

Sudnow, D. 1967: *Passing On: The Social Organization of Dying.* Englewood Cliffs, NJ: Prentice Hall.

Vetter, N. 1995: *The Hospital: From the Centre of Excellence to Community Support.* London: Chapman and Hall.

Whittell, B. and Ramcharan, P. 2000: 'The trouble with kids: an account of problems experienced with local children by people with learning disabilities.' *British Journal of Learning Disabilities,* 28, 21–4.

Part IV

Policy Influences on Health and Health Care

When thinking sociologically it is important to recognize that private concerns are public troubles. Relationships between patients/clients and health care workers, and happenings on the hospital ward, are not isolated concerns but are connected socially, culturally and structurally. What this means is that nurses should recognize policy influences on experiences of health and ill-health, the provision of nursing care and the organizational structure and culture within which care takes place. This part focuses specifically on health policy, the management and organization of health care and the impact of wider environmental issues on health.

In chapter 13, 'Health Policy', you are introduced to the development and implementation of health policies. Whilst health policy may seem far removed from nursing, it is central to modern societies worldwide and important for nurses. This chapter examines the policy process, policies relating to treatment and health care, and policies relating to public health, health improvement and the prevention of ill-health. The chapter also considers how where you work, what you are able to do for patients/clients and the ways in which your work is monitored and assessed are shaped by policy, and encourages you to think about how changes in health policy can affect your practice.

Chapter 14, 'The Management and Organization of Health Care', sheds light on the role of management in the complex organization and delivery of health care. The term 'management' is defined and its significance for nurses, and the role of nurses as managers, are discussed. Some key sociological concepts are introduced, including 'bureaucracy', 'negotiated order' and 'power', and the significance of sociological research methods for understanding organizations is highlighted. This chapter asks you to reflect on how management continues to influence patient/client care and the role of nurses.

A wider perspective is taken in chapter 15, 'Health, Housing and the Environment'. Following on from the discussion of the biomedical and social models in chapter 3, the chapter contrasts the medical and public health models. It outlines recent trends in housing policy and discusses the relationship between housing and health. In particular, it discusses the significance of the 'fitness standard' and shows how poor housing conditions and homelessness affect health. Overall, this chapter asks you to develop an awareness of the importance of housing and environmental threats to health and to think about the wider role of nurses in health improvement and the prevention of ill-health.

This part provides only a brief introduction to some of the wider sociological and policy issues that influence nursing. Its purpose is to show that nursing work (and all other health work) is influenced by a range of factors that affect who becomes ill and who dies, and by the conditions within which nursing care takes place.

Health Policy

David Cox

Key issues within this chapter

- Health policy and the nurse.
- Policy and the NHS.
- Policies on the organization and management of health care.
- Health policies and the process of treatment and care.
- Policies and public health.

By the end of this chapter you should be able to . . .

- Understand how nursing is affected by changing health policies.
- Appreciate how health care has become a central issue for government policy.
- Understand the way in which policies on organization and management, treatment and care and health promotion have evolved over time.
- Discuss and analyse health policy changes and their effects on your practice.

1 Introduction

This chapter is about how the health services in which nurses work are developed and shaped through the political system and the development and implementation of policies.

At first this might seem far removed from the immediacy of learning about patients' needs or nursing skills. You may come home after a placement shift too tired even to watch the TV news or to pick up a newspaper! You might, however, be surprised to find how much coverage is given to health service and policy matters in the media – both the human stories and the policies about health care are widely covered. As your training and professional career develop, understanding the policy context of your work may help you when faced with difficult situations and problems, such as the delay in discharging one of your patients to community care. This individual's personal problem is also part of a wider national policy debate which as a citizen and as a professional you may be able to influence.

Activity 13.1   **Media watch**

Do a 'media watch' on health issues preferably in the week in which you read this chapter.

(a)   Choose a week and try to listen to a daily news broadcast and monitor a local or national paper.
(b)   What health care issues arise? Who speaks for the NHS on these issues? What are the implications for individual nurses and for the nursing profession more generally?

---

2   Health policy and the nurse

Health policy refers to the laws and directions from governments that seek to affect health and to regulate private or to supply state-run health care services. In industrial countries health policy is a major area of political interest and public debate. Governments seek to respond to changing patterns of ill-health, the needs of ageing populations, new diseases (for example, HIV or variant CJD), the availability of new and expensive treatments, drugs and therapies, the maintenance costs of old and inadequate buildings and the rising expectations of a more critical public. The most dramatic examples of health policy are probably when it fails. Waiting lists and times in particular became dominant themes in British health policy discussion and governments put both money and direction into trying to solve this problem.

Let us look briefly at how the working context of nurses has been shaped by health policy. A third of all NHS buildings were built before the NHS was established in 1948 and, as the Audit Commission (2002, p. 26) says, 'the age and state of repair of some hospitals adds to the difficulty of providing pleasant and clean surroundings for patients'. Buildings are physical evidence of past health policies and a large hospital site will contain evidence of a succession of policy initiatives designed to improve the physical resources for patient care.

Private Finance Initiative
(PFI)   a method of
raising money for
developments like new
hospitals from private
investors

Currently, the Government is using a number of **Private Finance Initiatives** (PFI) to build new acute hospitals, while various policy drives like day-case surgery, community-based psychiatric care, non-institutional homes for people with learning disabilities, etc. mean that health services are less dependent on large institutional buildings than they were in the last century. All nurses and especially those in mental health and learning disability branches are now much more likely to be working in the community, visiting clients at home or working in community centres and clinics than in the past.

Policy is about how the powers of government are used to shape the world in which we live and work. How are policies developed? Where do they come from? Governments are not all-powerful – they have to raise money from tax-payers and live with the realities of economic constraints. They are accountable to the voters for the success or failure of their policies. Their every move is scrutinized by powerful and critical media. Moreover, they have limited influence over the behaviour of individuals, private companies and even their own governmental organizations. Many policies do not get fully implemented because other influences affect decisions and actions or because of problems in the organizations that are charged with carrying them out. So while there may be policies about switching to public transport, they have not included sufficiently strong incentives or prohibitions to stop the growth in car use. Policies may be frustrated by events outside a government's control or be delayed and diverted by the problems of implementation through complex organizations. Modern governments not only issue priorities, instructions, advice and guidance to the health service, they have become more determined to see their policies implemented. They set tight targets on key issues like waiting lists and times and monitor them closely. NHS Trusts that fail to implement policies will be subject to investigation, a 'no star' rating, or 'naming and shaming', and senior managers may be replaced.

As a nurse, where you work, what you are able to do for your patients and clients (for example, the expansion of nurse prescribing), the nature of health services (community-based care, day cases, etc.), and the ways in which your work is monitored and assessed are all shaped by the policy process and subject to change.

Activity 13.2   **Influencing the policy makers**

Access the Department of Health website (www.doh.gov) and locate a current consultation or health policy which interests you and relates to your future practice.

(a)   Using the summary section, outline to a colleague what the main issues are.

(b)   Try to form your own opinions about the policy you have chosen.

3   Policy and the National Health Service

Discussion of health policy in the UK since 1948 has been dominated by the problems and opportunities of government-led NHS funding, 'reform' and 'modernization'. The idea of a national, comprehensive health service, funded out of general taxation and largely available free at the point of delivery on a basis of need, has been central to popular experience, professional work and public discussion.

modernization the imposition of national standards in health care, encouragement of local managerial and professional initiative, more public involvement in health issues and NHS organizations, improvement in buildings, equipment and IT, more streamlined ways of diagnosing and treating illness, and new ways of working which break down barriers between professions

As comparative studies of health policy in different countries show (see Baggott, 1998, pp. 105–7), a National Health Service is not the only way to organize and provide health care in a modern society. Other approaches include that of the USA, which has a variety of private and public hospitals and services with mainstream funding from private health insurance underpinned by Medicare and Medicaid federal schemes for the elderly and the poor. (Medicare is a national insurance programme for the elderly and disabled established in 1965. Medicaid provides medical benefits and health care for certain low-income groups who are on welfare programmes.) In continental Europe the norm is for health services to be funded through compulsory health insurance schemes paid for by employers and employees. Both these types of systems involve higher administrative costs but can produce very good services for those who can afford to pay or who have good insurance cover. But as chapter 8 shows, such people are less likely to need health care and represent a good risk for insurers. Private insurance schemes mean that the poor, the chronically ill, anyone who is considered a high risk (or who becomes one), is much less well provided for. At the time of writing, no major political party in the UK has included a move towards a more privatized or insurance-based health care system in its election manifesto. Even the radical governments of Baroness Thatcher, which introduced managerialism, competition and an **internal market**, were

internal market A policy whereby a large public sector organization is broken down into smaller, more independent provider hospitals or community units and they compete for contracts from a commissioning or purchasing body

concerned to reassure the public of their basic commitment to NHS principles. More recently, in 2002, the Labour government, also committed to NHS modernization and change, asked leading businessman Derek Wanless to review the basic funding model of the NHS and compare it to systems elsewhere. His report (Wanless, 2002) reiterated the benefits in terms of economy and efficacy of maintaining the tax-based, free-at-point-of-delivery model of the NHS. This important report cleared the way for the government to increase NHS spending to bring UK health spending up to average European levels and to enable sustained investment in the new facilities and staff that would be needed to achieve the targets set out in the NHS Plan (Department of Health, 2000).

It is important to be aware that in the UK not all health care is provided by the NHS. As chapter 10 shows, much health care in Britain, as throughout the world, is provided informally through self-care, through families and neighbours. Furthermore, there is a

Activity 13.3   **The 'bottomless pit' argument**

Consider this extract from the Audit Commission Report (2002, p. 8):

'Every year 15% of total Government expenditure is spent on healthcare. This is more than is spent on education and more than twice the amount spent on defence. Only spending on social security is higher.

Spending on health has almost doubled since 1980. Reasons for this include:

- The introduction of new treatments and advances in medicine and surgery;
- Patients and carers' higher expectations and greater awareness of healthcare issues have led to increased demands;
- An increasing population; and
- Longer life expectancy and an increase in the number of elderly people needing treatment.'

Debate with a colleague the idea that 'health care spending is a "bottomless pit" which will never be filled'.

significant private sector made up of hospitals, private medical practices and nursing homes which takes up 16 per cent of UK health care, funded through direct payment or private health insurance (King's Fund, 2001). In 1999 the Labour government decided to foster collaboration with the private health sector, and there is support for treating NHS patients in private hospitals where necessary and for inviting private and overseas suppliers to carry out some of the treatments needed by NHS patients.

The NHS has been a central feature dominating health policy in the UK. Government has to pay close attention to its funding, effectiveness and efficiency while ensuring that it continues to satisfy the public that use it. While the NHS remains popular overall, successive governments have tried to 'reform' the way it operates.

4 The policy process

Governments are elected in part on the basis of party manifestos which outline the policies or courses of action that they intend to carry out. This will be done through acts of Parliament, annual decisions on expenditure (public spending round), budgets and much administrative detailed guidance issued by government departments like the Department of Health. In a democratic society policies are widely discussed, with political parties and independent 'think-tanks' making proposals, and pressure groups (like professions, patients' associations, etc.) giving their views and lobbying or persuading governments and the public to their way of thinking. The press, TV and radio give extensive coverage to these debates, and there will be national and local consultations about service developments and changes.

Health policy is a major political issue, featuring daily in media coverage and political debate. However, it should not be forgotten that many other areas of policy (economic, regional, transport, housing, environment, education, and so on) affect the health of the population in very fundamental ways.

How are policies changed?

A read of previous chapters will suggest that some groups in society have less influence than others. This is a key aspect of inequality and factors like class, race, gender, age and disability are dimensions of powerlessness (see chapters in part II). Excluded groups have to organize and overcome structural difficulties if they are to have any influence on policies or challenge the status quo. Hence campaigns for equal rights for women, the labour and trade union organizations, movements for race equality, campaigns by pensioners or the disability rights movement; all have tried to reshape the way decisions are made and resources allocated and to influence policy, with varied success.

Chapters 3 and 4 show how important medical dominance has been for a century and a half in shaping health policy both by influencing government and societal thinking about health and by ensuring medical control of key institutions, activities and practices. Nursing has for many years found itself to be in a subordinate position constrained by medical power and medical attitudes. However, this can change, and as professionals and as citizens, often by working through pressure groups, nurses have opportunities to influence policy and reshape health policy in a way that emphasizes the values of nursing and care.

The care of sick children in hospital and in the community is one aspect of health policy that provides a good example of this process and of the influence of independent pressure groups who seek to influence and improve policies which affect their area of concern and interest. Action for Sick Children is a major charity which aims to improve services for children with health problems. It began over 40 years ago and was earlier called the National Association for the Welfare of Children in Hospital (NAWCH). Many policies that we as parents or child health nurses now take for granted were the result of the efforts of this campaigning organization to influence government and NHS bodies. Research in the 1950s, and notably the work of John Bowlby (1967) on maternal deprivation, seemed to show that separating young children from their parents could have long-term effects on their health and well-being. NAWCH brought together parents, journalists, sociologists and health care professionals to campaign for overnight rooms for parents, specialized children's wards, more specialist children's nurses and doctors and a greater recognition of children's emotional and psychological needs.

Policy with regard to the care and health of children is likely to engage public and media interest, and the campaign to improve the care of children in hospitals had access to good research evidence and influential professionals, and the support and patronage of relatively wealthy and influential members of the public. Campaigns for the 'normalization' of care for people with learning difficulties and the eventual closure of the isolating 'colonies' of special hospitals took many years to implement (for a definition of normalization see chapter 12). Even though the professional argument had been won, funding for suitable teams of multi-professional staff and the building of suitable homes in the community took some years to come through.

Through pressure groups and professional bodies, nurses and members of the public can seek to change and modify policies and, where there is a determined effort on behalf of particular patient groups, this can be very successful.

5   Evolution of policy on health care organization and provision

Rob Baggott (1998) describes how policy has evolved and the key issues in the funding, organization and management of the British health care system. If you talk to people who have been involved as managers or nurses in the NHS for some time then you will probably hear complaints about too many changes and targets being handed down from central government. UK governments of different political parties often say that they wish to leave the professionals, such as the doctors and nurses, to get on with treating patients. Yet politicians feel compelled to intervene, reorganize, develop new policies and closely monitor their implementation.

Policies on the organization and management of health care

The British NHS was founded in 1948. Major structural reorganizations were initiated in 1974, 1982, 1990, 1997 and 2002. These policies have been concerned with improving the management, efficiency and quality of service in the NHS through different patterns of organization, often reflecting ideas and practice from the private sector. Detailed accounts of these changes can be followed up elsewhere (see Baggott, 1998).

While on placement it should be possible to seek out some of the more experienced members of staff and ask them their views. Let us consider someone appointed in 1974 as a mental health nurse (probably in a large mental hospital) and now perhaps considering retirement. She or he would have been trained in a small hospital-based school of mental health nursing and have worked initially in the same hospital. The hospital was within an Area Health Authority which provided all secondary, hospital and community care for its area. The new nurse's role would have been near the bottom of a nursing hierarchy which was led by a Director of Nursing Services. Professions were all-important and at each level there were committees made up of senior representatives of each profession determining how the service should be run. The 1982 reorganization removed a layer of bureaucracy above the new District Health Authority (DHA), but this would not have impacted much on our nurse.

In 1983, however, the Thatcher government commissioned a report from Sir Roy Griffiths, managing director of Sainsbury supermarkets. The Griffiths Report (1983) brought the introduction of 'general' management, 'regardless' of professional discipline, into the NHS. Still part of the DHA, the mental health hospital now became a Unit with a Unit General Manager reporting to a District General Manager. The new general managers and a number of processes of co-ordination and control began to challenge the full autonomy of the teams of professionals. The service became more cost-conscious, better financial and performance information was required and, while overall expenditure continued to rise, efficiency savings had to be made each year and 'cuts' might result from spending reviews when budgets were in danger of being overspent.

Between 1990 and 1997 the Conservative government's new policy of the internal market had an effect on the mental health service as elsewhere. The local mental health service became an 'NHS Trust' a bit like an independent company, although still in the NHS and not allowed to make a 'profit'. To treat patients and survive the Trust had to attract funding contracts through a commissioning or purchasing process from the District Health Authority. Financial discipline was increasing: only patients covered in the main contract or from specially agreed 'extra-contractual referrals' from other districts could be treated.

A new Labour government in 1997 promised to end the internal market, improve funding and encourage partnership working in the NHS. However, the NHS Trusts continued with a modified system of contracting through 'Service and Financial Frameworks' negotiated by District Health Authorities and more recently the new Primary Care Trusts, thus perpetuating a modified form of internal market.

The main features of these managerial changes are discussed in the next chapter. From a health policy perspective they demonstrate the pressure on successive governments to implement health care policies which control costs and meet public expectations and a restless search for new structures and a growing reliance on management processes. A variety of factors forced health care onto the government's social and economic agenda. Increased costs resulted from new medical technologies and treatments, an ageing population with greater health needs, rising expectations amongst users of services and an accumulation of old and poorly maintained buildings. This, combined with the impact of wider pressures on government expenditure from tax-payers, brought the NHS, like all other aspects of public services and welfare, under close scrutiny. The changing political and ideological climate means that all governments are confronted with similar dilemmas.

Health policies and the process of treatment and care

Alongside these reorganizations, there has been a steady growth of policy initiatives concerned with the actual processes of treatment and health care and the patient experience. These policies have a much more direct impact on what happens to patients in terms of access to services and the treatments they experience, while they also impact on the way nurses and other health professionals work. For example, policies have been developed and implemented on how long patients wait in accident and emergency departments. Successive governments have tried to reduce the time spent waiting for outpatient appointments and elective operations and, more recently, tight targets have been set for access to general practitioners and health care professionals (mainly practice nurses) in primary care practices (see chapter 11). These matters become part of health policy because in the national and centralized NHS, governments are held directly responsible for such standards of service. Delayed treatments rapidly become matters of political controversy; governments set targets and then have to put pressure on local NHS managers and clinicians to achieve them or be seen to fail. In any one year there are 13 million visits to accident and emergency departments and almost one in 12 people will have a hospital stay (Audit Commission, 2002). Each of these episodes exposes the government to the risk of criticism if anything goes wrong.

What happens to patients is of course important to them, and traditionally this was determined by resources available locally and the clinical discretion of trained professionals deciding on priorities and using their expertise and judgement. Since the development of the Patient's Charter (Department of Health, 1996) under John Major's government and many promises made by later Labour governments, patient expectations, treatments, targets, and ◄ performance monitoring have become subject to direct political involvement. The organizational and managerial changes discussed

performance monitoring regular checks on key targets like financial balance, waiting times and discharge delays, by superior bodies within the NHS hierarchy

above have made this much more possible but it is the way that health policy has become much more 'up close and personal' that is interesting.

Quality of care is in part defined by the ability to meet the satisfaction of patients and clients in terms of waiting lists, patient information, cleanliness of facilities and attitudes of staff. The mental health nurse is now much more involved in consulting users and carers and designing services around their needs and aspirations. You will find that this commitment to working in partnership with clients or patients and their carers is now an integral part of modern nurse training.

In *The New NHS: Modern, Dependable* (Department of Health, 1997), the incoming government laid out its plans for the NHS. One important theme was the idea of common national standards implemented locally. The objective was to ensure that best practice was available throughout the country and to set standards for the 'quality' of service delivered by the NHS. There are a number of dimensions to this set of policies but they were outlined in a Department of Health paper, *A First Class Service* (1998), which made clinical quality a top priority for NHS Trusts. The concept of **clinical governance** was introduced along with two new institutions: the **National Institute for Clinical Excellence (NICE)** and the Commission for Health Improvement (CHI), now the **Health Care Commission.**

Clinical audit, a method of comparing patient outcomes whereby fellow professionals critically assess practice, had been instituted in the NHS since the 1990s but the information was confidential (mainly within the medical profession). A number of scandals, notably the Bristol child heart surgery investigation, and research which showed that patient outcomes varied across the country, for example in cancer treatment, meant that a coherent set of policies about the process of treatment and care could be introduced.

NICE was established as a government-backed expert body which began to evaluate the efficacy, cost-effectiveness and patient acceptability of new drugs and treatments. It issues guidelines which, while not mandatory, set the standards against which local health care practice will be evaluated. At the same time comprehensive and compulsory National Service Frameworks (NSFs) have been developed by the Department of Health using expert opinion. These set out the standards to be achieved within a number of key service areas. The origins of this approach were in the Calman Hine report on cancer services in 1995 which determined the optimum balance between local and specialist care (spokes and hubs) and established the state-of-the-art pathways for the treatment of various cancers. The object was to bring cancer services nationwide up to the standards of the best and improve survival rates in the UK, which were falling behind in international comparisons. Subsequent NSFs have been

clinical governance the process whereby a health care organization works to ensure a high and rising standard of treatment and care for patients and users

National Institute for Clinical Excellence (NICE) a body of experts who evaluate the evidence on new and existing treatments, drugs and clinical procedures and determine whether they are worthwhile clinically and economically

Health Care Commission the independent regulatory body for health care

issued for mental health, care of the elderly, chronic heart disease, and diabetes.

These are powerful health policies which guide practice, investment, training and local policy and give a strong sense of direction to critical areas of health care. For example, the NSF on chronic heart disease has led to much-increased prescribing of cholesterol-reducing drugs called statins, which in turn has put a strain on primary care prescribing budgets. There is no doubt that aspects of your own syllabus and placement experience will have been affected by NSFs and the guidance from NICE.

However, as discussed earlier, issuing policy does not guarantee implementation within very complex organizations. For example, there has been considerable media coverage of complaints from cancer specialists and mental health charities that aspects of policy have not been fully implemented across the country and that investment earmarked for cancer care or mental health has been siphoned off into meeting other priorities or to cover previous deficits.

To complement NICE, the government set up the Commission for Health Improvement which in 2003 was replaced by the Commission for Health Audit and Inspection. This powerful body carries out a process of checking, enforcement, inspection and performance monitoring for all NHS Trusts. The Health Care Commission sends expert teams in to visit Trusts regularly and inspects both their performance and their internal clinical governance arrangements and processes. Are waiting list targets being met? Have relevant NSFs been implemented? Are staff appropriately trained and retrained? Are arrangements for clinical governance in place? Are treatments and practices reviewed regularly? Are these quality matters regularly reported to the Board?

Governments will defend such policies of inspection on the grounds of 'accountability'. Health care professionals and managers are responsible for spending large amounts of public money and carry out work which is of the utmost importance to patients and their families. How else can the government and thus the public be assured that standards are being upheld and the best possible practice is being carried out across a large and complex system? To encourage improved performance, Trusts are evaluated on a star ranking system, with extra opportunities and money going to successful '3-star' Trusts whilst those with no stars will be subject to greater intervention and scrutiny with the possibility of new managers being brought in from elsewhere.

Policies on public health, health improvement and prevention

Thus far we have concentrated on health care policies – how best to ensure treatment for people who fall ill. However, there is an important aspect of health policy concerned with preventing illness and trying to ensure the good health of the population.

These policies are associated with prevention through measures to enhance individual and community health and interventions like vaccination or smoking cessation clinics. Finding ways to shift thinking and behaviour from treatment to prevention has been the holy grail of health policy. Research by McKeown (1979) suggests that the major improvements in the health of populations in the industrialized world have been the result of environmental improvements, especially to water supplies and housing, together with economic prosperity, rather than the remedial intervention of medicine and health care systems (see chapter 3 for a further discussion of the social causes of ill-health). If all the population lived in warm, dry, well-lit housing in a cleaner and safer environment, if economic policy improved household incomes and greater equality reduced stress, then there would be less pressure on the health service and people would enjoy healthier lives. Similarly, from a more individual perspective, if health education encouraged people to stop smoking, eat sensibly, breastfeed their babies, reduce alcohol intake, practise contraception and safer sex, drive more carefully and take regular exercise, then fewer people would suffer from cancer, chronic heart disease, diabetes, accidents, mental health problems, obesity, and HIV and other sexually transmitted diseases.

Health education and promotion campaigns have been a feature of health policy for many years, with organizations like the Health Development Agency producing materials and encouraging behavioural change through advertisements, training programmes, support to teachers, advice to companies, and so on. Some of this will have permeated your nursing course; for example, you will be encouraged to use your influence as a nurse to advise and support patients and clients in search of a healthier lifestyle. Activity 13.4 asks you to consider health promotion for young people.

Key documents like *The Health of the Nation* (Department of Health, 1992) and *Saving Lives: Our Healthier Nation* (Department of Health, 1999), from Conservative and Labour governments respectively, have sought to emphasize health promotion and set targets for improving health. While not having the immediacy and popular impact of policies on health care and never attracting the level of funding and professional interest that responding to ill health requires, health promotion remains a significant aspect of health policy.

Furthermore, the Blair government has given some emphasis to health promotion and improvement in the way the NHS and partner agencies are directed, in the setting of targets and in monitoring and evaluation. PCTs are tasked to enter into partnership with other agencies, especially the local authority, schools and voluntary organizations, in working towards health improvement. Thus activity to cut smoking or avoid heart disease might be coordinated across an

Activity 13.4   **'Our future?' Health and young people**

Drinking and
smoking is
widespread
among teenagers

(a)   Brainstorm a health promotion strategy for young people living
on an outer-city housing estate with poor services, few leisure
facilities, high teenage pregnancy and high unemployment.

(b)   Consider a health promotion strategy for young people with *either*
learning disabilities *or* mental health difficulties. How would this
strategy differ from (or be similar to) the strategy identified for
question (a)?

(c)   Should you aim to spread 'health messages' amongst young
people regarding safer sex, obesity, smoking, and so on, or try to
persuade local and central government to target the estate's
underlying problems?

area or a particular estate, and projects around diet, exercise and
support programmes introduced. PCTs have Directors of Public
Health, part of whose job is to direct strategies for health
improvement. Similarly the monitoring and star rating of PCTs will
include scores on the number of people who have quit smoking, the
incidence of venereal disease or the rate of teenage pregnancies.

Once again we can see how the context of health care and the
work of nurses is directly affected by the health policies adopted by
successive governments, and how the desire to ensure
implementation drives down to directing the work of local
practitioners. Community and practice nurses are involved in work
around smoking cessation, sexual health and advice on diet and
exercise. While this is fully in line with good professional practice,

they are aware that their results are being assessed and will be one of the factors that leads to a successful or unsuccessful star rating of the local PCT.

This section has classified health policies into three major categories: those concerned with the organization and management of the health care system; those concerned with directly affecting the way health care and treatment are carried out; and those concerned with enhancing health and trying to prevent the onset of disease. The nurse has a role to play in all of these policy areas, and knowledge of how your personal work is located within these major public issues can give you confidence and enhance your effectiveness in working on behalf of your patients and clients.

Summary and Resources

Summary

- Health policy is of major importance in British politics and the nurse's professional practice is carried out within a legal, organizational, financial and health care system determined through the policy process.

- The NHS has been central to health policy in the UK since 1948 and there have been successive reorganizations in pursuit of a better and more efficient service.

- Policies are the product of a political process to which as a citizen and as a professional the nurse can make a contribution.

- Health policies have been increasingly about the detailed management of the health service, about improving patients' access to treatment and the very process of clinical care itself, trying to ensure universal best practice and patient satisfaction.

- There is a long-standing emphasis in health policy on trying to improve the health of the population through public health measures and health promotion so as to enhance well-being and prevent illness.

Questions for Discussion

1   Should nurses leave all policy issues to the politicians and concentrate on giving good care to patients?

2   Children, people with learning disabilities, the very elderly and people with severe mental health problems are relatively powerless in society; can nurses be influential advocates both for individuals and for the broader development of policy?

3   Is government policy getting 'too close for comfort' by seeking to determine how doctors, nurses and other health care workers carry out their work for patients? Should policy at this level be left to the professionals?

Further Reading

R. Baggott: *Health and Health Care in Britain*. 2nd edn.
Basingstoke: Macmillan, 1998.
Extremely thorough and well-referenced guide to all aspects of health policy, ideal for exploring issues in depth or obtaining an understanding of how the NHS and health policy have developed.

C. Komaromy (ed.): *Dilemmas in UK Health Care.* Buckingham:
Open University Press, 2001.
Part of a long-established and respected Open University course in
health and disease, this is a reader with articles about the various
dilemmas facing the public, health care workers, managers and
policy makers. It covers economic constraints, management,
professions, evaluation, technology, disease prevention and poverty.

References

Audit Commission 2002: *The Performance of the NHS in England:
Developing an Independent Commentary.* London: Audit Commission.
Baggott, R. 1998: *Health and Health Care in Britain*, 2nd edn.
Basingstoke: Macmillan.
Bowlby, J. 1967: *Child Care and the Growth of Love*, 2nd edn.
Harmondsworth: Penguin.
Calman Hine Report 1995: *A Policy Framework for Commissioning Cancer
Services: A Report by the Expert Advisory Group on Cancer to the Chief
Medical Officers of England and Wales: Guidance for Purchasers and
Providers of Cancer Services.* London: Department of Health.
Department of Health 1992: *The Health of the Nation: A Strategy for
Health in England.* London: HMSO.
Department of Health 1996: *The Patient's Charter and You: A Charter for
England.* Leeds: DoH.
Department of Health 1997: *The New NHS: Modern, Dependable*, Cm
3807. London: Stationery Office.
Department of Health 1998: *A First Class Service: Quality in the New NHS.*
London: Stationery Office.
Department of Health 1999: *Saving Lives: Our Healthier Nation*, Cm
4386. London: Stationery Office.
Department of Health 2000: *The NHS Plan: A Plan for Investment*, Cm.
4818. London: Stationery Office.
Griffiths, R. 1983: *NHS Management Enquiry*, London: Department of
Health and Social Security.
King's Fund 2001: *General Election 2001 Briefing*, 8. London: King's
Fund.
McKeown, T. 1979: *The Role of Medicine: Dream, Mirage or Nemesis?*
Oxford: Blackwell.
Wanless, D. 2002: *Securing our Future Health: Taking a Long-Term View:
Final Report.* London: HM Treasury. At
www.hm_Treasury.gov.uk/consultations_and_legislation/wanless/
consult_wanless_final.cfm.

14 The Management and Organization of Health Care

Alistair Hewison

Key issues in this chapter

- What is management?
- The contribution of sociology to our understanding of the management and organization of health care.
- The need for nurses to engage with management.
- Organizational aspects of health care including interprofessional relationships, clinical governance and the NHS Plan.
- The application of sociological concepts to the reality of contemporary practice.

By the end of this chapter you should be able to . . .

- Define the term management.
- Use sociological concepts to examine the activities contained in the chapter.
- Summarize the main components of the structure of a typical NHS organization.
- Discuss the role of the nurse as a manager.
- Recognize the continuing influence of management in health care.

1 Introduction

When a football club is relegated who is sacked? If a business is failing who is deemed to be responsible? When an error is made in an NHS Trust who is expected to explain the circumstances to the media? In most circumstances the answer to these questions is: the manager, or, to use a more recent title, the chief executive. How does this observation relate to nursing and health care? Essentially all organizations, both large and small, need to be managed in some way. In the case of health care if the service is to be delivered, certain people within the organization need to make sure things are done on time and in the right way. However, this is not as straightforward as it might appear. Things go wrong, people make mistakes, sometimes a ward or department is so busy that information concerning patient care is not passed on and patients do not receive appropriate care. What sociology can offer that would help explain how such situations occur and provide an indication of how things can be improved is the focus of this chapter.

2   What is management?

The term 'manage' derives from the Italian word *maneggiare*, which means to control or to train, and was originally applied to the management of horses (Grint, 1995). One of the foremost writers on management summarizes a view that many have of this activity: 'Management is a curious phenomenon. It is generously paid, enormously influential, and significantly devoid of common sense' (Mintzberg, 1996, p. 61). Yet without management and organization would it be possible to provide patient care? If nurses do not know who is in charge, which patients they are looking after on a particular shift, which patients are for surgery that day or going out on a visit, problems will ensue.

   The aim of this chapter is to offer a working definition of management and to examine the contribution of sociology in increasing our understanding of the management and organization of health care. For the purposes of this chapter management is

agency the capacity individuals have to shape their social life ◄ defined as: an expression of human **agency**, the capacity to actively shape and direct the world, rather than simply react to it. The process of management therefore has five elements:

1   deciding/planning what is to be done, and how;
2   allocating time and effort to what is to be done;
3   motivating or generating the effort to do it;
4   coordinating and combining disparate efforts;
5   controlling what is to be done to ensure that it conforms with what was intended. (Hales, 1993, p. 2)

This is applicable to people working in all organizations, including health care. As Iles (1997, p. 1) observes: 'As soon as we ask someone else to do something, rather than undertaking it ourselves, we become managers. We rely on someone else to perform that task in the way we would do it.' Nurses soon find they have to ask others, such as care assistants, parents, carers, and members of the multidisciplinary team, to undertake a range of tasks, and so are involved in management from an early stage in their career.

3   Management in health care

It has been argued that from its inception in 1948 until the introduction of the recommendations arising from the Griffiths Report (Department of Health and Social Security, 1983), the NHS was 'administered' rather than managed (Connelly, 2000; Harrison, 1988; Harrison et al., 1992). Management was not a term that was widely used and the role of administrators within the service was to enable health professionals, primarily doctors, to undertake the care and treatment that they determined the patient needed. There were attempts to introduce more management controls and limit expenditure; however, these were often diluted by compromises that were necessary to ensure the co-operation of the professions (Ranade, 1997). The Griffiths Report ushered in a structure in which there were 'general managers' and an 'executive' board. The managers were seen as fulfilling the role that a manager in a commercial company would play, that is, undertaking the five key aspects of management identified earlier, to ensure the service was delivered. The impact of the Griffiths Report has been assessed by a number of researchers employing a sociological approach, which examined the origins and implementation of the Report (see for example Cox, 1991; Owens and Glennerster, 1990; Strong and

ethnography   a research ◄ Robinson, 1990). The approach they used was **ethnography**. They
approach which involves found that the Report had a profound effect on nursing. Many of the
the direct observation of most senior nurses lost their positions, and those who were retained
the activity of members of were given advisory posts. The overall authority over the nursing
a group or organization workforce they previously enjoyed was removed, and they were there simply to provide advice to whoever was now managing nursing. Furthermore, in a third of health districts senior nursing advice was dispensed with altogether (Strong and Robinson, 1990). It caused widespread disruption and uncertainty, particularly in the higher levels of the nursing hierarchy, and most units were reorganized in such a way that nursing management was eliminated (Owens and Glennerster, 1990). The Report itself was very respectful of medical power and sought to co-opt doctors into management, whereas it hardly referred to nursing at all (Cox, 1991). Consequently this was a traumatic period for nursing management.

The Griffiths Report was followed by the White Paper 'Working for Patients' (Department of Health, 1989), which led to the establishment of an internal market in health care in which contracts between providers of services, such as hospitals and clinics, and purchasers of services, such as health authorities and general practitioners, formed the basis of the organization and structure of the service in the 1990s (Salter, 1998). More recently, the publication of the NHS Plan (Department of Health, 2000b) indicated the way the Government envisaged health care being managed for at least the following five years. Some of the key elements of this ambitious plan for reform which are particularly pertinent to nurses are outlined in box 14.1. It is anticipated that nurses will take on significant leadership and management responsibilities within the NHS. This is reflected in the creation of the **modern matron** posts and the establishment of the national **nurse leadership programme**.

Box 14.1 indicates that it is important that nurses have an understanding of the nature of management in health care. In the following section some of the concepts from sociology which can provide useful insights on the way health care organizations function will be considered. As Hunter has observed: 'Medical sociologists, with their traditional preoccupation with macro and micro themes and issues in health care, are well placed to bring a distinctive and well informed perspective to bear on policy, implementation and management issues' (1990, p. 215). Similarly, as Albrow (1997) argues, sociology regards organization as the outcome of social

modern matron a nurse who is easily identifiable to patients, accountable for a group of wards and in control of the resources necessary to organize the fundamentals of care

nurse leadership programme a programme of leadership development for nurses at ward and senior level instituted following the NHS Plan

---

Box 14.1   **The NHS Plan: some key issues for nurses**

Changes for nurses

Plans	Details
Staff	20,000 more nurses to be recruited. New payscales (*Agenda for Change*), (NHS Executive, 2001).
Improvements in the working environment	(*Improving Working Lives* initiative) (Department of Health, 2000a).
New skills and roles for nurses	Removal of barriers between professions. Interprofessional training. 1,000 nurse consultants by 2004.
£140 million to develop staff skills	Continuing professional development. £150 annual learning account for all staff
Modern matrons	Nurse leaders. NHS leadership centre. Leadership programmes at all levels.

Source: Department of Health, 2000b.

activity. Organizations are human creations and sociology studies their origins and continued existence, which can never be taken for granted.

4   Sociology and the management of health care

This 'distinctive and well informed perspective' derives from a number of concepts that can be employed to make sense of how organizations and the people within them function. Three of these will now be examined to demonstrate this.

Bureaucracy

This term is often used to describe rule-bound organizations where it is difficult to get any explanation or response because of red tape. If a process or person is referred to as being 'bureaucratic' it is generally intended to indicate that this is negative and unhelpful. In an extreme form bureaucratic organizations fail to do what they are supposed to because rules and regulations are applied so rigidly that employees lose sight of what their job is. For example, if it is Trust policy that injections of analgesics for pain can only be given if pain is monitored by the use of a pain scale and the severity of the pain recorded, a nurse may adhere so rigidly to this policy that pain relief is not given. If the pain chart has items such as 'moderate', 'intense' and 'unbearable' to indicate the level of pain being experienced, but the patient describes his or her pain as an 'ache', the nurse may refuse to give an injection because the patient's response does not fit in with the form. This results in a situation where a procedure is introduced to ensure pain is monitored and managed appropriately in order to provide a good standard of care to the patient, and yet in following the 'procedure' to the letter the nurse feels unable to deliver that care.

bureaucracy   a structure found in large organizations, based on specialization of tasks, rules and regulations, systems and authority

Bureaucracy, as a sociological concept, was originally developed by Max Weber, one of the first sociologists to consider the role of individuals in relation to the structural determinants of social action (see also chapter 1). Much of his work was concerned with the notion of 'rationality', which he used to explain the development of Western society which was increasingly based on science and calculation (Jary and Jary, 1991). This, combined with the growth of large organizations throughout the nineteenth century, led Weber (1947) to conclude that the decisive reason for the advance of bureaucratic organization was its purely technical superiority over any other form

ideal type   a model of a phenomenon which identifies its essential elements

of organization (p. 214). In short it was a description of an ideal type of organization. Not ideal in the sense that it was perfect or one that should be aimed for, rather that its structure contained specific

Box 14.2   **Main components of a bureaucracy**

- Rules govern the exercise of authority.

- There are boundaries of specialism and areas of competence within which authority is exercised.

- People within the organization hold an office within the hierarchy.

- Staff or office-holders lower in the hierarchy are responsible to staff at a higher level.

- Staff undertake training that prepares them for their specific role within the hierarchy.

- Administrative acts, decisions and rules are formulated and recorded in written form.

- The office-holder is expected to act objectively and administer in compliance with the rules.

Source: Adapted from Blundell and Murdock, 1997 and Weber, 1947.

elements that characterized it as a bureaucracy and which were necessary to manage the organizations of the day (see box 14.2).

In many respects, the hospital is a crucial illustration of Weber's analysis of rationalization (Turner, 1987). Health care organizations can be described as 'professionalized bureaucracies'. Not only do they have a large number of personnel working in designated roles, governed by rules and procedures, they also employ autonomous professionals. Although Weber's concept of rational bureaucracy does not form the definitive framework for the study of hospitals, it can be used to help explain organizational failure and conflict (Hillier, 1987). It can take a long time for decisions to be made as any proposal for change has to be considered by several committees.

For example, it is now generally accepted that the best time to give many types of tablet is at meal times. Medication is usually dispensed in caring institutions during medication rounds of one form or another. If the nursing staff wished to change the time of the medication round to coincide with meal times such a proposal would need to be considered and agreed by a wide range of staff. Medical staff would have to change their prescribing habits; the pharmacy staff would need to alter their system for ensuring ward or department stocks of medication were up to date; the mealtime routine would have to be changed. This would also involve gaining the agreement of the catering staff and the way the drug round was conducted would have to be changed. All of these actions are likely to require discussion by a range of groups of staff in different meetings and examination of

Activity 14.1   **Introducing self-medication in a bureaucracy**

As part of the treatment programme it has been decided by clinical staff that clients need to manage the administration of their own medication.

(a) Think about this and identify the potential barriers to the introduction of a self-medication scheme for clients in a psychiatric unit.

(b) Who would need to discuss such a proposal? Can you think of any committees that would be required to rule on this?

(c) How would a bureaucratic structure affect the speed of decision making in this case?

the implications of the change before it occurs. This all takes time and there are many potential barriers to the change.

Once you have thought about the issue in this way it becomes clear how the concept of bureaucracy can be useful in explaining seemingly strange rules and procedures in health care. These include midwives escorting a mother and baby about to be discharged to the hospital entrance and then handing the baby over to the mother, because this is the hospital policy. A work order form may have to be completed in order to get a faulty light bulb replaced, because unless a form is completed there is no way of tracking the work and paying the appropriate person for doing it. This occurs in part because public bureaucracies sometimes perceive themselves as guardians of the national interest: there is the idea that they embody ideals that transcend the policies of particular governments; they can develop a character of their own and become set in their ways and difficult to change. In these circumstances professionals can be more concerned with their own survival than with the broader aims of providing for the needs of the consumers of their service (Owens and Petch, 1995). This can be observed in the barriers that can exist between different wards and departments and the lack of co-operation that ensues. Differences of opinion over whose role it is to provide a counselling service for clients with mental health problems can delay the provision of the service. Prolonged discussion concerning patients' hygiene needs can result in the development of a whole classification system to determine whether patients being cared for in the community require a 'nursing' or 'social' bath. At a more basic level, nurses can become so concerned with completing all of the forms that need to be filled in when a patient is admitted that they have less time to spend with the patient delivering care. This is not a criticism of the individual nurse who is trying to complete her work, it is an indication of how an understanding of the concept of bureaucracy

Activity 14.2   **Organizations as bureaucracies**

(a)   Describe the structure of an NHS organization you have knowledge of. Who is the chief executive? Is there a board? How many levels are there in the hierarchy above ward/department level?

(b)   Identify the rules and policies that are deemed to be the most important.

(c)   When you have done this try to assess to what extent the organization matches Weber's ideal type of a bureaucracy. In what ways does this help you understand how the organization functions?

can help explain some of the more puzzling aspects of nursing practice. Activity 14.2 further illustrates how it can be applied to make sense of the organization as a whole.

Bureaucracy is helpful in explaining how rigid organizational structures can affect the way nursing care is delivered. However, there are other concepts that reveal other aspects of the management and organization of care. One of those which were developed, in part, to account for the limitations of bureaucracy is the **negotiated order** approach.

negotiated order   a means of organizing the outcome of interactions between people

Negotiated order

In contrast to the ideal type of bureaucracy, the concept of negotiated order emphasizes the importance of the informal organization, arising out of negotiation between individuals. Bond and Bond (1986) locate the concept of negotiated order within a broad interactionist tradition. This is that social phenomena, particularly organizational arrangements, emerge from the ongoing interaction among people. It involves negotiation and renegotiation over actions and decisions, and stresses the fluidity and uncertainty of social arrangements. For example, when starting work in a new placement it is unlikely that a nursing student will know all of the rules and procedures. Similarly she or he will not know the patients/clients and their needs. The information relating to policies and rules will be passed on by a mentor, colleagues and others gradually as the placement progresses. There may be a requirement to record this information in a continuous-assessment-of-practice document; however, this does not guarantee that the student has read all of the relevant policies. Indeed, it is unlikely that the permanent staff have read them all. In this instance the information is passed on and discussed and can be adapted in the process. So the policy may state, 'All patients will have their risk of developing pressure sores assessed using the Douglas score (or Waterlow, or Norton score)' (tools for calculating pressure sore risk). However, the student may be informed, 'We do not do that here because we have a lot of day cases and it does not apply to them'. The way care is delivered deviates from the policy. In the case of patient handovers, the way the information is conveyed determines the way the care is organized and delivered. The patients' care plans ostensibly contain all the information necessary to care for them; however, during the verbal handover report the care the patients receive is negotiated and renegotiated. For example: 'The doctor says he can now take a light diet but it's a bit soon; we'll start him on sips of water first and see how he goes.' In this situation direct instructions are adapted by the nurses on the basis of their experience of post-operative care and knowledge of the individual patient.

Two classic pieces of sociological work, which illustrate the application of the negotiated order approach to understanding health care, have been conducted by Strauss and his colleagues and Leonard Stein and are examined below.

From work conducted in psychiatric hospitals Strauss et al. (1963) found that the way care and treatment were organized was the outcome of constant negotiation on the part of the people involved. Whereas bureaucracy would suggest that all that is necessary is to follow the rules, Strauss et al. (1963) discovered that this is only part of the picture. For example, in the hospitals they studied they found that there were different ideologies of treatment advocated by different doctors ranging from medication and electric shock-based approaches at one extreme through to psychotherapeutic or counselling-based ones at the other. As Strauss et al. (p. 154) observed:

> On occasion the diagnosis and treatment of a given patient runs against the judgement of the nurses and aids, who may not go along with the physician's directives, who may or may not disagree openly. They may subvert his therapeutic programme by one of their own. They may choose to argue the matter. They may go over his head to an administrative officer. Indeed, they have many choices of action – each requiring negotiative behaviour. In truth, while physicians are able to command considerable obedience to their directives at this particular hospital, frequently they must work hard at obtaining cooperation in their programming.

This situation is compounded by the fact that in many situations there is a lack of certainty concerning the patient's illness. There is still a great deal that is unknown about psychiatric illness in particular and illness in general. This creates the space for disagreement and negotiation about care and treatment. Discussion of treatment programmes and decisions about the most appropriate way to treat patients are not fixed and are often unsystematic. They are the outcome of negotiation between various interested parties including nurses, doctors, patients, carers, social workers and so on. Each of these people will have different levels of influence on different occasions depending on their status, the other people involved in the ongoing negotiation and the needs of the patient. For example, a first-year student nurse is likely to be more hesitant in demanding that a patient receives antibiotic treatment for an infected pressure area than an experienced staff nurse.

As Strauss et al. (1963) conclude, the hospital is a locale where staff are enmeshed in a complex negotiative process in order to accomplish their individual and organizational objectives. The dynamics of how this is accomplished on a day-to-day basis are illustrated in the work of Stein (1967) who characterized it as the 'doctor–nurse game'. This is described in chapter 4 and is a particular type of negotiation. In playing the game the intention is that the work can be done without creating too much friction. The role of the nurse has moved on a good deal since 1967 and in 1990 Stein et al. noted that in an increasing number of hospital settings nurses feel free to confront and even challenge physicians on issues of patient care. A good example of this in acute Trusts is when new junior doctors start their first six-month clinical experience. They have to rely heavily on experienced nurses to guide them through the ward routine and treatment regimes, and if they fail to heed the instructions and advice of the nurses they can make serious errors. Although rooted in its time vestiges of the 'game' persist and illustrate the enduring relevance of negotiated order approaches in understanding the way health care organizations function. There may be rules and structures yet the day-to-day work is negotiated between individuals in the setting.

Activity 14.3   Negotiating patient care

The next time you are involved in a handover report or case conference on one of your clinical placements, think about the way decisions are being made about patient/client care.

(a)   To what extent are they the outcome of a formal decision-making process and based on 'objective' clinical evidence, and to what extent are they the outcome of informal discussion?

(b)   Whose views prevail and why?

---

power the ability to control or influence other people with or without their consent

Inherent in this process of negotiation is the way **power** is exerted. This is another concept which is central to sociological analysis. One of the elements of the negotiated-order approaches is the relative power of people in the setting and indeed the power of the setting to shape or influence events.

Power

The notion of power is extremely complex and, as Johnson and Gill (1993) note, despite its obvious importance the literature on power seems to suffer from ambiguous definitions and applications deriving from conflicting philosophical assumptions. Also, debates about power are often conducted in highly esoteric language. However, detailed discussions concerning the nature of power which are useful sources for further study in this area include Clegg (1979; 1989), Etzioni (1975), Lukes (1974), and Mintzberg (1983). Consideration of the nature of power is also a particular concern of many of the sociologists referred to in other chapters in this book. Central to much of the work of Weber and Marx, for example, was the analysis of organizations as social settings characterized by power struggles. It is beyond the scope of this chapter to examine this work in detail; rather, the intention is to use an example from sociology that can be applied to health care organizations and used to increase understanding of the way they function.

Individuals have power over others for all sorts of reasons such as their gender, social class and ethnicity (see chapters 5, 8 and 9 respectively). The focus here is on the nature of power as a social resource in organizations. French and Raven (1959) produced a useful typology of social power which has continued relevance in the context of contemporary health care. They identified five sources of power within organizations which can serve as a basis for people to exert 'social power' (see box 14.3).

Different people within health care organizations have power over others arising from the sources identified by French and Raven. Within a ward team there is a ward sister or charge nurse who is the appointed leader and should possess legitimate power. Members of the ward team will defer to the ward manager's right to exert influence over them. But what if members of the team do not believe that the manager is equal to the task? If there is a perception that the individual concerned has been appointed without having amassed sufficient experience and knowledge (expert power) and is not a popular individual (lacks referent power), team members are less likely to accept his or her authority. This can result in a dysfunctional team.

The importance of the ward sister/manager as the crucial determinant in the quality of care delivered and the atmosphere on the ward or in the department has been identified in several studies (Fretwell, 1982; Ogier, 1982; Orton, 1981; Pembrey, 1980) and the importance of nurse management has been recognized in the NHS Plan (Department of Health, 2000). In order to be a skilled manager it is necessary to be able to use these sources of power in a balanced and constructive way. For example, coercive power, if not used sparingly, will very quickly have detrimental effects on any team. If a

Box 14.3 **The sources of social power**

Reward power is based on a person's perception that his or her leader or supervisor has the ability and resources to confer rewards of various kinds on those who comply with directives. These may be pay rises, promotion, increased responsibilities or the granting of privileges.

Coercive power is based on fear and the employee's perception that the leader or supervisor has the capacity to punish or bring about undesirable outcomes for those who do not follow directives. This can include withholding of privileges, allocation of undesirable duties or responsibilities, withholding of support, and use of disciplinary procedures.

Legitimate power is based on the person's perception that the manager or supervisor has a right to power because of his or her role or position in the organization. It is a recognition of the authority vested in managers at particular levels of the hierarchy of the organization.

Referent power is based on the employee's identification with the manager. The manager exercises influence because of the perceived attractiveness or popularity he or she has. Other terms which can be included in this form of social power include respect, esteem and charisma, which all convey the way the manager is regarded by others.

Expert power is based on the recognition by the employee of the specialist knowledge or expertise of the manager or supervisor. It arises from perceptions on the part of employees of the credibility of the manager. Evidence of this can include particular qualifications and skills.

Source: Based on French and Raven, 1959 and Mullins, 2002.

ward manager seeks to blame an individual when errors occur and punishes him or her with a public rebuke, the individual concerned is less likely to report any errors in the future for fear of being treated in a similar manner. This can have serious consequences. If a drug administration error is not reported because the nurse is worried about being told off and humiliated the patient concerned is at risk. The need to have systems whereby risk and potential errors are identified and discussed to avoid harm to patients is central to clinical governance (Department of Health, 1998), the government's strategy for quality in the NHS. However, if power is misused within the ward such disclosure will not occur.

Another set of power relationships that it is important to be aware of are those which exist between nurses and their patients. Nurses can exercise power over patients because in many situations they are perceived as experts and in possession of legitimate power. There is an emphasis in current approaches to nurse education on communication and working in partnership with patients/clients. The expectation is that nurses will discuss the needs their patients have and then construct care plans to meet those needs. This is not always possible: patients may feel that 'nurse knows best' and defer to the perceived expert and legitimate power. Also, nurses may use the power they have to 'control' the activities of patients (May, 1992a; 1992b). One of the most stark examples of this was the scandal of the Ely hospital (Klein, 1995) where nursing staff were complicit in the abuse of long-stay residents. There were other organizational factors that contributed to this situation, but the lack of power on the part of the residents was a key issue.

It is vital that all those involved in the management and delivery of care understand the power relationships that exist, as they must be managed if the needs of the patients are to be met. Hospitals are large, powerful institutions with a complex division of labour, and sociology has a major part to play in the understanding of health care organization (Green and Thorogood, 1998). Nurses constitute the largest group of employees within health care organizations (Salter, 1998) and so have the potential to exert considerable power by sheer dint of numbers. This alone would suggest that it is worth considering the nature of power within health care. As nurses take on more management responsibilities, insights from sociology can help ensure that these duties are performed in pursuit of the patient's interests, rather than for the purposes of internal organizational power struggles.

Activity 14.4   **Power relationships at work**

When you are on placement, take a little time to observe how power relationships operate. Focus primarily on the nursing team and assess who is able to exert power and why.

(a)   Which of the staff do you recognize as having 'expert' power? Is coercive power used? If so, why? How is power exerted over patients?

(b)   Consider how a knowledge of social power may influence your approach to managing the nursing team in the future.

Summary and Resources

Summary

- Health care organizations are large and complex and will not function unless they are managed. The importance of management in the organization and delivery of health care is reflected in the structure of NHS organizations.

- Key concepts from the study of sociology such as bureaucracy, negotiated order, and power can provide useful insights into the way health care organizations operate. Similarly, research methods developed in the discipline of sociology have been used to shed light on important aspects of health care organizations.

- Nurses are increasingly involved in management from an early stage in their careers and so an understanding of how organizations work is important. The study of sociology is necessary to help develop the composite knowledge base all managers need.

- Management is a prominent feature of the government's plans for health care over the next few years. Health policy is predicated on notions of the NHS being effectively managed and organized. Sociology provides a means of studying this development.

Questions for Discussion

1. Why is it important for health care organizations to be managed effectively?

2. What are the advantages and disadvantages of nurses being managers in health care?

3. Are people born managers or can they be trained?

4. Is it possible to manage the National Health Service?

Further Reading

D. Allen: *The Changing Shape of Nursing Practice: The Role of Nurses in the Hospital Division of Labour.* London: Routledge, 2001.
An examination of nursing work from a sociological perspective which draws on detailed observation of the reality of practice. The relationship between nursing and management is explored in chapter 6 and provides useful insights on its complexity and effects.

D. Allen and D. Hughes: *Nursing and the Division of Labour in Healthcare.* Basingstoke: Palgrave Macmillan, 2002.

This book examines the organization and delivery of nursing care from a sociological perspective. It includes reports of research on a range of issues, including team work, expanded roles and continuing professional development. It draws on sociological theory to explain and illuminate different aspects of practice.

J. Green and N. Thorogood: *Analysing Health Policy: A Sociological Approach.* London: Longman, 1998.
This examines broader health management concerns from a sociological perspective. It is an accessible text which uses examples from research to examine issues in health policy and management.

T. J. Watson: *Sociology of Work and Industry.* London: Routledge, 1995.
Do not be put off by the title; this is a comprehensive text which applies sociology to organizations. It is written clearly and demonstrates how ideas and concepts from sociology can be used to understand work and organizations.

References

Albrow, M. 1997: *Do Organizations have Feelings?* London: Routledge.

Barley, S. R. and Kunda, G. 1992: 'Design and devotion: surges of rational and normative ideologies of control in managerial discourse.' *Administrative Science Quarterly,* 37(3), 363–99.

Blundell, B. and Murdock, A. 1997: *Managing in the Public Sector.* London: Butterworth Heinemann.

Bond, J. and Bond, S. 1986: *Sociology and Health Care.* Edinburgh: Churchill Livingstone.

Clegg, S. R. 1979: *The Theory of Power and Organization.* London: Routledge.

Clegg, S. R. 1989: *Frameworks of Power.* London: Sage.

Connelly, J. 2000: 'A realistic theory of health sector management: the case for critical realism.' *Journal of Management in Medicine,* 14(5/6), 262–71.

Cox, D. 1991: Health service management – a sociological view: Griffiths and the non-negotiated order of the hospital. In J. Gabe, M. Calman and M. Bury (eds), *The Sociology of the Health Service,* London: Routledge, pp. 89–114.

Department of Health 1989: *Working for Patients* (Cm 555). London: HMSO.

Department of Health 1998: *A First Class Service: Quality in the New NHS.* London: HMSO.

Department of Health 2000a: *Improving Working Lives Standard: NHS Employers Committed to Improving the Working Lives of People Who Work in the NHS.* Leeds: HMSO.

Department of Health 2000b: *The NHS Plan: A Plan for Investment a Plan for Reform* (Cm 4818–1). London: HMSO.

Department of Health 2001: *Agenda for Change: Modernising the NHS Pay System*. Leeds: NHS Executive.

Department of Health 2002: *Improving Working Lives and Accreditation for Strategic Health Authorities and Workforce Development Confederations*. London: DoH.

Department of Health and Social Security 1983: 'NHS Management Inquiry' (Griffiths Report). Press Release no. 83/30, 3 February.

Etzioni, A. 1975: *The Comparative Analysis of Complex Organizations*, 2nd edn. New York: Free Press.

French, J. R. P. and Raven, B. 1959: The bases of social power. In D. Cartwright (ed.), *Studies in Social Power*, Ann Arbor: University of Michigan Press, pp. 150–67.

Fretwell, J. E. 1982: *Ward Teaching and Learning*. London: Royal College of Nursing.

Green, J. and Thorogood, N. 1998: *Analysing Health Policy: A Sociological Approach*. London: Longman.

Grint, K. 1995: *Management: A Sociological Introduction*. Cambridge: Polity.

Hales, C. P. 1986: 'What do managers do? A critical review of the evidence.' *Journal of Management Studies*, 23(1), 88–115.

Hales, C. P. 1993: *Managing Through Organisation*. London: Routledge.

Harrison, S. 1988: *Managing the National Health Service: Shifting the Frontier?* London: Chapman and Hall.

Harrison, S., Hunter, D. J., Marnoch, G. and Pollitt, C. 1992: *Just Managing: Power and Culture in the National Health Service*. Basingstoke: Macmillan.

Hillier, S. 1987: Rationalism, bureaucracy, and the organization of health services: Max Weber's contribution to understanding modern health care systems. In G. Scambler (ed.), *Sociological Theory and Medical Sociology*, London: Tavistock Publications, pp. 194–220.

Hunter, D. 1990: Organizing and managing health care: a challenge for medical sociology. In S. Cunningham-Burley and N. P. McKeganey (eds), *Readings in Medical Sociology*, London: Tavistock Routledge, pp. 213–36.

Iles, V. 1997: *Really Managing Health Care*. Buckingham: Open University Press.

Jary, D. and Jary, J. 1991: *Collins Dictionary of Sociology*. Glasgow: HarperCollins.

Johnson, P. and Gill, J. 1993: *Management Control and Organizational Behaviour*. London: Paul Chapman.

Klein, R. 1995: *The New Politics of the NHS*, 3rd edn. London: Longman.

Lukes, S. 1974: *Power: A Radical View*. London: Macmillan.

May, C. 1992a: 'Nursing work, nurses' knowledge, and the subjectification of the patient.' *Sociology of Health and Illness*, 14(4), 472–87.

May, C. 1992b: 'Individual care? Power and subjectivity in therapeutic relationships.' *Sociology*, 26(4), 589–602.

Mintzberg, H. 1983: *Power in and around Organizations*. Englewood Cliffs, NJ: Prentice Hall.

Mintzberg, H. 1996: 'Musings on management.' *Harvard Business Review*, July–August, 61–7.

Mullins, L. J. 2002: *Management and Organisational Behaviour*, 6th edn. Harlow: Financial Times/Pitman.

NHS Executive 2001: *Agenda for Change: Modernising the NHS Pay System*. Leeds: NHS Executive.

Ogier, M. E. 1982: *An Ideal Sister? A Study of Leadership Style and Verbal Interaction*. London: Royal College of Nursing.

Orton, H. D. 1981: *Ward Learning Climate*. London: Royal College of Nursing.

Owens, P. and Glennerster, H. 1990: *Nursing in Conflict*. Basingstoke: Macmillan Education.

Owens, P. and Petch, H. 1995: Professionals and management. In P. Owens, J. Carrier and J. Horder (eds), *Interprofessional Issues in Community and Primary Health Care*, Basingstoke: Macmillan, pp. 37–55.

Pembrey, S. E. 1980: *The Ward Sister, Key to Nursing*. London: Royal College of Nursing.

Ranade, W. 1997: *A Future for the NHS? Health Care for the Millennium*. London: Longman.

Salter, B. 1998: *The Politics of Change in the Health Service*. Basingstoke: Macmillan.

Shafritz, J. M. and Ott, J. S. (eds) 2001: *Classics of Organization Theory*, 5th edn. Fort Worth, TX: Harcourt College Publishers.

Stein, L. I. 1967: 'The doctor–nurse game.' *Archives of General Psychiatry*, 16, 699–703.

Stein, L. I., Watts, D. T. and Howell, T. 1990: 'The doctor-nurse game revisited.' *New England Journal of Medicine*, 322(8), 546–9.

Strauss, A., Schatzman, L., Ehrlich, D., Bucher, R. and Sabshin, M. 1963: The hospital and its negotiated order. In E. Freidson (ed.), *The Hospital in Modern Society*, Basingstoke: Macmillan, 147–69.

Strong, P. M. and Robinson, J. 1990: *The NHS: Under New Management*. Milton Keynes: Open University Press.

Turner, B. S. 1987: *Medical Power and Social Knowledge*. London: Sage.

Weber, M. 1947: *The Theory of Social and Economic Organization*. New York: Free Press.

Whitley, R. 1984: 'The development of management studies as a fragmented adhocracy.' *Sociology of Science*, 23(4/5), 775–818.

Whitley, R. 1989: 'On the nature of managerial tasks and skills: their distinguishing characteristics and organization.' *Journal of Management Studies*, 26 (3), 209–24.

Willmott, H. C. 1984: 'Images and ideals of managerial work: a critical examination of conceptual and empirical accounts.' *Journal of Management Studies*, 21(3), 349–68.

Willmott, H. C. 1987: 'Studying managerial work: a critique and a proposal.' *Journal of Management Studies*, 24(3), 250–70.

15 Health, Housing and the Environment

Douglas McCarrick

Key issues within this chapter

- The effects of housing on health.
- Housing status and health.
- Housing and environmental issues.
- Housing, environment and the role of the nurse.

By the end of this chapter you should be able to . . .

- Understand the contrasting perspectives of medical and public health models.
- Have an understanding of trends in housing policy.
- Recognize how housing conditions and homelessness affect health.
- Discuss the significance of the 'fitness standard'.
- Be aware of the importance of housing and environmental threats to health for nurses.

---

1 Introduction

public health largely preventive health measures targeting populations and environmental improvements (in contrast to individual, curative medical approaches)

◄ This chapter is concerned with two major aspects of **public health** – housing and its environment – and recognizes that the relationship between health and housing is a complicated but nevertheless crucial one. The effects of housing and other environmental factors on health and the significance of housing provision for particularly vulnerable social groups will be considered; the latter requires a review of housing policy. The chapter will also consider the importance of these issues for nursing.

The perspective taken here is not a typical view for those who work in our health services. The dominant way of thinking about health in modern Britain is in personal and medical terms rather than in environmental terms. The medical model has been extremely influential (see chapter 3) in shaping not only how individuals perceive their health, but also health policy and health services (see chapter 7). Medical constructions of health have brought advantages – they encourage intervention, aim at achieving cures and have improved some physical conditions – yet it has been argued that they are also given credit for improvements to health to which they are not entitled (McKeown, 1979).

There are ways of thinking about health other than the medical model. The public health approach addresses issues as they relate to communities or populations. Public health often takes a more preventive position towards ill health, seeking to avoid its causes in communities, and thus is often concerned with health threats in the environment. Public health views of health are typically **salutogenic** since they focus on health rather than illness, take a wider focus on a population or a community, and are concerned with epidemiological perspectives and prevention. These contrast with the medical approach, which is largely individualistic, concerned with the signs and symptoms of disease and oriented towards cure. The public health perspective therefore leads to an examination of how housing and other elements of the environment contribute to causing ill-health.

salutogenic focusing on health as positive and on resources for maintaining health rather than on factors which threaten morbidity and mortality

2   The effects of housing on health

There are several ways in which housing can be seen to influence health: if a house has no clean water supply or has holes in the roof these defects will clearly pose health threats to those who live there. Yet houses are much more than this (Davey Smith et al., 2001). You might have noted those psychological aspects of housing as well as the threats to physical health that poor housing can pose. Houses have meanings in our social lives and are bound up with our sense of identity and our security. They can be particularly important for those who spend long periods of time at home, for example, mothers with young children, carers, unemployed, sick and disabled people (Blackburn, 1991).

Therefore while our homes can be an asset to our well-being, they can also present risks to our health. The places we live in can pose physical threats to health through their condition, their design, or the

Activity 15.1　　**Housing and health?**

Inner city
terraced housing

Ben Thomas /
istockphoto.com

(a)　　How might housing affect health? Write down three ways in
which you think it might.

materials of which they are constructed. Residents can face dangers
from overcrowding or from the people who share their homes or even
from the creatures which also inhabit them. Insecure homes, in terms
of tenure or crime, can mean psychological or physical threats. Gas
and electricity services attached to our homes can carry their own
menace. The location of housing is also important in shaping the
quality of life and health of those who live there. Each of these aspects

Activity 15.2 The significance of housing conditions on health

Consider the following graph, compiled by Stevenson, the Medical Officer of Health for Liverpool in 1911.

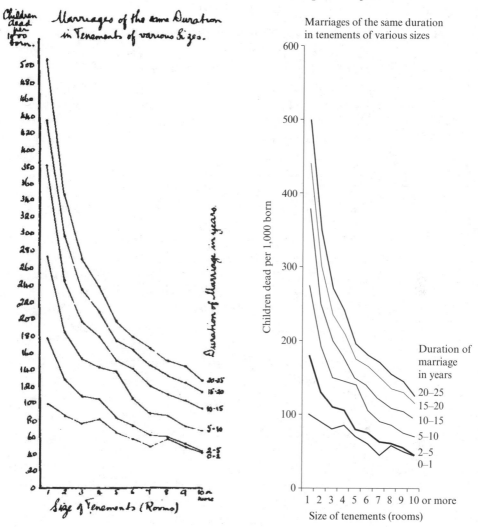

Marriages of the same duration in tenements of various sizes: diagram drawn by Stevenson to show child mortality, tenement size and duration of marriage, based on data from the 1911 Census (Fox and Goldblatt, 1982, figure 5.1, p. 65), alongside a redrawing to show data more clearly

(a) Describe the horizontal and vertical axes and note the additional information on the right-hand side of this graph. What does this tell us about health?

(b) How else might the size of tenements have affected health in 1911? Do you think the same is true today?

of housing merits the attention of health professionals who need, at least, to be aware of the hazards in people's homes and, at best, might be in a position to help do something about them.

Researching health and housing

Yet while it seems common sense that houses in poor condition will affect the health of the people who live in them, it is also important to recognize that while living conditions have long been reported to affect health, demonstrating that relationship has considerably challenged researchers. Are poor people who live in poor housing unwell because of their housing conditions or because of factors related to their poverty? Social life is a complex phenomenon and some have suggested that 'it is almost impossible to show a clear causal link between bad housing and ill health largely because of the "confounding variables" problem; it is almost impossible to separate housing out from such linked factors as poverty and poor diet' (Burridge and Ormandy, 1993, p. 72).

Nevertheless, the Acheson Inquiry (Acheson, 1998), which the government established to review the association between social exclusion and health (and which is discussed in relation to social class in chapter 8), confirmed the belief that there were links between cold, damp houses and ill-health. Such conditions are also especially threatening to those already vulnerable; babies, the sick and older people.

In spite of the difficulty of researching the relationship between housing and health, various researchers have identified strong and significant links between them, which are independent of other variables such as smoking, income and employment status. Some of the key research findings are summarized in box 15.1.

The condition of the people's homes is the main housing

fitness (for human habitation) the legal standards for minimum requirements in housing services and conditions ◄ influence on their health. The fitness of a home for human habitation is established in law. Hygienic toilet and food preparation areas, some form of heating and a water supply are among the requirements for fitness. The current fitness standard includes many housing features and implies a high quality of accommodation (see activity 15.3). Unfortunately many homes do not meet that standard. Conway comments that 'In spite of the slum clearance programmes, today over 1.5 million homes are unfit and one in five requires over £1,000 of urgent repairs. At the current rate of demolition, every new home will have to last 3,500 years' (Conway, 2000, p. 11). More recent figures suggest some improvement: 900 thousand homes are 'unfit' (Office of the Deputy Prime Minister, 2003, p. 2). However, the government's higher standards for judging homes, 'Decent Homes', concludes that there are 7 million dwellings which fail to provide their inhabitants with a decent home (Office of the Deputy Prime Minister, 2003, p. 2) (see box 15.2). Local authorities have been

Box 15.1   **Key research findings: housing and health**

- Four million British households suffer fuel poverty (the need to spend 10 per cent of household income on energy to maintain an adequate standard of warmth), resulting in 25,000–45,000 winter deaths per year (*English House Condition Survey 1996, energy report*, cited in Olsen, 2001).

- The presence of damp causes emotional distress in women and reports of respiratory, gastrointestinal problems and infections in children (Davies and Kelly, 1993).

- Wheezing and other respiratory problems, aches and pains, nerves, diarrhoea, headaches and fever are more prevalent in children who live in damp and mouldy homes (Wilkinson, 1999).

- Damp homes cause overcrowding in the more habitable parts of the accommodation and increase psychological stress (Etherington, 1983).

- High-rise accommodation causes social isolation and provides no play space for children (Etherington, 1983).

- Poorly insulated homes can create noise and neighbour disputes, generating a sense of persecution and anxiety (Etherington, 1983).

Box 15.2   **Decent homes**

For a dwelling to be considered a 'decent' home it must:

- meet the statutory minimum standard for housing (i.e., be fit);

- be in a reasonable state of repair;

- have reasonably modern facilities and services;

- provide a reasonable degree of thermal comfort.

Source: Office of the Deputy Prime Minister, 2003.

funded to provide assistance with some of these matters, but the extent of central funding has been declining and the criteria for receiving help are becoming increasingly restrictive. Community nurses may face some of these conditions in their daily work.

It is likely that nurses will encounter poor housing conditions, as 25 per cent of households living in non-decent homes include someone who is long-term ill or disabled (Office of the Deputy Prime Minister, 2003, p. 11).

Activity 15.3   **Fit for human habitation?**

ITEM A: The fitness standard

To be fit for human habitation in Britain a house requires:

- A piped water supply.
- A washbasin with hot and cold water, a fixed bath or shower and an internal WC.
- Drainage and sanitation facilities.
- Cooking and food-preparation facilities, a sink with hot and cold water, waste disposal facilities.
- Adequate natural and satisfactory artificial light, heating and ventilation.
- To be substantially free from rising damp, penetrating damp and condensation.
- To be structurally stable and of adequate repair. (Ministry of Health, 1946)

ITEM B

Unfit for human habitation?

Stephen Gibson / istockphoto.com   Jan Tyler / istockphoto.com

(a)   Some houses have been classed as 'unfit for human habitation'. How would you judge a house to be adequate for human beings to live in?

(b)   What minimum standards of provision and quality do you think a house would have to fall below in modern Britain to make it 'unfit for human habitation'?

House design, construction and location

The condition of a person's home is not the only way in which that domestic environment can impact on health. Homes can also pose threats to health though their design, the materials of which they are made or the location they occupy.

Poorly designed, or inadequately lit, kitchens create risky environments. Stairs, especially if handrails are inadequate, also pose the obvious threat of falls for children and older people. In 2001 the Department of Trade and Industry reported that 76 people were killed in domestic accidents each week in Britain, and compared this to 66 deaths weekly on the roads. Among the casualties are the victims of scalding, fires, accidental collisions, carbon monoxide poisoning, falls and DIY accidents; again, the most vulnerable groups are children and older people (Department of Trade and Industry, 2001).

The risks from lead in paint and pipes, asbestos roofing and insulation, and radon gas are widely accepted (Wilkinson, 1999), although only a small proportion of homes are affected. Poor wiring is also a major contributor to the domestic fires which take hundreds of lives each year. With a bitter irony, among those most at risk are those already homeless and relying on accommodation in houses in multiple occupation (e.g. homeless hostels).

There are disputes about risk from proximity to electricity pylons and radio masts, with experts, including those commissioned by the government, disagreeing on the effects of radiation and electromagnetic fields. Asthma has been increasing, and among the suggested causes are car pollution and the effects of smoking at home. Roads, rivers and canals close to houses create threats, as does traffic congestion, especially to older people and children. Access to good transport systems, shops, parks or medical resources can be health-enhancing neighbourhood features. Global warming and the development of housing on low-lying areas have also led to much greater incidence of flooding in several areas of Britain, bringing the physical dangers of drowning and infection and the psychological insecurity of living in a vulnerable location.

Also, while the UK water supply is generally sound there have been incidents of that supply becoming contaminated, admittedly so rarely that they have been nationally reported (Huby, 1998). In some areas the water we receive from our taps may be fluoridated to improve dental health, and, while the **White Paper** *Saving Lives: Our Healthier Nation* strengthened this element of public health, it is worth noting that this policy is not uncontested: claims are made that fluoridation itself poses different health threats (Hillier et al., 1996).

White Paper a discussion document in which government proposals are set out and which invites more limited consultation than a Green Paper

Some households also are at threat from infestations of insects or rodents, although these are much less common in Britain than they have been in the past. Arblaster and Hawtin (1993) note increasing reports of rat problems in cities, suggesting these are the result of poorly maintained sewers and poor food-disposal practices. They say, 'Because they often live in drains their bodies are a source of food poisoning and other disease-causing organisms. They also transmit leptospirosis through contact with their urine' (Arblaster and Hawtin, 1993, p. 22).

Housing and mental health

Conway (2000) has pointed out that mental ill-health and housing are related. She says: 'Mental illness can result in housing problems. There is also evidence that housing problems and homelessness in particular can lead to or exacerbate mental ill-health, particularly anxiety and depression. The physical condition of a dwelling can also undermine mental health' (Conway, 2000, p. 101). There is therefore a reciprocal relationship between housing conditions and mental health.

The difficulties of demonstrating in research the relationships between health and housing have been referred to above. The situation is even more complex, since 'the effect of poor housing on health may be indirect or take several years to manifest itself' (Marsh et al., 2000, p. 412). Housing can affect both mental and physical health in a number of ways. The condition of a house, where it is located, its design, the materials of which it is constructed can all impact on the health of its inhabitants. Government grants for houses which are 'unfit for human habitation' are available, but have been reduced. Homes are also the sites of many accidents because of poor design or maintenance. Poor housing is also related to poor mental health.

3   Housing status and health

Trends in housing provision

In Britain there are principally three forms of housing:

- owner-occupied homes;
- privately rented homes;
- the **social housing** sector.

social housing
housing provided by local authorities and housing associations to tenants with special needs usually unable to afford their own homes

Other forms of accommodation, including houses in multiple occupation, student halls of residence, and various residential institutions, make up a small proportion of the total housing stock.

The balance of provision across these sectors changed remarkably during the twentieth century, reflecting different political approaches to housing the nation. In 1914, 90 per cent of houses were privately rented, with only 10 per cent making up those in owner-occupation (Conway, 2000). The trend has been a massive increase of owner-occupied housing over the century, encouraged by successive

Activity 15.4   **Trends in housing provision**

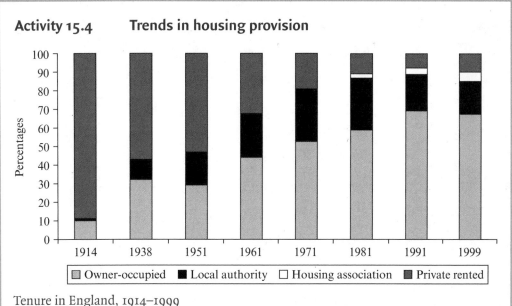

Tenure in England, 1914–1999

Source: House of Commons Research Report 99/11: 'A century of change', p. 12.

Consider the barchart above. It shows the shifts in housing provision in Britain in the course of the twentieth century. What trends can you identify in the changing nature of housing provision?

governments, with 70 per cent of homes falling into this category by 2001. Local-authority provision expanded as a central element of the post-war welfare state until it accounted for 29 per cent of housing in 1971. Despite the retreat from council housing under Thatcher's governments in the 1980s, led by the right-to-buy scheme of the 1980 Housing Act (Conway, 2000, p. 31), in 2001 council housing still made up 13 per cent of the nation's total housing stock. The attack on council housing has continued under subsequent Conservative and Labour governments. By 1997 private rented homes made up only 10 per cent of the total, and a new form of not-for-profit housing provision, social landlords, made up a growing 5 per cent. At the time of writing the present Blair government is encouraging the transfer of local authority housing into private or charitable ownership, though it has faced a major setback to these plans with their rejection by council house tenants of Birmingham City Council, Europe's largest landlord.

Defining homelessness

The 1977 Housing (Homeless Persons) Act had placed a statutory responsibility on local authorities to house the homeless. The

| Box 15.3 | **The continuum of homelessness** |

- Without a roof
- In homeless accommodation
- In insecure housing
- Shortly to be released from an institution
- Sharing accommodation in intolerable relationships
- Living in unsatisfactory accommodation
- Sharing involuntarily.

Source: Conway, 2000.

homelessness without appropriate accommodation; this can range from living in undesirable conditions to being roofless

definition of **homelessness** in the Act was extensive, incorporating ideas of overcrowding, of being in a home which was insecure, of being in a home where you were the victim of domestic violence or sexual abuse (see box 15.3). This wide view of homelessness came under pressure during the Thatcherite years, with the notorious comment of one Conservative minister that the real homeless were 'the sort you step over when you come out of the opera' (Sir George Young, Minister for Housing, reported in the *Mail on Sunday* during 1991). By the time this construction of homelessness had been articulated there had already been a diminution of the responsibility of local councils with the Housing Act 1985, which contained the concept of people making themselves 'intentionally homeless'. The Act absolved councils of their erstwhile statutory duty if applicants were judged to be responsible for their own plight. By 1990 about 5,500 households were denied assistance since they were deemed 'intentionally homeless' (Department of the Environment, 1991).

These policies have direct implications for health. The housing policies of the last twenty years have seen a reduction in the provision of social housing and an increase in homelessness and rooflessness with their consequent health threats.

Homelessness, rooflessness and ill-health

Homelessness affects health in several ways. People who are living on the streets face particular threats, but there are also threats to physical and mental health from living in hostels and in the restricted access to health services.

The condition brings isolation, stress and depression; rooflessness restricts access to proper food preparation and hygiene facilities as well as bringing vulnerability to cold and pollution. Rough sleepers, says Skellington (in Dallos and McLaughlin, 1993,

How do you think being homeless might affect someone's health?

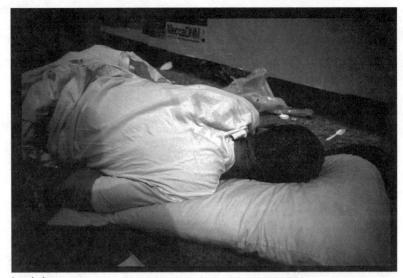

istockphoto.com

Annette Birkenfeld / istockphoto.com

Box 15.4   **Health problems and homeless people**

Families in temporary accommodation	*Single homeless people*
poor diet	chronic chest and breathing problems
infections	malnutrition/digestion
child accidents	infestation and skin complaints
poor child development and behaviour	musculo-skeletal and foot problems
dental, eyesight and hearing problems	stress and depression
obstetric risks in pregnancy	risk of violence/assault
low-birthweight babies	

Source: Conway, 2000.

---

p. 262), 'are especially vulnerable to diabetes and epilepsy [and] bad diet and living in poor environments has meant that homeless people become particularly susceptible to chest infections'. Problems with their feet, and a greater incidence of tuberculosis, have also been reported among the roofless. Additionally, the life expectancy of the homeless is far below the national average; homeless people are 150 times more likely to be fatally assaulted, 34 times more likely to commit suicide, 8 times more likely to die in an accident and 3 times more likely to die of hypothermia or pneumonia than the average person (West Midlands Health Research Unit, 1994).

Homelessness and mental ill-health have been shown to be related. Bines (2000) demonstrated that physical health problems were more common among the single homeless than in the population at large and that people in hostels and bed-and-breakfast (temporary) accommodation were eight times more likely to experience mental ill-health. For those sleeping rough the multiple rose to eleven.

Homelessness, diversity and inequalities in health

Risks of homelessness and to health are not proportionally distributed across society. The reduced opportunities to find alternative housing have meant that people who find themselves in unwanted situations have fewer escape routes. Diaz (2000) reports that in 1999, Shelter estimated that 400,000 individuals were accepted as homeless by local councils. Sixty per cent of the affected households had children. Twenty-five per cent lost their homes because of relationship breakdown. The people who become homeless are therefore often already vulnerable.

Darke (1989) argues that women are especially disadvantaged with respect to housing. She claims that women relate to houses differently to men, spending more time in that environment and giving it more social importance, yet house design rarely takes into account the domestic and caring tasks which often fall to women within them. The disadvantages faced by women (and children) are exacerbated by the lack of alternatives to abusive situations. Homeless people are at increased risk of injury and attack and Gilroy and Woods (1994) indicate that women will try to avoid sleeping rough because of the threat of sexual attack.

Oppenheim (1990) found that every indicator of poverty showed that black groups were more at risk of homelessness. For black women the situation may be even more acute since they are four times more likely to be homeless (Sexty, 1990). Gilroy and Woods (1994, pp. 107–14) suggest: 'Because of racist attacks/racial harassment, instead of the home being a sanctuary, for many Black women it is, or can be, a prison. . . . leaving a violent home may well mean embarking on a long ordeal of racism, homelessness, near destitution as well as fighting immigration laws.'

The homes they live in may also have especial significance for older people. It is likely that older residents will spend longer in their homes with a proportionate increase in the influence their housing conditions will have on their health. The community care policies developed over the 1980s and 1990s were largely welcomed as a shift from institutionalization; however, among the criticisms of under-resourcing of services there was also a claim that housing matters were inadequately considered. Heywood et al. (2002, p. 62) assert: 'Was the house in disrepair? Was it affordable? Did it need adapting as frailty and impairment increased? Was the house in a high crime area? Such questions were nearly always ignored by health and welfare professionals working with older people.' These are, of course, issues which must concern nurses involved in the discharge of patients into the community. Houses which are not appropriate for older people may pose health threats through cold, falls or isolation and depression.

Homelessness not only reflects and generates health problems; the situation is compounded by difficulties in engaging health services, which are critically required. Community nurses and practice nurses may find they rarely encounter homeless patients, in spite of their health care needs; indeed, research suggests that 37 per cent of homeless people are not registered with a GP (Diaz, 2000). Conway (2000) remarks on the difficulties of access to health services, explaining this in part by the mobile nature of the homeless population, but also commenting on the attitudes of doctors who may see homeless patients as more expensive to treat than housed patients. This can lead to a 'cycle of reluctance' whereby an unwillingness to treat homeless people leads to a reluctance to seek aid (Fisher and Collins, 1993).

The twentieth century saw increasing involvement of the state in ← housing provision and significant changes across the **housing sectors** away from private rented accommodation towards state housing and

housing sectors the forms of housing provision in Britain: social housing, private rented accommodation and owner-occupation

owner-occupation. More recently, governments have retreated from direct provision of housing and in the 1980s, in particular, this led to increasing homelessness. Homelessness can describe a range of inappropriate housing situations. Homelessness affects health, and rooflessness is especially health-threatening since it is compounded by poor access to health services.

4 Housing and environmental policies

Along with health, education and a minimum income, housing was recognized as a key element of the welfare state that was established after World War II. In the post-war consensus Labour and Conservative governments vied with each other to build more local-authority housing provision each year. This situation lasted until the 1970s when governments began the retreat from collective state provision of housing and other services.

Recent governments have also acknowledged housing and

Green Paper a discussion document issued by government as a first step towards legislation

environmental issues as important to health. The **Green Paper,** *Our Healthier Nation: A Contract for Health* (Department of Health, 1998b, p. 12), stated: 'The government recognises that the social causes of ill health and the inequalities which stem from them must be acknowledged and acted upon. Connected problems require joined-up solutions. This means tackling inequality which stems from poverty, poor housing, pollution, low educational standards, joblessness and low pay.'

In July 2000 the Labour government pledged to ensure all social housing meets standards of decency by 2010 but, despite politicians' aspirations towards 'joined-up' government, the new structures of the health services – the Primary Care Trusts (PCTs) – include social services representation by right but no housing representation.

housing policy government policy on housing provision and control

Housing policy has to deal with improving existing homes and encouraging the provision of new homes. However, government policy has been oriented towards fiscal conservatism and reliance on the private sector to provide housing and on housing associations to supply social housing. Government has provided grants to bring poor housing up to scratch, but these have also been facing gradual but significant reductions.

The Housing and Local Government Act 1989 did establish mandatory renovation grants, by which any home which was found unfit for human habitation was brought fully up to fitness, and minor works assistance, which helped home-owners over 60 get the work done which would allow them to remain living at home. The Act also endorsed home improvement agencies which acted as agents for householders seeking government help for improving their properties; they helped with the forms, helped tender for contractors, supervised work, and so on. There was also a disabled facilities grant to assist in the access to and adaptation of homes for residents with disabilities. The trend in housing policy since then, however, has remorselessly been towards less funding and grants provided only at the discretion of the local authorities. The 1996 Housing Grants, Construction and Regeneration Act even removed the right to a grant for people living in unfit homes. However, although critical of the limited nature of government help, Heywood et al. (2002) argue that the value of what is provided, especially to older people, should not be underestimated.

Nurses who work in the community should be aware of the provision in their local areas. Renovation grants are available for fitness matters, insulation, heating, fire escapes, roofs, gutters, windows, doors, drains, unsafe gas and water pipes, damp-proofing, installing an inside toilet or bathroom, improving ventilation or dealing with rot. Modernising Social Services (Department of Health, 1998a) announced a 'prevention grant' of £100 million over three years to help older people to stay in their homes. Home safety checks, handyperson schemes, speedier access to aids and adaptations may be available through local authorities. Insulation and draft-proofing are also presently available through other government schemes.

The White Paper Saving Lives: Our Healthier Nation cited housing and a polluted environment as environmental factors affecting health (Department of Health, 1999). Living on a run-down housing estate with poor facilities and a vandalized environment generates insecurity and despair. Some projects for urban areas have been created but evidence that these have had any long-term success in changing local environments is limited.

Health Action Zones do seek to establish health-promoting partnerships in areas of health inequality. They are trailblazers to tackle key health and social problems like the incidence of coronary heart disease, cancer, mental health, teenage pregnancies, drug abuse, and other issues including housing. Government has invested more than £270 million in this project and its evaluation is currently underway. Healthy Living Centres have also been encouraged to involve a range of local agencies in building better neighbourhood health. The Health Improvement Programme (HImP) requires each PCT to engage the local community in identifying its health needs for the plan, but the success of that involvement has also been limited.

Saving Lives: Our Healthier Nation (Department of Health, 1999) proposed the collection of good local information on health which would allow the assessment of how effective its health-promoting activities were. These 'public health observatories' are planned for each NHS region to identify and monitor local health needs, set up disease registers and promote research. The observatories have a virtual identity through the internet. Campbell describes them: 'The government claims that the eight new observatories will act as the "eyes and ears" in the battle against health inequalities across the country. The primary purpose of the observatories is to collect and analyse data on population and diseases, which will inform both local and national evidence-based decision-making in the public health arena' (Campbell, 2000, p. 2).

Much of the government's approach to local provision encourages local agencies to collaborate. However, there has not been as yet a great deal of extra funding for these ventures. It is arguable that area-based initiatives have a poor history of success, and the success of present area schemes for improving the health of disadvantaged communities has been mixed.

Housing is a crucial element of the healthy environment. The first intervention by the state in housing was in terms of public health objectives. Housing policy has continued to recognize the influence housing has on health and renovation grants were intended to create better home environments for the inhabitants of poor housing. Small adaptations to people's homes, and insulation grants, can have an effect on the quality of life of the most vulnerable. The government is keen to encourage agencies to collaborate to improve people's health and has established 'public health observatories' to provide accurate information on local health needs. There is some question, however, about the effectiveness of area-based initiatives.

5 Housing and the environment: the role of the nurse

As nursing has increasingly recognized the complexities of health and become committed to holistic care, the significance of housing has become apparent. New directions in health policy also require a widened public health role for nurses including community health assessment and a focus on disadvantaged groups (Department of Health, 1999).

There is a growing need for nurses, whatever their professional context, to be aware of the housing and community conditions of the people they care for. Those who work in hospitals, perhaps somewhat removed from the immediacy of people's lives, need some understanding of the living conditions of patients, the possible contributory factors to ill-health and the health threats which they may face on discharge. While it is understandable that hospital-based professionals may prioritize emptying beds, partnership with social services in setting up the support systems required for someone to return home safely might be more effective once the complications of establishing a healthy home are better understood.

Nurses who work in the community are likely to have a more immediate insight into the health issues of people's homes, though they may be unsure how far they regard these as their business. Nevertheless, there have been appeals for a wider approach to health care in nursing (see Fisk, 1998).

Housing is central to a healthy life. Poor housing contributes to ill-health and can jeopardize rehabilitation. The importance of the local environment has increasingly been acknowledged in legislation, and community nurses in particular are considered to have important health promotion roles. There are resources nurses might explore for help. Primary Care Trusts have budgets and responsibility for health-promoting activities in their areas. Local authorities control budgets for adapting houses and removing some of the health risks they pose. New technology, such as remote controls, timers and security lights may also help create safer homes. For those on low incomes, local-authority grants and private companies' remortgaging might provide funds older people need for house repairs. There may also be a nurse or health visitor dedicated to working with the homeless.

The debate about state intervention in health, and especially in housing, will go on. Nurses have a calling to care for the ill and will therefore continue to pick up the casualties if no good answers are found, and good housing has a huge potential for maintaining good health. Holistic nursing recognizes the limitations of the medical model and values the insights the public health perspective offers. Arguably, it is nursing's responsibility to understand the impact of housing on health as nurses are peculiarly placed to see the effects of poor health. They know better than most the needs for resources of the vulnerable. Nurses understand how social conditions shape health and, through practice and research, can extend their influence into those areas of policy which create healthier homes and environments for their patients.

Summary and Resources

Summary

- The chapter considered housing policy and focused on housing as a health resource and as a public health approach to health improvement.

- Our homes affect our health in many ways, from overcrowding, cold or pest-infested conditions to homes which isolate us and are detrimental to our mental health.

- Homelessness has been both a target for housing policy and a consequence of it. We have seen how homelessness affects health and the difficulties homeless people have often experienced in gaining access to health services.

- Nurses recognize the effects housing has on the health of patients being treated or facing discharge. Nurses can call upon local councils to provide assistance for residents, to improve homes and to adapt them for their health needs.

Questions for Discussion

1   Consider the situation of patients facing discharge to poor properties. What might nurses do about the problems they face? What could nurses do about the health threats poor housing poses to new babies going home for the first time?

2   In what ways should homes be suitable for the following people with special needs: women, older people, people with mental illnesses, people with learning disabilities?

3   What might be the advantages and disadvantages of state-provided housing (council housing)? As well as considering the interests of the householder, examine the advantages and disadvantages for society as a whole. Consider the same questions in the case of charitable provision of housing.

Further Reading

J. Conway: *Housing Policy.* Eastbourne: Gildredge Press, 2000. This chapter owes a lot to this excellent and eminently accessible book. It covers housing policy, homeless, and health issues, recognizing the range of social factors involved. It includes some useful internet sites.

P. Durden: Housing policy. In S. P. Savage and R. Atkinson (eds), *Public Policy Under Blair*, Basingstoke: Palgrave, 2001.
A useful chapter which covers the development of British housing policy and contains a helpful brief section on 'The Social Dimension'.

F. Heywood, C. Oldman and R. Means: *Housing and Home in Later Life.* Buckingham: Open University Press, 2002.
An excellent consideration of this specific sector of housing need. It considers the physical and psychological importance of housing to older people and raises critical questions for housing provision and interprofessional working for good community care.

References

Acheson, D. 1998: *Independent Enquiry into Inequalities.* London: Department of Health.

Allott, M. and Robb, M. 1998: *Understanding Health and Social Care.* London: Sage.

Arblaster, L. and Hawtin, M. 1993: *Health, Housing and Social Policy.* London: Socialist Health Association.

Bines, W. 2000: *The Health of Single Homeless People.* York: Centre for Housing Policy, University of York.

Blackburn, C. 1991: *Poverty and Health.* Buckingham: Open University Press.

Burridge, R. and Ormandy, D. 1993: *Unhealthy Housing: Research, Remedies and Reforms.* London: Spon.

Busfield, J. 2000: *Health and Health Care in Modern Britain.* Oxford: Oxford University Press.

Campbell, F. 2000: *Democratic Health Network Briefings 011/00.* London: Democratic Health Network.

Chinn, C. 1991: *Homes for People.* Birmingham: Birmingham Books.

Conway, J. 2000: *Housing Policy.* Eastbourne: Gildredge Press.

Dallos, R. and McLaughlin, E. 1993: *Social Problems and the Family.* London: Sage.

Darke, J. 1989: 'Problem without a name.' *Roof,* March–April, 31.

Davey Smith, G., Dorling, D. and Shaw, M. 2001: *Poverty, Inequality and Health in Britain, 1800–2000: A Reader.* Bristol: Policy Press.

Davies, J. K. and Kelly, M. P. 1993: *Healthy Cities: Research and Practice.* London: Routledge.

Department of the Environment 1991: *Homelessness Statistics.* London: HMSO.

Department of the Environment, Transport and the Regions 1996: *Housing Grants, Construction and Regeneration Act 1996.* London: HMSO.

Department of Health 1998a: *Modernising Social Services* (Cm 4169). London: HMSO.

Department of Health 1998b: *Our Healthier Nation: A Contract for Health* (Cm 3852). London: DoH.

Department of Health 1999: *Saving Lives: Our Healthier Nation.* London: DoH.

Department of Trade and Industry 2001: *Home Surveillance System Report.* London: HMSO.

Diaz, R. 2000: *Health and Housing.* London: Shelter.

Dibblin, J. 1991: *Wherever I Lay my Hat: Young Women and Homelessness.* London: Shelter.

Etherington, S. 1983: *Housing and Mental Health.* London: MIND/Circle 33 Housing Trust.

Fisher, K. and Collins, J. 1993: *Homelessness, Health and Welfare Provision.* London: Routledge.

Fisk, L. 1998: Housing primary care in the community. In M. Allott and M. Robb (eds), *Understanding Health and Social Care*, London: Sage, pp. 155–62.

Fox, A. J. and Goldblatt, P. O. 1982: *OPCS Longitudinal Study: Socio-demographic Mortality Differentials, 1971–75.* London: HMSO.

Gilroy, R. and Woods, R. 1994: *Housing Women.* London: Routledge.

Heywood, F., Oldman, C. and Means, R. 2002: *Housing and Home in Later Life.* Buckingham: Open University Press.

Hillier, S., Inskip, H., Coggon, D. and Cooper, C. 1996: 'Water fluoridation and osteoporotic fracture.' *Community Dental Health,* 13, 63–8.

Huby, M. 1998: *Social Policy and the Environment.* Buckingham: Open University Press.

Lee-Treweek, G. 1994: 'Bedroom abuse: the hidden work in a nursing home.' *Generations Review,* 4(1), March, 2–4.

Marsh, A., Gordon, D., Heslop, P. and Pantazis, C. 2000: 'Housing deprivation and health: a longitudinal analysis.' *Housing Studies,* 15(3), 411–28.

McKeown, T. 1979: *The Role of Medicine: Dream, Mirage, Nemesis?* London: Nuffield Provincial Hospital Trust.

Ministry of Health 1946: *Report of the Standards of Fitness for Habitation Sub-committee of the Central Housing Advisory Committee.* London: Ministry of Health.

National Institute for Social Work Black Perspectives Sub-Group 1983: *Residential Care: Positive Answers.* London: HMSO.

Norman, A. 1998: Losing your home. In M. Allott and M. Robb (eds), *Understanding Health and Social Care*, London: Sage, pp. 75–9.

Office of the Deputy Prime Minister 2003: *English Housing Condition Survey.* London: Office for National Statistics.

Oliver, M. and Barnes, C. 1998: *Disabled People and Social Policy.* London: Longman.

Olsen, N. D. L. 2001: 'Prescribing warmer, healthier homes.' *British Medical Journal,* 322, 748–49.

Oppenheim, C. 1990: *Poverty: The Facts*. London: Child Poverty Action Group.

Savage, S. P. and Atkinson, R. 2001: *Public Policy under Blair*. Basingstoke: Palgrave.

Sexty, C. 1990: *Women Losing Out*. London: Shelter.

West Midlands Health Research Unit 1994: 'Health and homelessness.' *Health Watch*, March.

West Midlands Health Research Unit 1999: 'Environment and health action in partnership.' *Health Watch*, July, 79.

Wilkinson, D. 1999: *Poor Housing and Ill Health: A Summary of the Evidence*. Edinburgh: Scottish Office.

Conclusion

Developing your sociological imagination

This book has sought to develop your 'sociological imagination' – something which we hope you will find useful, both in meeting the diverse needs of your patients and in your pursuit of a career within nursing. In this book, we have described sociology as multiparadigmatic. This means that sociology can provide you with a set of theories, concepts and methodological tools which you can apply to everyday issues within clinical practice. It does not usually provide you with an 'answer' but, rather, it provides you with ways of knowing, the ability to question everyday assumptions and the capacity to look beyond common-sense explanations.

Reading through the book you have probably found that some parts, or chapters, are more meaningful to you than others. This will, of course, depend upon your previous knowledge as well as your personal and clinical experiences. Each chapter has been written to ensure that its sociological relevance is applicable to all branches of nursing but you may find that some of the issues resonate more powerfully, and find some issues more interesting than others. For example, if you are pursuing a career in learning-disability nursing then chapter 7 may seem particularly relevant. Similarly, those of you wishing to pursue children's nursing may find chapters 6 and 10 of more interest, and those of you studying mental-health nursing may find chapter 12 of especial relevance. As you progress through your nursing career it is likely that this will change and that all of the issues raised within the book will take on a particular significance.

The sociology of health is an already vast, and increasingly growing area of study. It has been described by Sarah Nettleton as disparate and eclectic (The Sociology of Health, Cambridge: Polity, 1995), and the range of issues we have addressed are as much a reflection of the field itself as they are a reflection of our own preferences and expertise as editors and authors. The sociology of health has a very strong empirical tradition and most of the research in this area deals with issues that are familiar to us all, either as lay individuals or health professionals. However, it is precisely this which ensures that the sociology of health can be applied so well to clinical practice. The book is not exhaustive and, indeed, there are numerous omissions. It has not been our intention to provide such an account of the sociology of health, but to outline some of the key debates within sociology and to show how these are of relevance to the various branches of nursing. We hope that the book has provided you with a solid grounding in the sociology of health to enable you to continue thinking sociologically.

Each of the chapters within this book has been written as a springboard for supplementary study in that area. Further study of sociological theory, for example, will reveal a wider range of theoretical perspectives than those described in this book. Postmodernism is one such theory. It suggests that there is no one valid 'truth' or 'reality', and can very usefully be applied to the relationships between patients and so-called medical experts, and to the subsequent shifts in knowledge and power between the two. A detailed discussion of postmodernism and health can be found in Nick Fox's *Postmodernism, Sociology and Health* (Buckingham: Open University Press, 1993). Further exploration of feminist theory will also, in fact, reveal a choice of feminist theories, ranging from the radical to the reformist. There are many feminist texts available but you may find the book by Gayle Letherby – *Feminist Research in Theory and Practice* (Buckingham: Open University Press, 2003) – particularly useful.

This book has also introduced you to sociological research methods. These are useful not only because nursing is an increasingly evidence-based profession but because, one day, you too may engage in research and find sociological methods of value. A further study of research methods will enable you to better assess the research findings of others and, thus, be better able to evaluate the extent to which such findings should influence your own practice. Sociology also offers a rich set of methodologies that can be applied to help you understand the experience of being a patient. The book by Judith Green and Nicki Thorogood, *Qualitative Methods in Health Research* (London: Sage, 2004) is useful, as is *Research Methods in Health: Investigating Health and Health Services* by Ann Bowling (Buckingham: Open University Press, 2002).

A deeper study of public health will enable you to understand the effects that environment can have on your patients. In this book we have focused on the role of housing as a health resource and have considered issues of class and poverty, but these are only some of the facets of public health. It is worth considering other issues, for example, education and the concept of 'healthy schools', the workplace and occupational health, or the relationship between public spaces, leisure and health. *Public Health, Policy and Politics* by Rob Baggott (London: Palgrave, 2000) may be useful as it examines the relationships between health, food and diet, as well as smoking, alcohol and drugs. You may wish to pursue the study of risk and think about health promotion and the problem of risky behaviours. You may also wish to think about how nurses and other health professionals can manage the uncertainties of clinical practice. The dilemma of protecting sick and often vulnerable patients, whilst at the same time promoting empowerment and choice could also be usefully explored. The book by Andy Alaszewski and Larry Harrison, *Risk, Health and Welfare: Policies, Strategies and Practice* (Buckingham: Open University Press, 1998), is worth reading.

As we said at the beginning of this book, sociology can be applied to everything and, indeed, it is possible to have a sociology of anything. The different sociological theories, concepts and tools outlined within this book can be, and have been, applied to any area of nursing or clinical practice. We hope that you have enjoyed learning about the sociology of health and that you continue to apply sociology to your own nursing practice. We have included some further resources below that you may find useful.

Additional Resources

Web-based Resources

Dead Sociologists' Index (www2.pfeiffer.edu/~/ridener/DSS/ INDEX.HTML)
This index of sixteen sociologists provides brief biographical detail, a summary of their theories and extracts from original works. Of particular interest are the entries on Mead, Marx, Durkheim and Weber.

The National Statistics Office (www.statistics.gov.uk)
Described as the UK's home of official statistics. It has a useful section on health and care with searchable data, press releases and news stories.

Social Sciences Information Gateway (www.sosig.ac.uk:/)
A useful worldwide resource base. Here you will find links to journals, mailing lists, organizations, books and more.

The National Centre for Social Research (www.scpr.ac.uk)
The National Centre for Social Research (NatCen) is the largest independent social research institute in Britain. It has a useful search engine.

The UK Data Archive (www.data-archive.ac.uk)
The UK Data Archive (UKDA) is an internationally renowned centre of expertise and provides resource discovery and support for secondary use of quantitative and qualitative data.

Journals

Critical Public Health
Culture, Health and Sexuality
Diversity in Health and Social Care
Health: An Interdisciplinary Journal of the Social Study of Health, Illness and Medicine
Health and Social Care in the Community
Health Promotion International
Journal of Advanced Nursing
Journal of Epidemiology and Community Health
Social Science and Medicine
Social Theory and Health
Sociology of Health and Illness

Useful Organizations

The American Sociological Association (www.asanet.org/)
A useful organization with sections on general medical sociology and the sociology of mental health.

The British Sociological Association (www.britsoc.co.uk)
The British Sociological Association is the professional association for sociologists in Britain and the BSA website is a key resource for sociologists and students of sociology. It can tell you more about what it is that sociologists do. The BSA operates a large network of study groups; the Medical Sociology Group may be of particular interest.

The European Sociological Association (www.valt.helsinki.fi/esa/index.htm)
The European Sociological Association aims to facilitate sociological research, teaching and communication. It has research networks on medical sociology and health policy research and another on the sociology of professions.

More Books

We have already listed many useful books both within the text of each chapter and within our suggestions for further reading; it is important to read widely and we recommend that you follow up on these reading suggestions. However, there are also several useful sociology readers which bring together classic and contemporary excerpts in accessible collections.

M. Bury and J. Gabe (eds): *The Sociology of Health and Illness: A Reader.* London: Routledge, 2003.
This introduces classic texts as well as more contemporary pieces. It is organized into the following sections: health beliefs and knowledge; inequalities and patterning of health and illness; professional and patient interaction; chronic illness and disability; evaluation and politics in health care.

L. Mackay, K. Soothill and K. Melia (eds): *Classic Texts in Health Care.* Oxford: Butterworth Heinemann, 1998.
This text is specifically marketed for students on nursing and allied health care degree and diploma courses. It contains 56 readings organized into three sections: fundamental issues in health, the health professions, and the NHS.

S. Nettleton and U. Gustafsson (eds): *The Sociology of Health and Illness Reader.* Cambridge: Polity, 2002.
This text brings together contemporary readings on the sociology of health and illness. The book has a general introduction and is

organized into five sections, each with its own introduction. These sections are: bodies, health and risk, experiencing illness, social patterning of health and illness, and health care work.

M. Purdy and D. Banks (eds): *The Sociology and Politics of Health: A Reader.* London: Routledge, 2001.
This explores sociological and political issues in health and health care. It has 31 readings organized into four sections: ideology and policy; social stratification; professionalization; and the experience of health and illness.

Index